# The Visitor's Guide
## to
## EGYPT

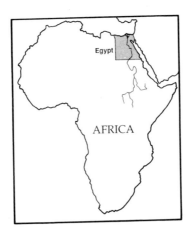

Egypt

AFRICA

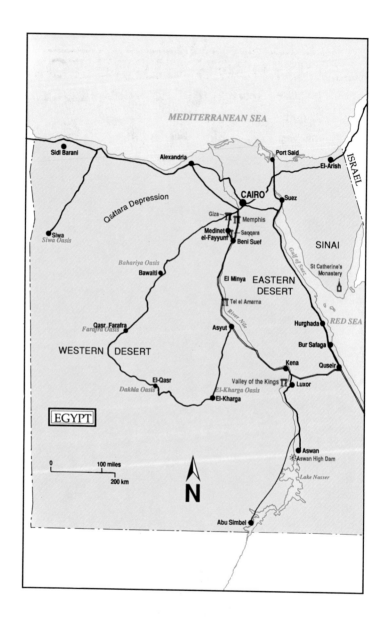

# THE
## VISITOR'S GUIDE TO
# EGYPT

## ANDY GERALD GRAVETTE

MPC

HUNTER
PUBLISHING INC

Published by:
Moorland Publishing Co Ltd,
Moor Farm Road West,
Airfield Estate,
Ashbourne,
Derbyshire DE6 1HD
England

British Library Cataloguing in
Publication Data:
Gravette, A. Gerald (Andrew
Gerald)
   The visitor's guide to Egypt.
   1. Egypt. Visitor's guides
   I. Title
   916.20455

ISBN 0 86190 369 2 (paperback)
ISBN 0 86190 368 4 (hardback)


Published in the USA by:
Hunter Publishing Inc,
300 Raritan Center Parkway,
CN 94, Edison, NJ 08818
ISBN 1 55650 267 2 (USA)


Colour and black & white
origination by:
Scantrans, Singapore

Printed in the UK by:
Richard Clay Ltd, Bungay, Suffolk

Cover photograph:
*Giza* (A. Gravette).

Acknowledgements
The author would like to thank the
following for assistance in the
compilation of the *Visitor's Guide to
Egypt*: The Egyptian Tourist Office,
London; Museum of Egyptian
Antiquities, Cairo; British Museum
and British Library; Abercrombie &
Kent; Top Deck Travel; Mark
Wright of Explore Worldwide;
Martin Dunn, James Croll and
Andy Chadwick of Transglobal;
3M Scotch Film and friends and
colleagues throughout Egypt.
   Special mention should be made
of Yvonne without whom I could
not have enjoyed our honeymoon
travelling the Nile and in Alexandria, and without whose support
this book could not have been
written.

# *CONTENTS*

## Key to Symbols Used in Text Margin and on Maps

 Pyramid

 Monastery

Mosque

 Building of interest

 Ruin/Place of historical interest

 Castle/Fortification

Birdlife

 Museum/Art gallery

Garden

 Beautiful view/Scenery, Natural phenomenon

 Other place of interest

## Key to Maps

═══ Main road

● Town/Settlement

─── Minor road

Lake/Oasis

City

 Country Boundary

# INTRODUCTION

E gypt, known as the 'Gateway to the East' is a land of absolute contrasts. Its lush Nile Valley cuts an emerald swathe through arid deserts and russet cliffs. The world's longest river supports a large percentage of the country's 50 million population whose rich ancestry ranges from dark Nubians to olive-skinned Mediterranean types. With a wealth of culture and history behind them, Egypt's people live mostly in or around Africa's largest city, Cairo. Commanding the headwaters of the fertile Nile Delta, Egypt's capital has earned itself the well-deserved title of 'Mother of the World'. Spectacular traces of Egypt's ancient cities and civilisations now attract millions of tourists to this land of colour and diversity.

The black mud of the Nile prompted Ancient Egyptians to name their land 'Kemi' after the dark, fertile silt contrasting it to the barren red sands of the deserts lying on either side of the country's 'lifeblood'. Egypt's modern name comes from the Greek word *aigyptos* also referring to the colour of the River Nile deposits. The Roman word *aegyptus* (dark) emphasises the overriding importance to the country's economy of its rich alluvial soil. In the fifth century BC, more than 2,000 years after Egypt's two ancient kingdoms were founded, the Greek historian, Herodotus, described the land as the 'Gift of the Nile'.

More than 966km (600 miles) of Egyptian Nile waters have nurtured a long tapestry of interwoven civilisations, cultures and religions, over a period of almost 15,000 years. With a variety of climates and terrain along the valley from the Sudan border in the south to the Delta on the Mediterranean coast, the ribbon of cultivatable land spawned numerous early settlements, many of which survive to this day. Other towns grew up around the many desert oases and along the coastlines of the Red and Mediterranean Seas. Toil on the land, battles with the elements and wars with a string of invaders over the centuries has produced in Egypt a fascinating country with a strange and wonderful history, peopled by a mixture of races, creeds, colours and cultures.

## GEOGRAPHY

From the air Egypt appears as a flat, barren, khaki waste, roughly rectangular in shape, bisected by a narrow sliver of green, fertile land and bordered by seas on two sides. This yellow-red corner of the African continent is desert, crumpled in places by brown mountain ranges. The silver-blue ribbon which divides two desert regions is the River Nile bounded by the bright green banks of the river's floodplain. Turquoise waters fringe white sandy beaches along a coastline which divides the bulk of the country from the triangular Sinai Peninsula — dark brown with mountain peaks. This is the long arm of the Red Sea, together with the narrow Gulf of Suez, a necklace of Bitter Lakes and the Suez Canal. Where the river meets the ultra-marine waters of the Mediterranean a triangle of low-lying viridian denotes the verdant Delta at the mouth of the Nile. Seemingly flat from the air, Egypt's landscape is surprisingly mountainous and its highest peak, Mount Catherine (Gebel Katherina), in the southern Sinai, soars to 2,642m (8,666ft) above sea level. Across the Nile from the Eastern Desert, the Qattara Depression is the mountain's antithesis, where land sinks to nearly 200m (656ft) below sea level. Although the majority of Egypt's 1,002,000sq km (385,168sq miles) are Saharan sand, this shifting desert is marked by tiny green oases, five of which are extensively developed and cultivated. Arranged around the Nile's south to north watercourse, five deserts, three plateaus and two great depressions, provide a contrast of terrains.

Politically the country has three borders which, because of their straight lines, emphasise the quadrilateral shape of Egypt. To the west the vast deserts of Libya border Egypt's own Western Desert. Sudan, in the south, skirts the Toshka Depression — the Eastern and the Nubian Deserts. The long waters of Lake Nasser, formed by the damming of the Nile, reach down to the Sudanese frontier and, in the far east of the country, Israel's border cuts a line across the east flank of the Sinai Peninsula from the Mediterranean Sea to the Gulf of Aqaba. Across this natural boundary lies Jordan and Saudi Arabia.

## FAUNA AND FLORA

Because of the country's climatic variations and the harshness of its terrain, Egypt's animal and plant life is limited in its diversity. One reptile and at least two animals are synonymous with the Egyptian landscape. Cleopatra's famous asp was the Royal Cobra or the Uraeus of the Pharaohs, a sacred serpent which decorated their royal crown and symbolised Upper Egypt. The camel, without which photographs of the Egyptian scenery would be empty, is the one-humped dromedary which, together with the donkey, is bred as a beast of burden and for riding.

Out in the relentless conditions of the desert reptiles like lizards, monitors and snakes survive on small rodents, insects and birds. The Egyptian vulture, amongst others such as hawks and falcons, dominate the desert skies and small herds of gazelle, scavenging hyenas and jackals and foxes wander through the drifting dunes. Scrub bushes and other drought-loving plants sparsely dot the shifting sands and the only sight of greenery in the interior is around oases where doom palm and date palm provide shelter for nomadic tribes and a harvestable crop. A variety of cacti and thorn — the curious stork bill bush, Egyptian sagebrush and honesty — provide scant shelter for ghekos, chameleons and scorpion in the desert sands. Small plots of land are cultivated in the oases where tamarisk, acacias and fruit trees are also grown. Herds of sheep, goats and a few cattle are husbanded around remote wells and isolated pockets of water. Once, as can be seen in the wall paintings of the ancients, lion used to roam the deserts but now, apart from small wild cats and a few leopards reported to inhabit parts of Sinai, the big cats of Egypt are extinct. The Sinai however is famed for its rare breeds, notably the Nubian ibex, the slender horned gazelle, the houbara bustard and the Arabian rock pigeon, all among the rarest of the world's protected species.

It is along the coastal regions and the Nile Valley that most wildlife can be seen, but the thrills of spotting a hippopotamus or a Nilotic crocodile are gone as both species are presumed extinct in Egypt. Wild boar, however, have been seen in the Nile Delta region. Most of the larger animals seen in these regions are domesticated — water buffalo, cattle, goats, sheep, mule, ass and the ubiquitous camel. It is the great variety of birdlife which makes the Nile Valley popular with ornithologists. Huge flocks of cattle egrets settle in date palm groves and heron dart amongst the giant bulrushes of Biblical times. Another famous plant, the papyrus (used by Egyptians of old to make their paper), chokes the river banks and spreads across lakesides providing shelter for the sacred ibis of Ancient Egypt which are now a rarity. Also along the water margins quail, stork and egret are common, the latter often seen in large flocks following the farmer's plough or dogging grazing cattle preying off the insects disturbed by the animals hooves. In the grasslands the hoopoe is common as are cuckoos, nightingale and green bee-eaters. White kite may be seen wheeling above, a rare sight for the bird-watcher but a bane for the local peasant farmers who keep pigeons and turtle doves — a delicacy for birds of prey. Monkeys, sacred to the ancients, and ostrich used to be prevalent in southern Egypt but have long since been exterminated.

In the Pharaoh's Egypt the lotus was a symbol of the flourishing Nile although this beautiful waterlily has now been decimated. The diminishing numbers of this once prolific flower is now more symbolic of the shrinking acres of cultivated land fringing the great river. It is on Kitchener's Island at Aswan, that one can see just how luxuriant plants and flowers can be when surrounded by water although located in the midst of a desert wilderness. Poinsettia, asters, gerbera, bird-of-paradise flowers and even roses bloom here together under the shade of acacia, mimosa, jasmine, eucalyptus and flamboyant trees, while majestic royal palms soar above fig trees and grape vines.

Throughout Egypt flies and frogs, locusts and lice (another four of the Ten Great Plagues of Biblical times), are prevalent. Similarly, the sacred scarab beetle, worshipped in Egypt's ancient civilisation, still inhabits its noxious abode. Records left in ancient paintings and mummified remains show that the cat and Egyptian hunting dog were constant companions of the Pharaohs. Domesticated creatures like the large-horned cattle, shaggy goats and hardy sheep seem not to have changed since stone masons of old carved their images in bas-relief on the walls of tombs and temples. Fish life, both of the lakes and the river, was also depicted in early inscriptions and Nilotic waterlife is still as rich as it has been for thousands of years. In the Red Sea and off the Mediterranean coast the fish are varied and numerous. Not only do the coastal people live from the sale of such fish as shark, tunny, swordfish and shellfish, but the shores attract a large number of visiting scuba enthusiasts who come to view the 800 species of tropical fish bringing trade to local boat owners.

*Historic events of Ancient Egypt were recorded on stelae*

## HISTORY

### Prehistory to 3000BC

Fishermen and hunters were the first inhabitants of the Nile Valley, converging on this rich and fertile region from Sudan, North Africa and from Asia. Traces of an early occupation dating back almost 2 million years have recently been found near Luxor. Three groups of nomads eventually settled around 12000BC and intermingled, setting up dwellings along the banks of the great river. By 5000BC an agricultural system had developed and Neolithic artifacts, household utensils, weapons and implements have been unearthed in Upper Egypt. At about the same time a twin kingdom similar to that of Upper Egypt emerged in the Delta — Lower Egypt. Known as the El Fayyum cultural period, this was followed by the Naqada cultures which survived until around 3200BC. It was about this time that the two distinct kingdoms of Upper and Lower Egypt were amalgamated. The white crown of Upper and the red crown of Lower Egypt were joined into one and this diadem was first worn by King Menes whose capital was Memphis. Menes began the first of Egypt's thirty dynasties which lasted from about 3100BC until 341BC — a total of 2,759 years.

## The Dynastic Period to 332BC

Thirty Egyptian dynasties moulded the country's development and culture into one of the most advanced and fascinating civilisations known to man. Over this period a succession of kings (Pharaohs) ruled in a series of kingdoms known as the Old, the Middle, the New Kingdom and the Late Period Kingdoms. The word 'Pharaoh' comes from the ancient word *pra o*, meaning great house. Thirty dynasties of Pharaohs ruled from the days of Mena in 4400BC to Seti's reign around 1300BC and that of the great builder, Ramesses II around 1200BC. To put the era of the Pharaoh's into perspective, it is thought that either Seti, or Ramesses name was linked with the exodus of the Israelites related in the Bible.

The period of the Old Kingdom began with Pharaoh Zoser whose tomb is known as the Step Pyramid at Saqqara. His was the Third Dynasty which lasted until 2575BC and he was followed by more than seventy-five Pharaohs. These include the famous names of Cheops, builder of the Great Pyramid at Giza and the Sphinx; Chephron and Mycerinus who built the two other pyramids on the same site; Antef, one of the earliest rulers of the Middle Kingdom; Amenhotep I and his mother Nefertari, the early rulers of the New Kingdom when the country's capital removed to Thebes; Tuthmosis I and his celebrated daughter Hatshepsut; Akhnaton, whose wife was the legendary beauty, Nefertiti; Tutankhamen, famed for the treasures found in this young king's tomb; the eleven Pharaohs named Ramesses and Nektharehbe, the last Pharaoh of the Thirtieth Dynasty and the last local ruler of Ancient Egypt. High priests took control of the country from 1080BC, ending the era of the three great kingdoms and for more than 600 years from 950BC Libyans, Sudanese, Assyrians Persians and Macedonians occupied the land.

## The Ptolemaic and Roman Periods to AD395

In 332BC Alexander the Great, when he was just 24 years old, invaded Egypt, announced himself king and founded the city of Alexandria on the Mediterranean coast. Peacefully, the Egyptian hierarchy accepted his brief rule of 8 years and when Alexander died in Babylon and was buried in Egypt, King Ptolemy I took charge of the country. From 305BC to 30BC fifteen Macedonian Ptolemies ruled Egypt. Along with the Ptolemies a series of Cleopatras participated in the 275 years of control until the fabled Cleopatra VII shared her throne with the Roman Anthony, 3 years after Julius Caesar was murdered. When Anthony committed suicide and Cleopatra succumbed to snakebite, Egypt reverted to Roman rule under an illustrious succession of governors and emperors. From 30BC to AD395 (425 years), such great names as Augustus, Tiberius, Claudius, Nero and Hadrian influenced the course of Egyptian development. Towards the end of Roman rule Constantine the Great officially introduced Christianity into the country. Theodosius the Great was the last Roman to rule Egypt.

## Byzantine to Turkish Rule

The advent of Christianity had a far-reaching effect on the pattern of Egyptian life from 395 to 638 during the Byzantine domination of the country. Patriarchal rule eventually gave way to an Arab intrusion which put Egypt under the control of the Caliphs from 640 to 968. During this period of Arab rule the Islamic religion slowly infiltrated the country and many people adopted the Arab language. A period of Byzantine and Caliphate influence threw Egypt into 573 years of turmoil with famines, wars and religious conflict. It was under the Caliphs that Cairo was founded but it was the Fatimids (leaders of the Islamic Shi'i sect), who established the city as the country's capital. Saladin, champion of the Muslim world during the Crusades, was the first ruler of the Ayyubid Dynasty which lasted until 1250 and introduced almost 80 years of artistic and cultural expansion. In 1168 Saladin championed the Islamic cause by repelling the Crusader's attempts to enter Egypt after their success in Jerusalem. For almost three centuries after the death of the last Ayyubid sultan (As-Salih in 1249) the Mameluke sultans dominated the country and brought yet another golden age to Egypt in their spectacular architecture. Repeated outbreaks of the plague finally undermined the power of the Mamelukes and both political unrest and economic decline dogged their rule until they were eventually incorporated into the plan of governing introduced by their new masters, the Turks.

## The Ottomans to Modern Times

With their base in Istanbul the Turkish Ottoman rulers (pashas), inflicted a gradual decline in the importance of Egypt as a political centre, and navigational breakthroughs by European discoverers in Africa and the Americas during the fifteenth and sixteenth centuries left the country vulnerable to economic and physical overthrow.

*The prolific Nileside birdlife attracts many ornithologists to Egypt*

Towards the end of the Turkish era of domination, the Mamelukes briefly returned to power only to induce a short civil war. In 1798 Napoleon led his troops to victory over the Mamelukes but, although his scientific exploits and archaeological surveys played a significant role in the preservation of Egyptian artifacts, Napoleon was forced by a combined Anglo-Turkish force to vacate the country in 1805. Admiral Horatio Nelson's contribution in restoring Egypt was rewarded by the installation of Mohammed Ali Pasha in 1811, whose efforts brought about the political and economic resurrection of Egypt. Mohammed Ali's achievements were legendary and, after his death in 1849, the dynasty he had founded survived another 103 years. After a short period of in-fighting from Mohammed Ali's demise until 1863, Ismail the Magnificent ruled until 1879. Most significant during Ismail's reign were the 1869 opening of the Suez Canal. The vast European debts which he ran up prompted the British to take control of Egypt. From 1882 until 1907 the most spectacular achievements were the construction of the Nile barrage in 1890 and the building of the first Aswan Dam in 1902.

Khedives like Tewfik and Abbas Hilmi (descendants of Mohammed Ali) ruled under the auspices of the British and the country went through another period of revival and prosperity. After Egypt's status as protectorate from the outbreak of World War I in 1914, the Wafd Party until 1922 negotiated independence from British rule and Fuad was appointed as the first king of Egypt since the last great Pharaoh, Ramesses, 3,000 years previous. King Farouk succeeded Fuad in 1936 but was soon ousted as a result of his lavish lifestyle, by General Neguib in 1952. Two years later Colonel Nasser became the country's first president followed after his death in 1970 by Anwar el-Sadat. During the first year of President Sadat's period in power the Aswan High Dam was completed. In 1981 President Sadat was assassinated and Air Marshal Hosni Mubarak appointed president.

## POPULATION, POLITICS AND ECONOMY

Standing at around 52 million, Egypt's population is the second largest in Africa and, with over 15 million living in and around Cairo, the country's capital is the most populous in the Islamic world. The rate of increase of Egypt's people is estimated at more than 3 million every 2 years. About 20 million Egyptians inhabit the Nile Delta region between Cairo and the Mediterranean coast.

Four-fifths of the total population of Egypt are poor farmers living along the valley and in the Delta area of the Nile. These are the Fellahin, descendants from the Ancient Egyptians and whose blood has been intermingled with that of the Arabs. A proud and nationalistic people, the Fellahin live off the land and till the soil much in the same way as their ancestors did more than 3,000 years ago. The Fellahin are predominantly Muslim as are 94 per cent of the country's population and the branch of Islam which they follow is known as Sunnite. The lives of these people are controlled by two dictates — that of nature,

*Egypt's ruler-gods were immortalised in stone*

in the cycles of the River Nile and the climate, and that man-made teaching, the Islamic religion. To understand Egypt and her people more closely one should have at least a brief knowledge of the country's official religion which plays such an important part in daily life and whose principles guide the nation. Egypt, however, is not as strict in its religious discipline as some other Islamic countries and there is a certain emancipation of women and waiving of some harsher teachings which is not found in more fundamentalist Islam.

Those Egyptians who retained their Christian beliefs, less than 10 per cent of the population, are known as Copts and these people are generally middle class and live in the urban districts of Upper Egypt. Some negroid people, mainly from Sudan in the south, have filtered into the country over many millennia and are known as Nubians (from the land the ancients called Nubia). Some Nubians mingled with the lighter skinned Egyptian races but the typical Egyptian is of the Mediterranean type. In the desert, as opposed to the Fellahin, the Copts and the Nubians who are true Egyptians with ancestries dating back to Pharaonic Egypt (the Berbers and Bedouins) are of pure Arab descent and live a generally nomadic life.

A socialist democratic country, Egypt is governed by the People's Assembly which nominate a president who serves a 6-year term. There are still the two major political regions of Upper and Lower Egypt and the country is divided into twenty-five governorates and frontier districts.

The economy of the Egypt harks back to the earliest days of civilisation and land cultivation has been carried on in the Nile Valley over 7,000 years. Agricultural activities in Egypt were governed by the regular flooding of the Nile which created a cycle of sowing and harvest — the Ancient Egyptians developed the first calendar (in modern Egypt the Muslim calendar is now in use), and they developed the earliest systems of irrigation. Today the great river does not flood its banks but the methods of cultivation and irrigation have remained unchanged for eons. The wide belt of floodplain on each bank of the Nile has now shrunk but the crops raised along the river and in the fertile Delta have altered little since the days of the Pharaohs. Rice, maize, millet and wheat are grown by the Fellahin who also cultivate plots of vegetables, fields of sugar cane and groves of date palms and fruit trees. Egypt is the world's largest producer of dates and cotton is the country's largest cash crop. Egyptian cotton is considered among the finest and the sale of raw cotton and textiles yields over one-third of the country's export income. New industries which include iron steel, glass, aluminium and chemical production, are benefiting from recent oil finds and tourism now contributes a substantial amount to the economy both in foreign currency earnings and the provision of much-needed employment.

## FOOD AND DRINK

Egypt's cuisine is as diverse as its chequered history; from the basic diet of the wandering desert Bedouin which includes dates, roast bitter apple seeds, camel and goat's cheese, beans and the occasional meat dish, to the riverside Fellahin, whose staple food is *ful*, made with broad beans, humus (made with chick peas) a selection of green vegetables and tomatoes often supplemented with lamb or fish. From each corner of the near East — Arabia, Turkey and the Mediterranean, from France, Italy and England, the cuisine of Egypt has received more than a soupçon of influence. In the rich soil of the Nile Valley and its Delta almost any and fruit and vegetable thrives and it is with this extensive larder that the national dishes have evolved. Ancient Egypt may have undergone 7 years of famine but the country is now one of the world's leading producers of vegetables and fruits, exports of which contribute to the country's economy.

Meats — either mutton, beef, poultry or goat — form the main dish of the day and this, generally grilled, is accompanied by pulses such as black beans, broadbeans or rice and a selection of salad vegetables. Traditional Egyptian kebab and *mosaka* are known worldwide but less familiar dishes might include *kofta* (grilled minced lamb meatballs), *hammam* (grilled pigeon, *dolmas*, or *wara inab* (minced meat and rice wrapped in vine leaves), *mashwi* which is whole roast lamb or *kalawi* which are kidneys grilled in herbs and spices. The Egyptian culinary arts are often accompanied by an extensive use of herbs like parsley, mint and garlic and spices such as tamarind, saffron, caraway and cinnamon. Flat, unleavened bread is served with all main meals and sometimes serves as a sandwich for *shish* kebab or *ta'miya*, a concoction sometimes known as *falafel*. *Mezzas*, or snacks may be served before the main course and might consist of *gibna*, which is cheese (either white or yellow); *makarona*, literally macaroni with meat and sauce; *babaghanoug*, spiced sesame seed paste with eggplant olive oil, garlic and lemon; *batarik* which is a local caviare, or *mashi*, which is a pottage of vegetables. Tomatoes, peppers, eggplant, and courgettes are usually served in a bread shell (*'esh* in Arabic). Vegetables are served with almost everything and pickled vegetables, or *turshi*, is also very popular.

Sweets, often with nuts, honey, syrup, shredded wheat and fruit are a delight. Visitors may know *baklava*, a favourite Eastern Mediterranean dessert but, more typically Egyptian is *om-ali*, a hot, cinnamon and coconut mix with corn flakes and milk. Custards are plentiful as are fruit juices, fools and ices. Although Egypt is an Islamic country, a religion which forbids strong drink, it produces a wide range of good wines (white, rosé and red) with enigmatic names — Queen Cleopatra, Nefertiti, Omar Khayyam and Pharaoh's wine. A local beer is also made in parts of Egypt and it varies in colour and strength. Date brandy is also produced as is *zibib*, the Arab answer to Greek *ouzo*, sometimes called *arak*. The unending coffee and tea pot may well have originated in Egypt, both served very hot and sweet in tiny cups. Spiced, hot drinks, *sahlab*, *erfa*, or cool infusions like *karkade*, made from the hibiscus flower, are available at almost every street corner. Egyptian mineral water is called *m'adaniyah* while normal water is *moyah*. It is advisable to keep to mineral instead of tap water, although water in most hotels is generally safe enough to drink. There is one source of water in Egypt which should be avoided at all costs. Nile water should be regarded with the utmost respect; the water should not be drunk, swam in, or used to wash fruits and vegetables.

## LEISURE AND ENTERTAINMENT
In Cairo the visitor can find a variety of excellent sports facilities, many of which are either part of leading hotel complexes or attached to country and sporting clubs. Golf can be played on the 18-hole course in the Gezira Club, Cairo, the Mena House Golf Club at Giza, or on the 9-hole at the Giza Oberoi Hotel. The Gezira Club has tennis courts as do most of the larger hotels and there are several tennis clubs in Cairo city. Football is a very popular sport and there are regular tournaments in the capital. Horse racing, every Saturday and Sunday during the winter months, takes place on Gezira Island and at the el-Shams club. At the Heliopolis Hippodrome, from October to May, horse races are held on the weekend afternoons. There are also several riding stables in Giza where mounts can be hired for rides around the pyramids or for further excursions.

Water sports facilities are particularly good in Cairo and on the Mediterranean or Red Sea coasts. Most large hotels have swimming pools as do several of the Cairo sports clubs. Alexandria and Mersa Matruh are favourite north coast resorts for swimming and sailing and Hurghada, Ras Mohammed, Sharm al Sheikh and Safaga are popular watersports and diving centres. Sailing on the Nile is an unforgettable experience and yachts or feluccas can be rented at

*In Egypt the craft of weaving dates back over 7,000 years*

*The Fellahin are descendants of the Ancient Egyptians*

some hotels and at the Cairo Yacht Club. The Nile cruise ships are almost all equipped with a swimming pool on the deck but it is important to remember that the Nile waters must be avoided at all costs because of pollution. There are three major rowing clubs in the capital and regattas are held on Fridays during the winter months. Gliding is becoming popular and one can take the opportunity to glide over the Nile or the pyramids from one of two flying clubs just on Cairo's outskirts. In the south, near Luxor, an organisation is offering balloon trips over the Valley of the Kings and other sites of interest.

The belly-dancing of Egypt is legendary and what better way to enjoy typical nightlife in Cairo or Alexandria than a visit to one of the night clubs on the Giza road to watch this traditional performance. Egyptians are enthusiastic musicians and singers and shows are organised almost nightly at most large hotels and at theatres in Egypt's main towns and cities. There is a symphony orchestra in Cairo and a ballet company, a national dance troupe which promotes traditional folk dancing, a puppet troupe and a national circus based in the capital. The Rida Troupe perform folk dancing at the Balloon Theatre and the Arabic Music Troupe puts on performances at the Gumhurriya Theatre. Near the Pyramids Road in Giza the symphony orchestra of Cairo occasionally make an appearance but are generally based at the Gumhurriya. Cinema's open at about 9pm and show an amazing selection of foreign and Egyptian films. *Son et lumière* performances at many of the ancient sites provide historic background and dramatic lighting effects which transform the monuments and transfix the audiences. Misr, the National Tourist Information offices across the country, have details of all performances and events. Some of the most interesting nightlife can be found in the street cafés and coffee shops of Egypt's towns and cities where one can observe the everyday bustle of the Egyptian evenings and, should the language be no problem, participate in the local's animated conversations. By dining out in one of the hundreds of excellent local restaurants in Cairo one can also share in the life of the capital after dark and the Nile by moonlight out-romances most of the world's classical sights. Egypt is a veritable magic carpet of diversions and the 'cradle of culture and civilisation' offers a Pandora's Box of delights.

In Cairo and Alexandria clubs and bars are particularly prevalent but other towns and cities of Egypt have their fair share of discothèques and pulsating nightclubs. Probably the most westernised of all club and restaurants in Cairo is The Four Corners in Zamelek, which attracts the young elite for its disco and video bar. Another popular music bar is B's Corner, also in Zamelek, or II Capo, next to the President Hotel. Many hotels have good clubs like Jackie's at the Nile Hilton, or Club 36 at the Ramesses Hilton. Out in Heliopolis, the Merryland, on al-Hijaz Street, is a popular nightclub with locals and foreigners alike. Pyramids Road is famous world-wide for its selection of nightlife and the Mena House Hotel has a spectacular music lounge out at Giza. The casino tables can be played at the Marriott, the Sheraton and the Nile Hilton hotels. For stunning scenes of the River Nile most of the modern hotels in Cairo have panorama bars and lounges like that at the famous Shepheard's Hotel.

Shopping in Egypt is a diversion in itself as this country lies at the crossroads of East and West. The most exclusive goods from Paris, New York, London and Hong Kong can be purchased in the arcades and boulevard shops of Cairo but the real joy is the plethora of specialist markets. One should be wary of 'antiquities' offered everywhere in the country but the traditional handicrafts of Egypt make excellent souvenirs at economical prices if one can maintain the hour-long haggle for a hand woven rug or brass coffee pot. There are markets for everything from spices and herbs to perfumes and jewellery. It is the very pleasure of wandering the markets and shopping arcades, the excitement of bargaining and the sights, sounds and aromas of the street bazaars which make shopping in the 'market place of the world' such an experience.

## EGYPT'S ANCIENT MONUMENTS

It may be wrong to suggest that Egypt's historic monuments are the sole reason the country attracts so many visitors from across the globe, but for most holidaymakers Egypt has two main attributes; its two spectacular coastlines and its numerous ancient sites which take prime place on the traveller's list of world-important sights.

The average holiday in Egypt, whether with an organised group or travelling independently, takes in at least four or five of the major archaeological sites, particularly those within easy reach of Cairo, the central base for most tour companies. More ambitious tours offer excursions to sites up and down the Nile, employing various forms of transport including the popular river cruises. More adventurous and more specialised are those tours organised for the visitor with a deeper than average interest in the country, its history, people and its monuments. These tours are usually confined to rather small groups led by an expert in Egyptology and often accompanied by a lecturer or two who provide specialist knowledge on particular sites. Apart

*Cairo has traditionally been the spice market of the Middle East*

*East meets West in an Egyptian market*

*Musicians playing the oud*

from the famous sites of interest along the Nile Valley, these specialist tours operate excursions to the outlying attractions of the country such as the Nile Delta, Alexandria, the Western Desert oases, the Red Sea coastline sites and those in the Sinai Peninsula. Often these companies combine their tours of Egypt with expeditions into Egypt's neighbouring countries, Jordan and the Holy Land, for example.

The most famous regions to visit in Egypt are Cairo, Giza, Saqqara, Luxor, Karnak, Western Thebes, Aswan and Abu Simbel. Today, if one includes 12 Old Kingdom pyramid sites, 8 royal tomb sites, 7 ancient temple sites and 24 ancient city sites (including Alexandria), the total sum of popular attractions for the travelling holidaymaker number just 51. Many visitors have time to view just a small percentage of these sites but if one sums up the important ancient sites from the Old to the Egypt of the New Kingdom, the total number exceeds 110. These comprise temples from the Middle and New Kingdoms; royal tomb sites from the Old, Middle and New Kingdom periods and Old and New Kingdom fortification sites. There are also city sites including royal capitals, palaces and some sites of major provincial tombs. Last but not least one should include the pyramid sites of the Old Kingdom. These sites do not include the hundreds of mines and quarries which, in themselves have become popular with visitors because of their prolific rock inscriptions and accompanying ancient artifacts. Turquoise, granite, alabaster, limestone, calcite, diorite, slate, flint, copper, tin and gold were mined throughout Ancient Egypt and some of these sites, like the turquoise mines in the Sinai, are now major features on the itineraries of some of the more enterprising tour operators.

Facilities for travellers have improved greatly in Egypt allowing easier access to the more obscure sites of antiquity. Although Egypt is primarily a tour-group destination, more independent travellers than ever are surmounting the traditional Egyptian exasperations of delays, pre-booking accommodation, searching out places to eat and places with a supply of petrol, avoiding itinerant hustlers and braving the extremes of Egypt's fearsome climate. Having overcome these, one can visit the country's remarkable variety of attractions at their own pace and within their own budgets. Numerous reliable tour companies however offer a wide selection of Egyptian excursions. Most popular among the various forms of travel available to Egypt's monuments are the selection of Nile riverboat cruisers. Many of these are run by the major hotel chains and have air-conditioning and swimming pools and offer all the luxuries necessary for one of the most romantic of river journeys in the world.

# 1
# *CAIRO*
# *GATEWAY TO THE EAST*

L ong before the present city of Cairo was founded the ancients focused their attention on a similar location just a mile north-east of the modern city in the district now known as Al-Matariyyah. A triangle of settlements were established at the point in the Nile where the great river branches out into its broad Delta. The earliest sites of the three, Memphis, Giza and Heliopolis, are now obscured by later monuments, temples and tombs. Heliopolis however, centre of the religious cult of the sun, was the hub of Egypt's ancient civilisation and survived as a rich township until its eventual downfall in around 30BC. It was around 1975BC that the Pharaoh Amenemhet I established Heliopolis as Ancient Egypt's greatest city. One of the earliest references to Heliopolis appears in the Book of Genesis where Joseph's father-in-law is described as a priest of the sun cult in the city of *Om* (the Coptic name for the city). In 24BC Strabo noted that the Heliopolis had been sacked and it was around that time that the Greeks began referring to a location halfway between Heliopolis and Memphis as Babylon. Little now remains of the city which flourished for almost two millennia but the two 'Cleopatra's Needles' which have been erected in London and New York originated in Old Heliopolis. It was from the pillaged remains of this 'City of the Sun' that today's Cairo evolved.

Babylon emerged on the site of an early battle and suffered several attacks and a great fire over a period of about 1,000 years until the foundations of present-day Cairo were set down. When the city was founded in 969 by the Islamic Fatimids it was named Kahira — The Triumphant One — after the planet Mars by the Fatimid com-

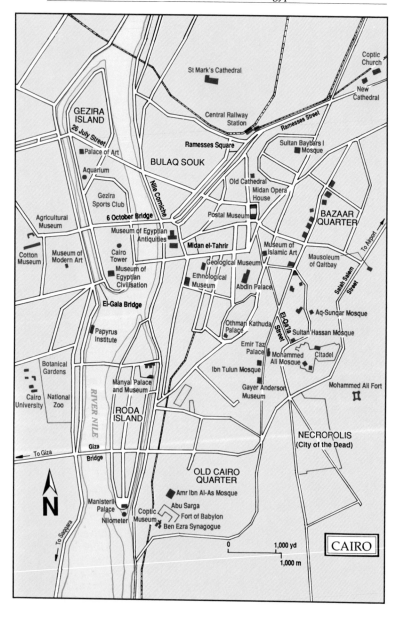

Coptic Church

New Cathedral

St Mark's Cathedral

Central Railway Station

Ramesses Street

GEZIRA ISLAND

26 July Street

Palace of Art

Ramesses Square

Sultan Baybars I Mosque

BULAQ SOUK

Aquarium

Gezira Sports Club

Old Cathedral

Midan Opera House

BAZAAR QUARTER

Agricultural Museum

6 October Bridge

Nile Corniche

Postal Museum

To Airport

Museum of Egyptian Antiquities

Midan el-Tahrir

Museum of Islamic Art

Mausoleum of Qaitbay

Salah Salem Street

Cotton Museum

Museum of Modern Art

Cairo Tower

Geological Museum

Museum of Egyptian Civilisation

Ethnological Museum

Abdin Palace

Aq-Sunqar Mosque

El-Gala Bridge

Othman Kathuda Palace

El-Gala Street

Sultan Hassan Mosque

Papyrus Institute

Emir Taz Palace

Mohammed Ali Mosque

Citadel

Ibn Tulun Mosque

Botanical Gardens

Manyal Palace and Museum

Gayer Anderson Museum

Mohammed Ali Fort

Cairo University

National Zoo

RIVER NILE

RODA ISLAND

NECROROLIS (City of the Dead)

To Giza

Giza Bridge

N

OLD CAIRO QUARTER

Amr Ibn Al-As Mosque

Manisterii Palace

Nilometer

Coptic Museum

Abu Sarga

Fort of Babylon

Ben Ezra Synagogue

To Saqqara

0    1,000 yd

1,000 m

CAIRO

mander Jawhar el-Saqally. However, General Goher, the Fatimid military leader, gave the city the name of Misr el-Kahira and Misr has survived as the name Egyptians now use when referring to their country and capital. Today the Arabic name for Cairo is El Qahira but the ancient sector of the city still survives south of the Cairo's heart and is known as the Old City. Between the Old City and the New stands Saladin's Citadel, on Moqattam Mount, constructed by the Muslim champion in 1177. New Cairo, a city of large squares, boulevards, offices, hotels, administrative buildings and parks, spreads mostly along the eastern bank of the Nile. Two islands, one known as Gezira and the other Roda (linked to both banks of the river by a number of bridges) are located in the centre of the city which

*Cairo, the most populous city in the Islamic world*

covers an area of around 21sq km (9sq miles).

Situated at the apex of the River Nile Delta, just 161km (100 miles) inland from the Mediterranean coast, Cairo commands a strategic position both geographically and economically. This 1,000-year-old city is the largest on the African continent and the most populous in all the Islamic world with more than 15 million residents. Being built on the crossroads of the East and the West, Cairo's checkered history has endured battles between rivals from both points of the compass and accommodated the two religions of Christianity and Islam. The city's twenty Coptic churches are outnumbered by more than forty major mosques which used to number many more, earning Cairo the accolade 'City of a Thousand Minarets'.

# Excursions in Cairo

The many museums, palaces, forts, universities, monuments, modern edifices, mosques and churches pose a problem for the average visitor who has a limited time in which to view the main points of interest in the city. For this reason Cairo is best divided into separate categories for ease of reference. Transport in Cairo is most comfortable by the black and white taxis, but some visitors prefer to hire their own car which is easy to arrange and economical. The red and white public bus service is a cheap form of travel around the city but buses are often crowded and stifling. An underground railway system is being completed for the capital. Cairo is a pleasant city to stroll in and one generally sees more by walking.

A small admission charge is made for entry into most of Cairo's important buildings and monuments. A certain amount of *baksheesh* is also necessary for the guide. Shoes should always be removed before entering any mosque. Women should wear head-covering while visiting mosques and care should be taken over ensuring legs and arms are suitably covered while touring in the city. Headscarves can be rented outside most of Cairo's main mosques.

A typical day's taxi trip to some of Cairo's sites might include the Citadel, Mohammed Ali Mosque and other interesting parts of the Citadel during the morning. Spectacular views of the city can be had from this lofty perch and there are many picturesque corners within its walls. In the afternoon one might visit the nearby Necropolis with its curious mausoleums, impressive tombs and glimpses of the dreaded 'City of the Dead' where even Cairo's authorities abandon criminals who stray there.

Old Cairo, with its Roman remains, Coptic churches and ancient excavation sites, together with a visit to the Nilometer which forms part of the complex, is a favourite half-day's trip by taxi. This could possibly be combined with a relaxing afternoon in the zoo and botanical gardens of El Urman, across on the west bank of the Nile. Quayside feluccas, moored along any available stretch of the river often offer transport across to the islands or opposite banks and can provide spectacular and unusual angles of the city's landmarks.

Another day could be spent visiting the twin islands of Gezira and Roda which provide more than a day's interest, entertainment and activity. The distance between the two islands could be covered by walking along the corniche but the islands are long. Taxis are

# Places of Interest On the Islands of Cairo

*Gezira*
**Aquarium**
Between Gabalayah and Hasan
Shari Streets on Gezira
Grotto and exhibition of sea life.

**Cairo Tower**
Southern tip of Gezira, south of 6
October Bridge
A viewing pylon dominating the
skyline rising to 180m (590ft).

**Cairo Exhibition Grounds**
North of Tahrir Bridge Road
Magnificent gardens and cultural
complex.

**Mohammed-Khalil Museum**
In the centre of the island
A storehouse of varied Egyptian
and European art.

**Mukhtar Museum**
On the tip of the island
Modern sculpture for comparison
of changing Egyptian styles.

**Museum of Egyptian Civilisation**
Situated in the exhibition grounds
off Tahrir Bridge Road
Exhibition centre for a panorama of
the people and their art.

**Parks**
Nile, Andelusian and Tahir.
Spectacular botanical wonderlands.

*Roda*
**Manisterli Palace**
Southernmost tip of island reached
by the Malik al-Saleh Bridge
Can be seen on a visit to the
ancient Nilometer, set in gardens
which are a botanist's delight.

**Manyal Palace and Museum**
Northern point of island
A wealth of foreign and Egyptian
artifacts housed in a museum with
architectural and botanical interest.

**Nilometer**
Tip of Roda Island, opposite Old
Cairo quarter
The device used for measuring the
rise of the Nile waters.

plentiful and are the best way to travel between the main sites. Great views can be had from the Cairo Tower and hours can be spent admiring the gardens and visiting the museums.

A day can easily be spent viewing the more important mosques of Cairo and one would definitely need transport to cover the distances between each site. Similarly one might choose to spend a complete half-day visiting a few selected mosques and the Museum of Islamic Art. Coptic sites in the city, including the Coptic Museum, might also take most of the day to see properly. It is certain that at least a half-day could be spent browsing in the world-famous Cairo Bazaar and souvenir hunters can lose themselves for hours among the stalls, the leatherworker's benches, antique souks and carpet vendor's pitches.

Just an hour or so driving around the streets of Cairo as a familiarisation excercise can be an exhilarating experience. The

*'City of a thousand spires'*

sights, sounds and aromas of bustling side streets and narrow alleyways combine to assail the senses. The magic of Cairo comes through after only a short time in the city and a small tour of acclimatisation soon allows Cairo to grow around as you begin to recognise landmarks and direction.

At night Cairo is a fairytale city, especially if viewed from alongside the reflective Nile. Lights sparkle in the river's mirror-like surface and the romantic can be truly transported as the velvet of a musky African night sinks its deep folds around the city. Nightlife in Cairo is unique and reminiscent of all those old movie clichés, fans slowly revolve on the ceilings of fly-blown bars, damask tablecloths are piled high in the city's cosmopolitan restaurants and dice roll in the casinos as belly-dancers tease the last of the hookah-puffing Cairo gentry. A tour of Cairo at night is an expedition into a mêlée of Eastern mysteries and delights. However, with all the expectation of visiting the city's sights, few travellers passing through Cairo have the time to burn the candle at both ends.

Many tour companies give their clients scarcely enough time to bustle through Cairo's Museum of Egyptian Antiquities and browse

*Cornerstone of empires*

through the main bazaar before embarking on set excursions out to Egypt's other major sights of interest. In order therefore, to appreciate the city which is the hub of Egypt, the independent traveller should schedule visits and certainly allow a few precious days to absorb the essentials that make up Cairo. In doing so, and by selecting some of the city's more fascinating attractions to explore, the visitor begins to understand the background behind not only the history of the country, its people and its architecture, but the cultural essence of Egypt which has pervaded this region for over 5,000 years.

## MUSEUMS

### Museum of Egyptian Antiquities

On the bank of the Nile, facing the lower tip of Gezira Island and at the end of the Ramesses Street, the museum is located on Midan el-

Tahrir (Liberty Square). Built at the turn of the century to house the collection of antiquities amassed by the Frenchman August Mariette over the latter half of the nineteenth century, the museum now contains the richest collection of archaeological artifacts in the world (over 16,000). The building, which is now being expanded, looks out over flyovers, the liberation monument and decorative gardens surrounding the square's fountain. The Nile Hilton is situated within a few minute's walk. In order to view the many exhibits properly, one should expect to make several visits to the museum whose collection comprises mainly of Graeco-Roman and Ancient Egyptian artifacts. Of all the numerous treasures contained in this imposing museum, none attracts visitors more than those found by Howard Carter and Lord Carnarvon in the tomb of King Tutankhamen during their 1922 expedition. These are to be found on the upper floor of the museum where the famous Mummy Room is also located. Pharaoh Cheops' mother's tomb furnishings, Roman coffins, gold jewellery, papyri, carved ornaments, statues of ivory and a display of typically Ancient Egyptian life, are also to be found on the same floor.

On the ground floor the museum exhibits the larger treasures of the Old, Middle, New and Late Kingdoms including stone sarcophagi, sphinx, immense statues, and a host of inscriptions, carvings and paintings. Antiquities from the Graeco-Roman and Coptic periods are also displayed in the ground floor galleries. The ground floor exhibits are arranged more or less in chronological order starting from the period of prehistory (3150BC), through to the period of the Ptolemys (332BC), in order to present the artifacts in context.

## Coptic Museum
On the same bank of the Nile as the Museum of Egyptian Antiquities, but opposite the southern tip of Roda Island in Old Cairo, the Coptic Museum has a fascinating collection of rare artifacts from one of the oldest Christian communities. These include funerary pieces, religious works, parchments and manuscripts, murals and craft items from the third century through medieval times almost to the present day. The papyrus codices known as the Nag Hammadi, are among the most important exhibits and date from the fourth century. The museum itself was founded early this century by Pasha Simaikah and stands within the walls of the Roman fortress of Babylon.

## Museum of Islamic Art
At the lower end of Port Said Street, on the crossroads known as Ahmed Mahir and next to the National Library the Museum of

# Places of Interest
# In and Around Central Cairo

**Abdin Palace**
Midan El-Gumhuriya
Nineteenth-century edifice of latter
day Egyptian rulers, magnificent
grounds.

**Aq-Sunqar Mosque**
In the El-Ahmar quarter, just below
the Citadel
Renowned for tiled dome.

**Art Gallery**
Midan El-Falaki
Testament to continuing art of the
Egyptian peoples.

**Bab Zuwaila**
Darb El-Ahmer Street
Ancient city gateway next to Sultan
Muayyad.

**Bazaar Quarter**
Near the crossroads of El-Azhar and
El-Muizz Din Allah Streets
Maze of hundreds of stalls, from
carpets to cosmetics!

**Bulaq Souk**
Cairo's local market for everyday
household goods.

**Citadel**
Set high on a hill to the south-east of
Cairo
Mohammed Ali Mosque, fortress and
ancient palace.

**Corniche**
This boulevard runs the length of the
city along the east bank of the River
Nile. Steamer cruises, Garden City
and hotels.

**El-Azhar Mosque**
End of El-Azhar Street
Early mosque with library and
columned courtyard.

**Ethnological Museum**
El Qasr El-Aini Street
Insight to background of the multi-
ethnic Egyptian peoples.

**Gayer Anderson Museum**
Next door to Ibn Tulun Mosque
Collection of typical household effects
from Mameluke period.

**Geological Museum**
Near city centre
Mineral information on resources of
past and future Egypt.

**Ibn Tulun Mosque**
Next to Gayer Anderson Museum
1,000 years old with special design.

**Midan el-Tahrir**
Modern Cairo. Government buildings,
gardens and fountain.

**Midan Ramesses**
Massive Ramesses statue and railway station.

**Museum of Egyptian Antiquities**
Bank of the Nile, facing lower point of
Gezira Island
Tutankhamen's treasures, mummies,
Greek artifacts and Roman antiqui-
ties.

**Museum of Islamic Art**
Lower end of Port Said Street
Largest collection of Islamic art and
artifacts in the world.

**St Mark's Cathedral**
Near Cairo's main railway station
Largest Christian church in Africa.

**Sultan Hassan Mosque**
End of El-Qa'la Street
Tallest minaret, stunning dome and
ceiling.

*The Citadel, begun in 1176 by Saladin*

Islamic Art was founded around 1880 by Khedive Ismail, but moved into the present building around the turn of the century. With over 80,000 exhibits this museum is thought to contain the largest collection of Islamic art in the world. Many of the treasures, pottery, glass and utensils of wood and metal came from Franz Pasha's collection. Exhibits dating from early Islamic Egypt, seventh century through to the nineteenth century, are exhibited in twenty-three galleries. Among its most treasured artifacts are an early fresco from El Fayyum of Adam and Eve, one of the earliest examples of printing ever found outside China and the forty-five wooden panels of St Barbara's icon-painted partitions.

The Egyptian Library is on the floor above the museum and contains almost 100,000 items from papyri of the sixth century to illuminated manuscripts from the *Koran* and books from around the world. A huge, handwritten *Koran* inscribed on antelope skin is a unique exhibit and the coin collection in the library, which was founded around the middle of the last century, is also of interest.

*Camel market
on the
outskirts of
Cairo*

*Cattle market
in a desert
village*

### Gayer Anderson Museum
Ask for the Ibn Tulun Mosque, south-east of the city centre. Right next door there are two ancient houses dating from the sixteenth and seventeenth centuries. This museum is also known as the Bayt al-Kritiliya, or Cretan Women's House. Anderson, an Englishman, in the 1920-30s, combined the two into a multi-storey exhibition centre housing a multitude of typical Arabic household effects dating from the Mameluke period onwards. An extension of the Museum of Islamic Art, a number of interesting *objets d'art* fill the corridors and galleries and the museum sports a classical *mishrabiya*, a carved wooden Islamic screen.

### House of Gamal al-Din
Situated behind Al-Muizz Street, this house is one of the finest surviving examples of aristocratic Ottoman sixteenth-century mansions in Cairo as many other examples have disappeared.

### House of Shuhaymi
Situated in the Darb Al-As district off Al-Gamaliya Street, this house is preserved as a jewel of Islamic architecture. Note the sixteenth-century courtyard, fountain and tiled wall on the upper floor.

### Mogamma al-Fenoun Centre of Arts
Located near the 26 July Bridge this former residence of Aisha Fahmy consists of two floors dedicated to exhibiting works of art by both Egyptian and European artists.

### Military Museum
Behind the Citadel, and just off the Saleh Salem Street to the southeast of the city, the Military Museum contains a spectacular collection of armour, weapons, uniforms and militaria. It is housed in Mohammed Ali's Harem Palace of 1827. Nearby is the Museum of Carriages where one can view a number of horse-drawn vehicles preserved from the palaces of Egypt's kings and some from early colonial days.

### Mukhtar Museum
Located on the very tip of Gezira Island this tiny museum commemorates the achievements of this famous Egyptian sculptor whose work has gained international acclaim.

### Museum of Modern Art
Across the El-Gala Bridge from Gezira Island to the west bank of the city, this important centre houses a collection which rates with those major modern art exhibitions around the world.

### Museum of Egyptian Civilisation
Part of the Gezira Museum on Gezira Island, the museum specialises in live performances showing the various Egyptian ways of life across the centuries. It also exhibits some of the artifacts from the Museum of Egyptian Antiquities and working models of Egyptian inventions and technology through the ages.

### Papyrus Institute
Situated on the Nile west bank near the 6 October Bridge, this institution is a study centre, containing the worlds largest collection of ancient papyrus scrolls.

## Mohammed-Khalil Museum
Almost central on Gezira Island this collection of artifacts and paintings, include some by Renoir, Degas, Monet, Rubens, Renoir and Van Gogh. It is housed in a 1927 building that was once the residence of a local *nabil*, an Egyptian notary.

## Manyal Palace Museum
On the northern point of Roda Island this museum complex consists of a reception palace, a private mosque, a hunting museum and one containing an assortment of Islamic furnishings. The palace was built during the nineteenth century by Mohammed Ali (see page 40).

## Agricultural Museum
Set in beautiful parklands and located in the western bank sector of Cairo, reached by one of the many bridges crossing Gezira Island, this museum and the Cotton Museum show clearly, by means of graphic exhibits, the importance of agriculture to the economy of Egypt.

## Cotton Museum
Situated at the end of 6 October Bridge this museum demonstrates the particular dependancy of the country on its cotton production and shows the development of the product in Egypt over the millennia.

## Postal Museum
Located in the head post office buildings near the centrally-located Midan Opera House and Ezbekiya Park, this exhibition of philatelic items is open every morning.

## Railway Museum
Part of the main railway station in the city centre, this impressive exhibition displays trains and carriages through the ages dating from the opening of Egypt's railway network in 1855. Among other exhibits is the private train of Said and other members of the Mohammed Ali dynasty.

## Carriage Museum
Located in the Bulaq area of the city this fascinating collection includes conveyances from the last century and earlier with carriages used by royalty and by colonial leaders.

## Transport Museum
This museum, on Gezira Island (near Cairo Tower), gives the visitor a rare insight into the various modes of transport used in the capital throughout the ages.

*The Museum of Egyptian Antiquities, Cairo*

Other museums to visit in Cairo include the Geological Museum near the city centre, the Ethnological Museum nearby, on the edge of the Garden City sector and the Police Museum in the Citadel. The Cairo Aquarium on Gezira Island exhibits fish typical of the Nile Valley and Delta. The National Zoo on the west bank, opposite Roda Island and in front of the university, contains animals from the African continent and the botanical gardens adjacent to the zoo houses trees, plants and flowers from Egypt and abroad.

## MONUMENTS

Wherever you go in the city centre you will see statues and stelae, obelisks and edifices which range in date from ancient to modern times. Most significant of these are the giant statue of Ramesses II in Midan Ramesses (Ramesses Square) dating from 1250BC; the 152m (499ft) high Cairo Tower built on Gezira Island in 1957; the statue of Ibrahim Pasha erected in the nineteenth century in Ezbekiya Park, (opposite the Midan Opera House in central Cairo) and the ancient Nilometer, on the tip of Roda Island, constructed to monitor the water level of the Nile and originally dating back to 861.

*'Tutankhamen's golden casket*

Although not monuments, the *babs*, or gates of the city are among the most impressive structures in Cairo. The seven main gates are as follows: the Byzantine-style Bab al-Futuh (Gate of Conquest) to the north-east, near the Al-Hakim Mosque; the Bab al-Nasr (Victory Gate) nearby and of similar age; Bab Zuwaila, built in 1092 as the south gate of Ancient Cairo; the huge tower of Bab el-Azab, opposite the Sultan Hassan Mosque; Bab el-Gedid, gateway to the Citadel, Bab el-Wastani (also in the Citadel) and the Bab el-Moqattam, under the Moqattam Tower in the Citadel. The last of the seven gates is the Bab el-Muzayyini (Gate of the Barbers), after the bracket entrance to the El Azhar Mosque which has its own gateways.

The *caravanserais*, or *wakalas* (inns) of early Cairo are also of interest as they were built for travelling merchants and had warehouses, camel or donkey stables on the ground level, a courtyard in the centre of the building and accommodation on the upper floors. Many have long since been pulled down but the prime example remaining include the Wakala of Qaytbey (Ousan) and the Wakala of Sultan al-Ghouri.

## PALACES

There are ten palaces in Cairo, all quite easy to reach from the city centre. Six of these are open to view or have gardens in which one can walk. These include the following:

### Abdin Palace (President's Palace)

Unmistakably dominating the Midan el-Gumhuriya and fronted by beautiful gardens and palm groves, this palace was built in the nineteenth century and was once the residence of King Farouk. It is now home of the Egyptian president.

### Manyal Palace

Located on the Geziret section of Roda Island and reached by crossing the Sayala Bridge at the lower end of Garden City, this palace faces the Nile Corniche. Now part hotel of the same name this complex, completed in 1926, is divided into six sections all open to the public and housing many interesting exhibits (see Manyal Palace Museum page 37). The tropical gardens are particularly attractive.

### Manisterli Palace

At the southernmost tip of Roda Island, and reached by the Malik al-Saleh Bridge along the Nile Corniche, this palace is usually seen on a visit to see the ancient Nilometer. The grounds are well laid out and contain a variety of interesting plants.

### Emir Taz Palace

Just around the corner from the famous Sultan Hassan Mosque, this palace has an imposing façade to hold the visitor's attention.

### Musafirkhane Palace

Behind the bazaar and near the Sayyidna el-Husein Mosque, this palace is tucked into a narrow street close to the Baibars Monastery and of passing interest.

### Gawharah Palace

Furthest from the city centre and inside the Citadel walls, this palace lies across the square from the Mohammed Ali Mosque. Built in 1814 but razed by fire in the 1970s, there is a museum in its restored remains.

### Othman Kathuda Palace

Located near the Citadel, part of this building dates from Mameluke times, around the mid-fourteenth century. The furnishings are of particular interest.

Other palaces in Cairo include the Er-Razzaz Palace near the Blue Mosque, the Qaitbay Palace near Bab Zuwaila, the Beshtak Palace opposite the Barquq Mosque and the remains of El Nasir Palace inside the Citadel.

## MOSQUES
With more than forty important mosques located throughout the city, Cairo's ancient places of worship are major attractions for the visitor. Mosques are not only centres of Islamic religion but they often house universities and libraries. There are several features to look for when viewing a mosque. Each usually has an impressive door or gateway, the minarets or spires and the *liwan*, which is the hall-like prayer room and is often supported by large columns. As water is necessary for washing before prayer, a fountain is sometimes provided in the courtyard and this can be surmounted by decorative, ancient wooden covers — the pulpit can also be old and intricately carved. Another feature is the *mihrab*, or prayer niche in the wall of the courtyard which directs the worshipper towards the holy city of Mecca. Lastly the dome is invariably richly adorned with painted tiles, mosaics, or carvings. You will note that no natural or living thing ever appears in the highly ornate decorations which sometimes include variations of the writings of the *Koran*. Decorations are stylised inscriptions or geometric patterns because the portrayal of living things is forbidden in the Islamic Sharia (Holy Law). It would be impossible to see all of Cairo's mosques in a short visit but ten are outstanding and warrant a brief description. Please remember that, on entering an Islamic place of worship, it is obligatory to remove one's shoes at the entrance. Women should check the local regulations regarding entry into some monuments.

### Mohammed Ali Mosque (Alabaster Mosque)
Probably the most visible of all Cairo's mosques from the city, this was built between 1830 and 1848 (the year before Ali died), and his tomb lies in the south-west corner. It was modelled on the Nur-el-Din Mosque in Istanbul with 'alabaster' covering its walls. The minarets which are remarkably slender, tower 84m (275ft) while the dome reaches 52m (170ft) above the courtyard. Located inside the walls of the Citadel, overlooking the city, it was completed in 1857 by Ali's descendent, Said.

### Sultan Mohammed Ibn Qalaun Mosque
Also inside the Citadel walls, this mosque is often known as the El-Nasir Mosque and took 17 years to build, being completed in AD1335. The Antiquity Department has attempted to restore its original glory, including the facing of the two Persian-Mongol style

*There are ten royal palaces in Cairo*

minarets. The variety of this mosque's columns illustrate the many influences on Egyptian architecture.

### Aq-Sunqar Mosque (Blue Mosque)
Down below the Citadel, to the north, this mosque was constructed by the Emir Aq-Sunqar Al-Nassari in 1347. Noted for the number of blue tiles casing its walls which were added in 1651, the mosque also contains a very rare marble pulpit.

### Sultan Muayyad Mosque (Red Mosque)
Next to the old city gate, Bab Zuwaila, and near the Museum of Islamic Art, this mosque (1410) is famed for its magnificent bronze gate and the painted ceiling of its sanctuary. The twin minarets of this mosque stand on the ancient city wall and were once used as the symbol of Cairo.

### Al-Aqmar Mosque (Grey Mosque)
Located behind Cairo's bazaar quarter, this mosque's façade was the first in Cairo to be built in stone, and is the oldest of its kind in the city, dating from 1125. It is one of the few remaining Fatimid edifices. The name means 'the moonlight' which captures the way the moon's light reflects off the mosque's stunning frontage.

### El-Azhar Mosque
Known as the 'most radiant' this first mosque of the Fatimid period was founded in 970 and houses an extensive library and a university. Entered by the Bab el-Muzayyini (Gate of Barbers) diagonally across El-Azhar Street from the bazaar quarter, the doorway to the main court dates from 1483. The prayer-niche to the right of the forecourt dates from 1309 and at least 100 of the impressive marble columns of the mosque's main *liwan* are from an even more ancient structure.

### Sultan Hassan Mosque
On El-Qa'la Street, this is one of the most beautiful of Cairo's mosques and was built in the mid-fourteenth century not just as a mosque but also a school and hospital. Mother-of-pearl decorates the dome which is unique in Egypt and gold embellishes the ceiling. The minaret in the south corner at 85m (279ft), is the tallest in the city.

### Al Rifai Mosque
In the shadow of the Citadel, at the end of El-Qa'la Street, this is a modern mosque and houses the tomb of the Khedive Ismail. Constructed in 1912, the body of the Iran's shah, Reza Pahlavi, who died in 1980, lies here.

## Ibn Tulun Mosque

This was the third mosque ever built in Egypt and lies adjacent to the Gayer Anderson Museum. It took 3 years to build and was finished in 879. The square design is modelled on the Muslim 'Holy of Holies' — the Kaabah at Mecca, and its gypsum wall coverings are important architecturally as is the minaret with its unique outside stairway.

## Amr Ibn Al-As Mosque

Located south of the city in Old Cairo (near the Mari Girges rail station) this was the first mosque in Egypt (and in Africa) built around 642. It was destroyed during the Crusades and rebuilt several times. A 900-year-old university is housed here.

Other mosques which are worth visiting include: the Maridarni Mosque, one of the largest in the city; the mosque of Al Hakim, completed in 1013 and restored 1980; the 1386 Barquqiya Mosque, now a university; Salih Talai Mosque, built as early as 1160; the Abu Bakr Ibn Muzhir Mosque and the Mameluke Sultan Barquq Mosque which has the typical *muqarnas*, or stalactite decorations to its portal. There are many mosques which have either been assimilated into more modern structures or are parts of mausoleums like the Sultan Qalaun's Mosque, begun in 1284, but now almost ruined and the funeral mosque of Al-Ishaqi, built in 1481. Other well-known religious edifices include Sultan Baybars I's mosque near Bab al-Futuh, with Crusader connections and used as a fort in Napoleon's occupation.

Mausoleums, often linked to places of worship, are also fascinating places to visit as their grandeur often nears that of the traditional mosques. For instance, the more significant mausoleums in the city of Cairo include those of Sultan al-Ghouri, which lies adjacent to his *wakala* and madrasah; that of Saiyididya Hussein and the Saleh Ayub Mausoleum. The eleventh-century Sultan Qalaum Mausoleum is quite spectacular and next door is the mausoleum of Al-Nasir Mohammed (1304).

However, out in the Necropolis, to each side of the Citadel and to the east and south of the Old Town walls, there are other mausoleums and mosques such as the Qait Bey, or Guiishi tombs. This area is known as the City of the Dead — ancient cemeteries inhabited by the overspill of Cairo's vast population. The region is divided into the Northern and Southern Cemeteries. Here, in the Northern Cemetery, there are the tombs of the Mamelukes and through the Gate of Qait Bey one can view the elaborate tombs of the Sultana Umm Anuk (1348), Princess Tolbey's tomb, the 1456 mausoleum of Barsbey al-

# Places of Interest On Cairo's West Bank

**Agricultural Museum**
End of 6 October Bridge
A collection of irrigation and farming exhibits.

**Cairo University**
Near the zoo and Botanical Gardens

**Camel Market**
New city of Imbaba
Truckloads of desert camels, sold and bought.

**Cotton Museum**
End of 6 October Bridge
Economical and agricultural interest in the production of cotton in Egypt.

**Museum of Modern Art**
End of El-Sad al-Ali Street
World important collection of art.

**National Circus**
Opposite northern end of Gezira Island on El Nil Street
Permanent circus site.

**National Zoo**
End of El-Gama'a Bridge
Vast park and zoo area including El-Urman Botanic Gardens.

**Papyrus Institute**
Opposite southern tip of Gezira Island. Contains the largest collection of ancient papyrus.

Bagasi, that of Amir Suliman, and Sultan Barquq's giant edifice constructed in 1400. In the Southern Cemetery are the tombs of Shagarat al-Durr constructed in 1250, that of Imam Al-Shafii, dating to 1211, an 1160 shrine to Sayyida Ruqayya and other tombs of the Abbasid caliphs. The caliph tombs date from the late fourteenth to the early sixteenth centuries. However, this Necropolis is a no-go area for individual travellers, and a reliable guide should be sought to enter this 'town within a cemetery'.

The main Saleh Salem Street runs past most of the famous mausoleums, tombs and funery mosques in this part of town and there are magnificent views of the city from the cliff-side motorway as it winds below the Mohammed Ali Fort on the Moqattam Hills. This road through the City of the Dead can be joined either near Roda Island on the Nile side embankment, by most of the main roads leading south-east, or by driving out along Al-Aazar Street past the mosque and Al-Azar University to the highway and then turning right, taking a tour around the city outskirts.

## MAUSOLEUMS, MOSQUES, MADRASAHS
## AND MARISTANS

Inside Cairo's city boundary, not including the Necropolis, there are
seven important mausoleums — domed tombs which are often a
place of pilgrimage and usually near a place of worship. Most
magnificent of these is the mausoleum of Qalaun in the Sultan
Barquq Qalaun Mosque. Built around 1290, this is said to be the most
splendid Arab building in the city. Other examples worth visiting are
those of Emir Salar and Sanjar, the Al-Sayyida Zeinab, Saleh Ayub,
Shagarat al-Durr and El-Ghuri Mausoleum. Many mausoleums can
be mistaken for mosques, so elaborate are the structures, as might be
the madrasahs. The mosque which the Sultan Hassan school belongs
to was built in the mid-fourteenth century and stands opposite the
Rifai Mosque in Qa'lah, or Mohammed Ali Street. This mosque is a
fine example of a Mameluke Islamic complex which includes a
mausoleum, madrasah with integral library and four *liwans* (open
halls), which lie to each side of the *sahn* (square courtyard). Each of
these has its *riwaq* (arcaded porch), a *fisuya* (fountain), in the main
courtyard; a *mirhab* (prayer niche) in the eastern *liwan* surrounded by
a *qibla*, or frame to the *mirhab*; a *minbar* (pulpit) can also be seen along
with a *dikka* (platform) where the imam acolytes stand; a *maqsura*, or
screened off area from where the caliph can worship in seclusion and
two minarets from which the muezzin broadcasts the beginning of
prayer to the faithful. Some mosques also have a *kuttab* (boys school),
adjacent and a *zawiya*, or small chapel attached.

The decorative features of the mosque are often immensely
ornate but adhering to geometric shapes and patterns as it is forbidden in Islam to portray any living thing in art. Mosaics are a popular
decoration, often incorporating calligraphic messages in minute
detail of alabaster, marble, plaster, glass, enamelled ceramics, onyx
and other exotic stones and often precious metal. A method of
decoration known as *ablaq*, or a banded stonework, was often employed in the embellishments around the arches in the mosques
façade or main gateway. Religious woodwork was often exquisitely
carved and the *mashrabiya*, or lattice screenwork around the *maqsuras*
are good examples of this. Inlaid, incised patterns and fretwork often
surround many features of the mosque, such as that around the
canopy of the *fisuya*. Even the lighting in mosques can be ornate such
as the *tannur* (chandelier), which often hangs from the ceiling of the
main *liwan*. Mosques are of two types, the *gami*, for ordinary commu-
nal prayers, and the *masgid*, for the more devout such as that of Sultan
Hassan. It is possible to date some mosques by the shape of their

*Cairo is a 'melting pot' of architectural styles*

minarets. Early mosques had no minarets but when they were adopted they all had little kiosks at the top for the muezzin to call prayer time from. Various features of minaret design were adopted over the centuries, like the addition of a dome, or the trend from a round, to a square, then to an octagonal shaft and back again to a round shaft. In early Mameluke times, as with the Sultan Hassan Mosque, the crescent moon symbol of Islam was generally added to the tip of minarets.

The Sultan Hassan Madrasah is opposite the Sayyidna al-Hussein Mosque, behind the Bazaar sector of Cairo. One of the greatest Bahri monuments with massive walls which facilitated its use as a fort both in the fourteenth and fifteenth centuries, the remaining minaret of the madrasah is Cairo's tallest and most impressive at 85m (279ft) high. Other madrasahs of note include that of Sultan Shaapen, El-Ghuri, Qani Bey, El-Gei those in the El-Azhar Mosque and the Sheikhu Madrasah.

The maristan is a hospital invariably attached to a mosque and often a school of medicine. A classic example is that in the mosque of Ibn Tulun, in the shadow of the Citadel. The hospital generally forms part of a walled complex which can contain schools, markets, baths, harems, and a number of houses.

## CHURCHES AND SYNAGOGUES

The churches of Cairo are mainly of the Coptic religion which, in English, means 'Egyptian Christian'. The foundation of this religion dates from 451 and today in Cairo there are around twenty major Coptic churches. About six of these deserve special mention as monuments which are of great interest. Primitive Coptic churches were generally concealed in the maze of doorways in Cairo's streets by provision of a small doorway entrance in an undecorated wall. Later, places of worship became more elaborate and things to look for in these churches are ancient frescoes, the colonnades which divide the nave, the altar, the throne, the usually richly-carved screens and religious paintings.

### Al-Muallaqa (St Mary's Church)

Usually referred to as 'The Hanging Church' as it appears to be suspended over the ruins of the two Roman fort towers at the Babylon site in Old Cairo, this church dates from the fourth century. Rebuilt in the ninth century there are interesting screens dividing the three chapels and many icons on the walls.

# Places of Interest In Cairo's Outskirts

**Abu Sarga**
Between two towers of Babylon, Old Cairo
Important for pilgrims, early murals and screens.

**Al-Matariyyah**
North-east of Cairo
Obelisk of the Sun Temple of Old Heliopolis.

**Al-Muallaqa**
Near Mar Girgis station, Old Cairo
Ancient Coptic church, fine screens.

**Amr Ibn Al-As Mosque**
Outskirts of Old Cairo
First mosque on African continent, important university.

**Ben Ezra Synagogue**
Old Cairo, alongside Babylon
Oldest Jewish place of worship in Egypt.

**Coptic Museum**
Old Cairo, opposite the southern tip of Roda Island
Fascinating treasury of early Christian life in Egypt.

**El Fustat**
South-east of Old Cairo
Earliest Arab settlement, excavations.

**Fort of Babylon**
Near Mar Girgis Station
Roman fortress complex, ancient towers.

**Necropolis**
South-east of Cairo
City of the Dead, interesting tombs and mausoleums.

**Sitt Barbara**
Beside Abu Sarga
Ancient carvings and artifacts.

## Mari Girges (St George's Church)

Also within Old Cairo just outside the Roman fortress, this church was founded in the seventh century and is renowned for its murals.

## Abu Sarga (St Sergius's Church)

Founded in the fourth century, this church is located at the end of the passage between the two Roman towers of Babylon and its crypt dates from the fifth century. Unusual in its architectural mixtures, its wooden screens are of importance as are the painted columns. As this church is associated with the Holy family's flight to Egypt, this monument has traditionally been a place of both Catholic and Orthodox pilgrimage.

## Sitt Barbara (St Barbara's Church)

Almost next door to Abu Sarga, the chapel here contains relics of St Barbara who was beaten to death by her father for her faith. The church dates from the fifth century and the wooden architraves around the columns are of interest as are the carved crosses.

*Cairo's forts date from AD30 to the present day*

### Coptic Cathedrals
Other Coptic churches in Old Cairo include the Al-Adra (Church of the Virgin) dating from the ninth century, St Peter, St Paul's, St Cyril and St John's. In Cairo there are two Coptic cathedrals. The Old Cathedral is located just off the Midan Ramesses, not far from the YMCA, near the city centre. The New Cathedral can be found at the far north-east end of Ramesses Street, further up than the Midan Ramesses in Abbasiya district.

Cairo has almost thirty synagogues. The most important is the Ben Ezra which is the oldest in Egypt (1115) and was built on a site, sold to the Jews, of a much earlier Church of the Archangel. Ben Ezra Synagogue is located inside the Old Cairo walls alongside Roman Babylon. Excavations in the courtyard have revealed a Roman archway here. Ben Ezra is the only functioning synagogue in Cairo today.

### FORTS

### Citadel Fortress
The structure dominating Cairo's skyline is the ancient Citadel, begun by Saladin in 1176. Originally the old wall was 1,200m

*There are souks or bazaars for every imaginable commodity in Cairo*

(1,320yd) in length and built of blocks from some small pyramids. After expansion over the centuries the wall is now double that length and incorporates three main gates. Inside the wall is the Military Museum and inside the Citadel itself is the Mohammed Ali Mosque (Alabaster Mosque) and the El-Nasir Mosque. The ruins of El-Nasir's Palace, the Bijou Palace of Mohammed Ali, the Moqattam Tower and Joseph's Well are further points of interest inside the extensive structure.

### Mohammed Ali Fort
High up in the Moqattam Hills, this military fort looks down on the Citadel and Cairo and is still in use. This area is therefore not usually on a visitor's itinerary but can be viewed from Saleh Salem Street.

### Fort of Babylon
Down in Old Cairo, next to Mar Girgis Station, the Ancient Roman battlements of Babylon were constructed around AD30 during Augustus Caesar's time on the older Persian site occupied some 2,500 years ago. Only the twin towers are left of the original structure and these were once a watergate entrance to the fort from the Nile. Recently a third tower to the fortress was discovered but not exca-

vated and archaeologists have also found a Roman arch, part of the early settlement of Old Cairo, in the courtyard of the Ben Ezra Synagogue. The Fortress of the Beacon, now the site of the Coptic Museum is located inside the Roman walls as is Al-Muallaqa.

## BAZAARS

Just as the El-Azhar Mosque has its trade gates, the bazaar sector of Cairo, at the end of El-Azhar highway and to each side of Muski, or Gohar el-Qait Street, has its many trade divisions. Famed throughout the world, Cairo's bazaar offers anything from jewellery to carpets, from copper and brass to spices and perfume, from tea and fruit juices to kebabs and sandwiches. The bazaar, or souk can provide practically anything and a day will not suffice to breathe in the aromas, absorb the colours or taste the tangs of the varied products on offer in this vast market place.

It is impossible, as with Cairo itself, to suggest any stringent tour or define a specific route for the visitor. The whole ambiance of Cairo's markets and bazaars are geared to aimless drifting through a wonderland of sights, sounds and smells. Cairo is the ancient trading centre which binds the goods of the West with those of the East. Ivory, slaves, animals, spices and exotic wares became the mainstay of Cairo's commerce over many centuries and today little has changed. Before haggling with the merchants and stall-holders of the market it is best to enquire from an old-hand, the sort of prices one might expect to pay. One can be pleasantly surprised by the bargains to be had if one is prepared to spend valuable time negotiating a price.

The *kasbah* is the local term for the city's main bazaar and it lies in the middle of what was the medieval city centre. The central part of the market dates from the fourteenth century and is known as the Kaln Al-Khalili. This section is noted for its copper, brass and textiles. Other markets include the Flea Market by the 26 July Bridge in the Bulaq area of the city opposite Gezira Island. Out near Imbaba Airport, on the outskirts of the west bank section of the city, the Camel Market makes a colourful and highly aromatic deviation from visiting Cairo's monuments and ancient buildings. Camels are brought here mainly from Sudan and many tribesmen still wear traditional garb. This is held only on Friday mornings and can be reached by bus from Ataba Square. Visiting this market gives an insight into the age-old tradition of Africa's nomadic traders who have been converging on the site with their livestock for centuries.

# The Outskirts of Cairo

Few visitors have time to see much of the suburbs of Cairo except maybe to make a cursory trip of the Necropolis. Here there is the opportunity to see the tombs of the caliphs, the tombs of the Mamelukes, Qait Bey's Mosque and the mosque of Imam el Shafii — all located on the south-east side of the city below the Moqattam Hills.

Driving into Cairo from the airport the early nineteenth-century town of **New Heliopolis** is bisected and its modern, spacious layout contrasts sharply with the cramped streets of the city. Old Heliopolis is almost devoid of antiquities as the site has been built over. This discourages visitors but, should one make the quarter-hour trip north-east of Cairo, a solitary obelisk is all that remains of this most ancient of Egyptian cities. In the village of **Al-Matariyya**, a short drive from Old Heliopolis, the Virgin's Tree, abounding with Biblical legends, is to be found outside the tiny village chapel.

The city of **Nasser**, south-west of New Heliopolis, contains the vast national stadium, sports facilities, exhibition halls and the tomb of the late President Sadat.

Just to the south-east of Old Cairo's suburbs are the ruins of **El Fustat**, the first Arab capital of Egypt. Historians are desperately trying to excavate the ancient site before buildings swamp the area. Although there is now little to see of El Fustat, one monument remains on the edge of Old Cairo in the shape of the Amr Ibn Al-As Mosque, dating back to the mid-sixth century. Treasures and artifacts from excavations at El Fustat can be seen in the Islamic Museum.

**Helwan**, a good half-hour drive south from Cairo, is a health resort and large holiday centre. There is little to see of particular interest in the town but the road provides pleasant views as it runs along the east bank of the Nile.

# 2
# MEMPHIS, SAQQARA, GIZA AND THE PYRAMIDS

It is the west bank of the Nile which has attracted visitors to this part of Egypt since time immemorial. Within easy striking distance of the capital the two major sites are the Giza plain and the further and larger location of Saqqara. Most tours heading for these monuments from Cairo's city centre cross Gezira Island and follow the embankment of the Nile, passing Roda Island on the left, or cut through the grounds of Cairo's National Zoo, to link with the Al Ahram highway in the Giza suburb. Here lies the dilemma, as this road heads directly out to the Giza monuments and the other forks off towards Memphis and Saqqara. However, the layout and chronology of the monuments on the edge of the Western Desert is important to understand as it can affect the way they are viewed. Saqqara is the oldest site and is best seen first as the structures there illustrate the development of pyramid geometry. An all-encompassing 2-day tour of the sites near Cairo, for example, will not start at the more famous sites in Giza, but at Memphis, 22km (14 miles) south of Giza.

In order to reach **Memphis** turn to the left as soon as you join the Al Ahram highway in the El Giza suburb of the city and the road follows both the railway on one side and the river on the left, through El-Hawamdiya town, past El-Badrshein, inland to the ancient capital. Although there is little to see here, the history of this site is captivating and dates back to the time of the first legendary king of Egypt, Menes, around 3000BC. Excavations are still continuing at Memphis but the two most important discoveries were found near the road leading to Saqqara. These are the colossal statues of Ramesses II — only one has been left here and that is the twin of the one in

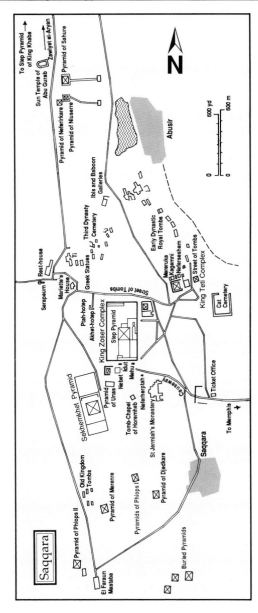

Ramesses Square in Cairo — and the Alabaster Sphinx which was also unearthed here. Both are more than 3,000 years old.

In the distance, to the west, a line of pyramids stretch across the horizon. The nearest of these to Memphis are the pyramids of **Saqqara**, the cemetery of Ancient Memphis. A ticket office to the Saqqara sites is located to the right of the road from Memphis (admission is LE3). Most impressive of the tombs is the **Step Pyramid** of King Zoser, dating around 3000BC. Part of the huge enclosure wall still exists and the entrance to the pyramid itself can be seen through a subterranean tunnel. The Great North Court and Great South Court are of particular interest. Special permission is needed to visit the inside of the tomb which is not lit and can be a claustrophobic 2-hour tour. Zoser's tomb design, the earliest of Egypt's pyramids, is based on the classical, low, platform-shaped mastaba which was the conventional tomb in use at that time. The six or seven stages of the pyramid suggest diminishing sizes of table-like mastaba piled on top of each other, so creating a revolutionary shape. The revered architect of this pyramid was also the first documented alchemist, astronomer and scientist in history, Imhotep, King Zoser's administrator. The **Pyramid of Unas**, which can be entered, has brilliantly decorated chambers and in the main vestibule (in 1881), archaeologists found the famous funerary 'Pyramid Texts'. In front of the south face of the Pyramid of Unas is the entrance to Egypt's deepest subterranean tombs, the **Persian Tombs** of the nobles Psamtik, Peleese and Zenhebu. Beyond the Unas pyramid is that of Zoser's successor, Sekhemkhet, whose step tomb remains unfinished.

Other sites within the Saqqara necropolis region are the numerous **mastabas**. In the Zoser complex are the mastabas of Princess Idut, Nebet, Mehu's mastaba and that of Neferherptah — (Tomb of Birds). Along the causeway are the tombs of Niankhkhnum and Khnumhotep. Further back towards the entrance are the ruins of the sixth-century Coptic monastery of St Jeremiah. The Tomb-Chapel of Horemheb lies behind the monastery.

Near the pyramid of King Teti, to the right as one enters the site from Memphis, are the mastaba tombs of Mereruka, Kagemni, Ankhmahor and Neferseshem. The first three contain delightful bas-relief frescoes which could lead them to be known as the 'Tombs of Hunting and Fishing'. Beyond Teti's tomb is the curious Cat Cemetery. The Street of Tombs and Queen Iput's mastaba run out from the same complex. A short walk to the east, passing the scattered Early Dynastic Royal Tombs, the Ibis and Baboon Galleries and the Third Dynasty cemetery. Far out to the left are the tombs Ptah-hotep and

# Places of Interest
# In Memphis and Saqqara

*Memphis*
On the west bank of the Nile 24km
(15 miles) south of Cairo

**Ramesses II Statue**
Near the road leading to Saqqara
Prone massive statue of the
Pharaoh.

**Alabaster Sphinx**
To left hand side of Saqqara road
Huge ancient, well-worn carving.

*Saqqara*
22km (14 miles) south of Cairo

**Step Pyramid**
Dominating Saqqara cemetery site
King Zoser's famous early pyrami-
dal tomb.

**Pyramid of Unas**
Located south of the Step Pyramid
Famed for hieroglyphic 'Pyramid
Texts'.

**Persian Tombs**
Front of south face of Pyramid of
Unas
Deepest tombs in Egypt.

**Serapeum**
On far west side of the Step Pyramid from the Saqqara site entrance
Subterranean burial caverns of
sacred bulls and tombs.

**St Jeremiah's Monastery**
Near entrance to the Saqqara site,
south of the Step Pyramid

Ruins of early Christian complex.

**Cat Cemetery**
Right hand side of road from
Saqqara to Step Pyramid
Burial grounds of animals and
birds.

**Sekhemkhet Pyramid**
South-west of Step Pyramid complex
One of a number of pyramid complexes at Saqqara, including those
of Teti and Unas.

**Mastabas**
South of King Zoser complex
Ptah-hotep, Akhet-hotep, Ti, Idut,
Nebet, Mehu and many other basic
early tombs.

**Mariette's House**
North-west of King Zoser complex
Early French archaeologist's base.

*Dahshur*
A short distance south of Saqqara

**Coloured Pyramids**
2km (1 mile) south of Saqqara
The White, Red and Black
Pyramids plus 'Bent' and 'Brick'
Pyramids.

*Abusir*
North-east of King Zoser complex

**Sun Temples**
A trio of pyramids plus two ruined
temples.

Akhet-hotep, crammed with carvings. Flagging visitors will be
relieved to learn that a rest-house has been built a little further on,
past the mid-nineteenth-century house of the archaeologist, Mariette. The **Serapeum** should not be missed as its strange contents

*Step Pyramid of King Zoser, Saqqara*

revealed twenty-four mummified bulls in separate coffins to startled archaeologists. These are known as the Apis Bulls, entombed in connection with the ancient's cult of bull-worship. There are also four important sarcophagi in the tomb's corridors. Nearby are a number of Greek statues and the mastaba of Ti with its depictions of everyday working life of the Old Kingdom.

Taking the road south, towards Saqqara proper, a number of pyramid complexes can be seen such as those of King Phiops I and Phiops II, the Pyramid of Merenre and those of Djed-kare, all dating from between 2500BC to 2184BC. Near Phiops II pyramid is the great mastaba of Faraun. If one can reach the furthest south group of pyramids at Dahshur, a good 15-minute trek by donkey or camel hired at the rest-house in Saqqara, some of the most striking pyramids of the region can be viewed. The five main tombs here include the Black Pyramid of Sesostris III; Sneferu's tomb, known as the Red Pyramid because of the colour of its blocks; White Pyramid of Amenemhet II, Amenemhet III's Southern Brick Pyramid and the Bent Pyramid, so called because of its irregular shape, with its adjacent little pyramid, causeway and temple.

Travelling back through Saqqara, past the Zoser site, one can visit the triple pyramids of Abusir although the full site contained fourteen tombs. Here the pyramids of Niuserre, Neferirkare and Sahure are complemented by Niuserre's Sun Temple a little further on at

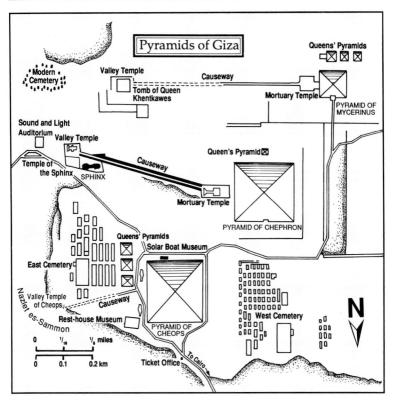

Pyramids of Giza

Queens' Pyramids

Modern
Cemetery

Valley Temple

Causeway

Tomb of Queen
Khentkawes

Mortuary Temple

PYRAMID OF
MYCERINUS

Sound and Light
Auditorium
Valley Temple

Temple of
the Sphinx    SPHINX

Causeway

Queen's Pyramid

Mortuary Temple

PYRAMID OF CHEPHRON

Queens' Pyramids

Solar Boat Museum

East Cemetery

Nazlet es-Sammon
Valley Temple
of Cheops

Causeway

Rest-house Museum

PYRAMID OF
CHEOPS

West Cemetery

N

0        1/16      1/8  miles

0        0.1       0.2 km

Ticket Office

To Cairo

Abu Gurab. There were said to be six temples at this site but only
those of Abu Gurab and Userkaph remain. Less than 15 minute's ride
further north, off the secondary road back to Giza, are the two last
pyramids in this region of the Nile's west bank. These monuments at
a site known as Zawiyet el-Aryan, are the Step Pyramid of King
Khaba and a Fourth Dynasty tomb known as the Northern Pyramid.
The six major sites, Memphis, Saqqara, Dahshur, Abusir, Abu Gurab
and Zawiyet el-Aryan, should provide an itinerary for a full day's
excursion.

# Giza

Reached by taking the same route as that across the capital to the Giza suburb, the Al Ahram road runs straight out to the desert's edge. Considered the major site, the monuments of Giza have captured the imagination across millennia, from Herodotus to the present day and probably for another 2,500 years. Erected by the rulers of the Fourth Dynasty of the Old Kingdom (2575BC to 2465BC), all that Giza seems to consist of is a long boulevard, rather like a 'sunset strip' with high-rise flats, hotels, restaurants and nightclubs. Past the Acadamey of Arts on the right, the straight road cuts across the narrow swathe of low fields and, as one nears the magical site of the pyramids, more modern hotels line the highway. After a 15-minute drive from Cairo's centre one is in the desert and confronted with the question of how to plan a days visit in Giza.

Early morning is the best time to arrive at the Giza pyramid site in order to take advantage of the coolness of the day and to allow enough time to see as much as possible. With only a day in which to see the sights this can be the longest and hardest day ever spent on an Egyptian visit — especially if you include the evening *son-et-lumière* show and remain to enjoy the sight of the monuments bathed in floodlight at night. There are twenty-five important features to the Giza necropolis complex. Each of the three main pyramids are integral structures which consist of a pyramid, a Mortuary Temple, a causeway linking the Mortuary Temple with a valley temple, smaller pyramids for the Pharaohs' queens and fields of mastaba tombs for officials and priests. Pits for 'solar boat' craft designs in traditional Nile galley style can also be seen. The dead Pharaoh was transported across the sky to the underworld in a 'solar boat'.

The pyramids here are those of the Kings Cheops, Chephron and Mycerinus. Immediately upon arrival a thousand postcards, pictures and films come to life and the two most prominent sites are instantly recognised as the Great Pyramid of Cheops and the Sphinx.

'Think, soldiers, from the summit of these pyramids, forty centuries look down upon you.' So spoke Napoleon to his troops at the Battle of the Pyramids in 1798. Two thousand years earlier, another military leader, Alexander the Great, had been similarly struck by these awesome structures. Today it is the turn of the visitor to gasp at the sheer size, power and majesty of these ancient royal tombs.

Known as the **Great Pyramid of Cheops** (Khufu) the tomb was created by the architect Hemiunu and is part of a complex which includes the rock tomb of the king's mother, Queen Hetepheres. This is the only tomb in the complex untouched by grave robbers who

# Places of Interest In Giza

**Pyramid of Cheops**
Dominating the Giza funerary site
Largest of Egypt's pyramids.
Entry permitted.

**Pyramid of Chephron**
South-west of Cheops Pyramid
Second tallest of the Giza trio of
pyramids.

**Pyramid of Mycerinus**
South-west corner of Giza site
Well-preserved and smaller of the
trio. Entry permitted.

**Sphinx**
South-east of Cheops pyramid
Famous Pharaoh-headed
'lion couchant' statue.

**Queens' Pyramids**
Located in various sites throughout
Giza complex

Seven small pyramids of queens
and princesses.

**Solar Boat Museum**
South side of Cheops pyramid
One of the ancient funerary boats
excavated and housed here.

**Mortuary Temples**
Located in various sites around
Giza complex
Remains of temples and
causeways.

**Cheops Papyrus Exhibition**
Near the Sphinx
Exhibition of papyrus and other
interesting artifacts.

**Dr Ragab's Papyrus Institute**
On El Nil Street
A fascinating collection of ancient
scrolls and souvenir shop.

desecrated the necropolis well before the year 2000BC. It contains
rich funerary treasures, an alabaster sarcophagus, but no mummy;
two more small pyramids for Cheop's favourite queen, Meritites and
a daughter, a royal cemetery of mastabas and two 'solar boats'. The
main pyramid now stands 137m (450ft) high but was originally 140m
(459ft) from base to summit. This pyramid is not, however, even half
the bulk of that at Cholula, Mexico. Originally clad in a coat of fine
Tura limestone, weathering and pilfering by various invaders has
eaten away at the covering which once smoothed the sides of the
great stone construction blocks. Each of the 2.3 million blocks weighs
an average of 2.5 tons. The outside blocks vary in size but most
measure more than two-thirds of the height of a man, making a climb
a marathon task. Special permission is needed for the arduous and
precarious climb to the stunning view from the pyramid's peak but
one can enter the tomb itself by means of an entrance in the north face
17m (56ft) above ground level. Little except the appreciation of the
pyramid's massive scale can be derived from the exploration of the
monument's heart — perhaps also an aching back because of the

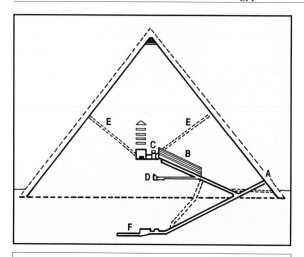

*The Great Pyramid of Cheops*
A Entrance
C King's Chamber
E Air Shafts
Height 137m (450ft)

B Grand Gallery
D Queen's Chamber
F Old Tomb Chamber

narrowness of the tunnels! Inside there can be seen the King's Chamber, Queen's Chamber, the Old Tomb Chamber and the Grand Gallery. The design of the interior is thought to have been changed three times and no relics have survived inside the tomb except an empty, massive, granite sarcophagus, too heavy for the grave robbers to remove. A museum to the east side of the pyramid houses exhibits from all the Giza sites.

The two royal barques known as the solar boats, were found alongside the pyramid in 1954, sealed with 700 tons of limestone. These contained the disassembled ships which had a place in the king's funerary rites. One cedar and sycamore vessel, reassembled after 4,500 years, is now housed in a special museum on the pyramid's south flank, although there are plans to put both boats on show on an alternative site. Near the Solar Boat Museum the rock tomb of Cheops' mother, Queen Hetepheres, has been excavated.

Looking taller but not as large as that of Cheops, the **Pyramid of Chephron** (Khafra) rises to 136m (447ft) in height, once 143m (469ft). Characteristically capped by its remaining limestone coating, the

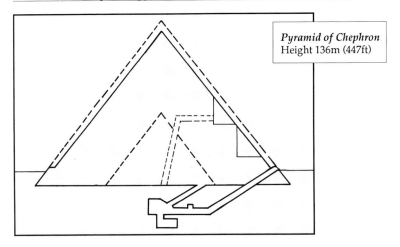

*Pyramid of Chephron*
Height 136m (447ft)

pyramid is built in a quarry but on higher ground than its mightier brother. A pyramid of the queen, a mortuary temple and a causeway connecting the pyramid with the Valley Temple and the monument of the Sphinx, with its own temple, complete the complex. Near the Valley Temple a tomb of Queen Khamerenebty I has been excavated as has a temple to Hauron-Haremakhet. The Valley Temple itself is exquisitely preserved and contains twenty-three statues of Chephron, but although the pyramid complex is the best preserved in the Giza site little, except an abandoned granite sarcophagus, has been found in the pyramid.

The enigmatic **Sphinx** holds the secret of one of the greatest historical mysteries in time. With the body of a lion and the head of a Pharaoh, said to be Chephron, the statue is 73m (239ft) in length and 20m (66ft) high. It is now thought that the original Sphinx could be much older than its assessed 4,500 years and many stories have been told of its mysterious powers. One such story relates to Tutmosis IV who is supposed to have dreamed of the Sphinx requesting the sand be cleared from its feet to show that it had not been abandoned. In return, the Sphinx promised the future Pharaoh a perfect kingdom. Waking from his slumbers in the shadow of the then 1,100-year-old monument, the prince had the paws of the Sphinx revealed and erected the 'Dream Stele', a granite obelisk in front of the statue. Tutmosis reigned for 10 years from 1412BC to 1402BC.

The third and smallest pyramid in the Giza area is the **Pyramid of Mycerinus** (Menkaure). Rising to just 62m (203ft) high the pyramid has a three attendant queens' pyramids, a mortuary temple and a causeway linking it with its Valley Temple, next to the Tomb of Queen Khentkaues. The main pyramid is open to the public but contains no relics as its sarcophagus, unlike those of Cheops and Chephron, was removed and now lies below the Atlantic waters off Spain. Unusually large blocks have been used to build the pyramid and its mortuary temple, some of which weigh up to 200 tons.

Near to the Sphinx is a museum called the **Cheops Papyrus Exhibition** where papyrus manufacture is demonstrated and souvenirs can be bought. The Sound and Light Auditorium is also located here, just in front of a modern-day cemetery. Throughout the Giza area it is possible to rent the ubiquitous camel for a souvenir photograph or for rides around the pyramid site.

The only other pyramid site is at Abu Roash, a 10-minute trip north of the Giza site. The two pyramids, that of Djedefre, son of Cheops, and his wife Henutsen, are the most northerly of all pyramids.

## PYRAMIDS

For more than 1,000 years the kings of the early Egyptian dynasties had pyramids constructed in which their mortal remains would be preserved in the afterlife. Even when the Pharaohs adopted a more secretive form of burial in rock tombs in the cliffs and mountains of Upper Egypt the pyramid shape was maintained in the architectural structure of their temples. The origin of this basic shape is simple in explanation and dates back thousands of years before the earliest Egyptian pyramidal-style tomb (the Step Pyramid of King Zoser), was erected. From Neolithic times in the Middle Eastern countries the traditional burial of leading figures was to entomb the body under a mastaba, literally a bench-shaped oblong above the actual burial pit. The first burials by this method exist no longer as soil displaced by the interment of the body, initially shaped into a flat platform. These eroded weeks after construction, leaving no trace on the surface. Today, in most Islamic countries, the tradition of the mastaba burial is maintained and the kings of Saudi Arabia are secretly interred in the desert in exactly the same way as their Neolithic ancestors.

Mastaba burials grew more sophisticated and the table-shaped platforms (measuring the conventional dimensions of the human form) were reinforced by constructing supportive edges of displaced soil to the oblong. At first the edging was sun-baked mud bricks, then bricks were used to fill the oblong creating a flat platform of bricks not much higher than the length of a hand. Erosion would crumble these structures within a very short period and, by early Egyptian times, more elaborate mastabas were being constructed. The earlier mastabas, when built any higher than one or two brick-widths, would fall apart if not staggered inwards, thus creating a flat-topped platform with sloping sides. Therefore the basis of a truncated pyramid, although oblong-based, was formed.

From primitive days when the mound of earth over a burial remained as the only evidence of a past life to later attempts at creating a more permanent memorial in the form of a brick platform, the earliest Egyptian dynasties began to shape their tombs. Eventually funerary priests developed a rude pyramid shape by constructing mastabas with sloping sides (to prevent deterioration) several bricks in height. Evolution and the desire for permanent tomb coverings, together with the trend to bury leading dignitaries in chambers in sarcophagi, necessitated much larger mastabas than the corpse-size norm. Rock or earth displaced by the excavation of burial chambers and heaped upon the gravesite required the construction of huge mastabas compared to the original simple design.

King Zoser's architect Imhotep, in around 2620BC, suggested that a series of diminishing-sized mastabas piled on top of each other would create a monument for the ruler which would last even longer than the flat structures of his predecessors. The fact that the Step Pyramid of Zoser at Saqqara stands firm after 4,600 years is testament to Imhotep's expertise. Each successive layer of the six stages of the pyramid-styled tomb is built at a height of about thirty dressed stone bricks and measures 60m (197ft) high. Still maintaining the tradition of underground interment, the king's burial chamber was excavated below the massive steps of the six mastabas. In the surrounding mastabas the rulers had extra chambers so that stored food and possessions could be transported into the afterlife with the soul, or *ka* of the deceased. In Zoser's tomb several chambers were created. As each mastaba layer was added the design changed and the size expanded. On the high plain of Saqqara, Zoser's monument could be seen for miles around and struck awe into any visitor to his empire until he eventually came to rest in its bowels in 2649BC.

It is easy to imagine how this gigantic structure was admired by King Zoser's successors who strove to emulate, if not improve on this original design. Many Pharaohs constructed their tombs along the lines of Zoser's pyramid until King Huni of the Third Dynasty constructed a huge, seven-tiered pyramid about 75 years after

Zoser's death. This is the famous **Collapsed Pyramid of Meidum**, much further south from the Saqqara site. The sides of each tall mastaba step were inclined inwards slightly like the early mastabas to ensure equilibrium and, at a later stage, the design was improved and altered. Eventually Sneferu, the first of the Fourth Dynasty Pharaohs, stylised the original design by expanding Huni's tomb around 2630BC. Upon completion the 'steps' of each side were infilled and the sides were rendered smooth and sloping, thus creating the original Egyptian pyramid. The pyramid at Meidum originally reached a height of 92m (302ft).

Famed beyond that of Huni and Sneferu are those later pyramids at the necropolis at Giza. The heap of rubble around the base of the Meidum pyramid indicates the dubious stability of Sneferu's work when improving the original core of the tomb. Around 2585BC the young Pharaoh Cheops was approached by his architect, Hemiunu. Aided by religious leaders, scientists, magicians and soothsayers, he told Cheops that he had devised a design for a far greater structure than that at Meidum which, he professed, would challenge efforts of competition by future generations. Four and a half thousand years later man has still not been able to reconstruct such a massive monument as the 'Horizon of Khufu' by the methods thought to

*The pyramids at Giza*

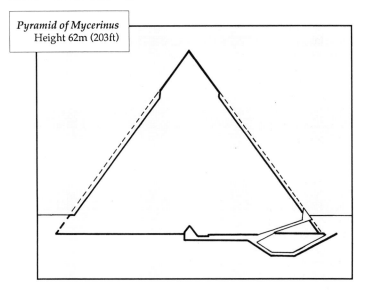

**Pyramid of Mycerinus**
Height 62m (203ft)

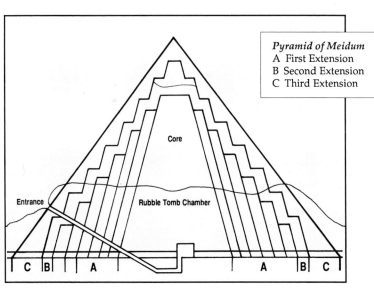

**Pyramid of Meidum**
A  First Extension
B  Second Extension
C  Third Extension

Core

Entrance

Rubble Tomb Chamber

C  B  A  A  B  C

have been employed in Ancient Egypt. So remarkable and revolutionary was the construction of the Great Pyramid of Cheops that experts and Egyptologists, since the historian Herodotus first penned his wonder of the tomb, still theorise on its origins. Such a controversial subject has drawn a mixture of amateur and expert individuals and bodies to put forward a bewildering variety of ideas about the pyramid's construction. From the days of Napoleon's Egyptian expeditions to futurists like science-fiction writers, the arguments have flown fast and furious.

Little has succeeded in altering the face of the monument. Analysing trapped air contemporary to the age of the pyramid's construction and attempts at X-raying and utilising modern mechanics to solve the mystery of how the edifice was built, have all produced near-negative results. Books, like Petrie's *Pyramids and Temples of Giza*, Daniken's *Chariots of the Gods*, Arthur C. Clarke's theories and Davidovits and Morris's *The Pyramids, An Enigma Solved*, have presented theories over more than 100 years which tend to make the question more complex. Did the builders use a forgotten formula better than that of cement to mould the massive blocks in situ, or did tens of thousands of slaves cut and haul the 2.5 million blocks, weighing from 2 to 70 tons apiece, without the wheel and without rollers? Why, also, did the architect deviate from the tradition by constructing burial chambers deep in the body of the pyramid instead of the simpler method of cutting burial rooms underground and building the monument on top?

Since 2,620BC, when King Zoser built the Step Pyramid at Saqqara almost 5,000 years of mysticism have added a supernatural element to the basic geometric shape. Cults have sprung up which revere the pyramid, worshipping the force that is supposed to be generated under a pyramid's apex. In modern times disciples of the cult have been known to build their houses in pyramidical style, even to place favoured articles and food under miniature pyramids in order that they might be endowed with the special properties this cult emanates from the shape itself. Some acolytes purport to gain powers and increase their intellectual abilities by remaining for long periods under pyramid-like constructions, even to the point of wearing pyramid-shaped hats. Their theories have certainly added a new dimension to the humble, flat mastaba from which the shape of Zoser's tomb grew!

## The Secret of the Sphinx's Smile?

There has always been a dilemma over the ultimate purposes of Giza's monuments especially on the riddle of the Sphinx. Chephron, the Pharaoh who had his pyramid built on a hill making it higher than that of his father Cheops, would certainly have known of the looting of his father's pyramid. It is possible that he considered that his own tomb would suffer a similar fate the moment he was interred, particularly as the structure, built during his lifetime, was so conspicuous. Having proof of the prevalent grave robbing in Saqqara, Chephron might have played one of the earliest deceptions in history by constructing the largest decoy on earth. Is it possible that Chephron built his own tomb without any intention of being buried in it?

Considering the fact that Cheops pyramid had been built in this isolated location (Giza) because his ancestor's tombs in Saqqara had been looted, Chephron may have sought a masterstroke which would elude subsequent pilferers. Cheops forerunners had chosen Giza as a sacred burial site because Menes, ancient king of *Om* (Heliopolis), had probably built his mastaba-shaped tomb here overlooking the Nile thus establishing a tradition and location. Is it possible that the remains of King Menes were buried under a great, flat, table-like grave and that this now forms the base of the Sphinx? It has been suggested many times that the base of the monument is very much older than its upper proportions. Earlier theories suggested that the entire Sphinx was carved from a solid outcrop of limestone. However, closer inspection reveals that the monument is constructed partly of man-made blocks cut at different times in history and then partly clad in man-made bricks. It is also thought that the edifice was once either painted in bright colours, or even, as some experts suggest, clad in a gold head-dress. Could Chephron have had an earlier mastaba structure embellished by adding the body of a lion, paws, and a head in his own likeness? What better place for Chephron to be interred than under an ancient tomb site, which had already been looted, and where no robbers would look? What better diversion than to build a decoy pyramid and even disguise the actual burial site as a guardian monument of statuesque importance — a grandiose memorial? Maybe it was a monument to scare off potential grave robbers. If this is a reason then it is of no surprise that the traditional name of the Sphinx is 'The Father of Terror' (abu'l-Hul).

The Pharaoh Tutmosis IV was told in a dream, 1,100 years after Chephron died, to clear the sand from the feet of the Sphinx. In

*The Sphinx standing guard over the pyramids at Giza*

return, he was promised the command of a rich and mighty king-dom. Was Tutmosis' dream related to the secret burial chamber of Chephron which might still lie beneath the Sphinx's feet?

### Sands of Time Running Out

Since Tutmosis had his dream while resting in the shade of the Sphinx's austere gaze, several million visitors have clambered over its paws and the tombs which he guards. Over those 3,300 years grave robbers have blasted into the pyramids, subsequent rulers have defaced the relics, soldiers have used the monuments as target practice and graffiti artists throughout the millennia have carved their messages in the ancient stones. Still these symbols of eternity appear almost unscathed by successions of desecration.

It is the hidden terrors of today's world which are now threaten-ing the 10,000 Egyptian monuments from the Mediterranean coast to the Sudanese border. Neither the utter mindlessness of those crea-tures who carve their names into the 3,000-year-old wall paintings in

Tutankhamen's tomb, nor the greed of the nineteenth- and twentieth-century 'archaeologists' have had the devastating effect that today's environment wreaks on Egypt's heritage. This is mostly noticable in Cairo city, Memphis, Saqqara and Giza, where monuments, which have withstood the ravages of nature and man for about 450 years are rapidly eroding.

*The awesome head of the Sphinx*

The Egyptian Antiquities Organisation say that all their ancient monuments are endangered but those at Giza are most at risk because of the proximity of roads and encroaching habitation which produces exhaust fumes and underground sewage pollution. In Helwan, across the river from the precious monuments of Memphis and Saqqara, the smog from its industrial complex can block out the sun as effectively as a Saharan sandstorm. Cars are now forbidden to drive up to the Giza pyramids but constant tourism and the rising water table underneath the Giza site threatens as much as air-bourne chemical pollution from Helwan.

Most noticable of the detrimental effects of toxic air on Egypt's monuments is the damage already affecting the Sphinx at Giza. The Sphinx's face is especially in danger of disintegrating. Once sporting a beard (now in the British Musem) the head-dress of the monument is crumbling and recently a large section fell from its place on the Sphinx's shoulder. Restoration work and preventative masonry designed to slow down the dangerous erosion is now being carried out on what is probably one of Egypt's most famous monuments.

In 1990, while repairing the sewer system in the village of Nazlet es-Samman, to the east of the Giza plateau, workers uncovered the long-lost remains of the **Valley Temple of Cheops**. Badly eroded by the rising water table it is being restored and will feature along with the famous Giza monuments.

# 3

# *THE NILE DELTA*

I n geographical terms, Lower Egypt can properly be described as the land encompassed by the Nile Delta triangle formed between Cairo and Alexandria on the west coast and Port Said to the east, at the head of the Suez Canal. This is an area of more than 18,500sq km (7,000sq miles) and is North Africa's most fertile land.

Because the region is blessed by such a rich alluvial deposit, this part of the country is the 'bread basket' of Egypt. By tradition, over millennia, the valuable silt which the Nile waters deposited across the Delta provided a deep layer of soil which promoted a vast agricultural economy. Today however, as the precious silt is now deposited behind the Aswan High Dam, some 1,500 km (930 miles) upstream from Cairo, erosion threatens the rich alluvial layer. Infiltration of saline water from the coast, because of the reduction in the volume of Nile water, has also affected crops in the Delta. The 'Gift of the Nile' which Herodotus wrote of in 450BC, is being eroded and fields of various crops are now showing the detrimental effect of the High Dam's strangle hold almost 2,500 years after the great historian's words.

Flat and inundated by a maze of waterways, irrigation channels, canals and crossed by at least two major arms of the River Nile , the Delta supports the majority of Egypt's vast population. Water dominates the life of the productive Delta and the Delta barrages, many erected in the early nineteenth century to divert the Nile into irrigation canals, carry water-bourne traffic. Agricultural workers, fishermen and traders on camel, donkey and in the felucca give the green landscape a Biblical air. Much of the region is papyrus swamp bisected by numerous waterways and broad fields, criss-crossed by irrigation channels. Many thousands of small towns and villages are located along the waterways and can be identified from miles away across the flat terrain by their mosque spires and inevitable clump of date palm trees which provide shade and food. The houses, mosques, schools and characteristic dovecotes of this area are constructed of Nilotic mud mixed with whatever stones are available naturally, and some rocks and stones which are often recovered from earlier sites of habitation. Mosques and their spires in this region are often whitewashed or painted in attractive pastel shades.

The primitive methods of irrigation are also a part of the typical Delta landscape and three examples include the *shaduf*, where water is drawn from the source by a leather bucket attached to a manually operated, counterbalanced wooden derrick and swung across to the irrigation ditch by hand; *saqiyas*, a vertical waterwheel of buckets geared to a horizontal cog-wheel turned either by camel, cow, bullock, buffalo or donkey, and which raises water continuously from source to irrigation gully as the beast circles the drive wheel and the *tanbur* or famous Archimedes Screw — a long, tubular device with a spiral internal compartment which, when turned by a hand-operated lever, draws water from one end of the tube, depositing it in the irrigation channel. Very early agricultural implements are also employed. Most of the small villages which dot the low, flat country-side throughout Egypt have a similar lifestyle to that of Biblical times employing early agricultural implements like the flail (an Ancient Egyptian symbol of royalty, together with the crook of the shep-herd). However recently there has been some modernisation in the form of mechanical water pumps and tractors.

Several large towns are located on the waterways of the Delta. **Damanhur** (Hermopolis, Parva, City of Horus) on the west side, is a typical example of a town which once was a provincial capital of Ancient Egypt. It is now a major cotton port, built over the silt which covers the once powerful city. **El Mahalla el-Kubra** lies almost central in the Delta and, to the east are the towns of **El Mansura**, an important commercial and industrial centre, and **Zagazig** (Tel Basta — Ancient Bubastis), another cotton and grain centre. At Zagazig the remains of a temple to the cat goddess and an underground cat cemetery can be seen. The Uragi Museum here houses artifacts  recovered from archaeological digs on the site. Many other sites of antiquity have been discovered in the Delta. Among these are Buto; San el-Haga (Ancient Sais) from which many early Egyptian statues  have been dispersed to museums around the world; Hathrib once the old city of Athribis where a large cache of treasure was discov-ered recently; Tel el-Rub (Ancient Mendes) and Tel el-Tmei (Ancient

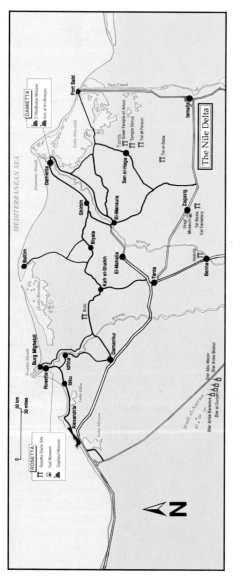

Thmuis), Tel el-Daba, Tel Faraun (Pharaoh's Hill), Daphnae, Kom Tinnis and Tanis, an important Tanite (Twenty-first Dynasty) site.

## TANIS

Tanis is a prime example of the importance of sites in this region. This was the capital of the Pharaohs who reigned after the New Kingdom period (1000BC) — the Twenty-first and Twenty-second Dynasties. The site was initially excavated during the nineteenth century and finds have included the Great Temple of Amun with its sacred lake, Royal Necropolis, the small Temple of Horus together with obelisks and colossal statues. The royal burials include that of King Psusennes I (Twenty-first Dynasty) whose tomb treasures of gold masks, silver sarcophagus and jewellery are now displayed in the Museum of Egyptian Antiquities in Cairo. Six tombs have been unearthed and the Royal Necropolis and that of Osorkon III are popular attractions. Outside the boundary wall of the Temple of Amun, a Syrian temple to the goddess Anat was discovered.

*A traditional Delta village from the air*

## ROSETTA

On the coast and the periphery of the giant Delta are towns and old  sites more likely to be visited by the casual traveller. Much of the coastal region of the Delta is covered by salty lagoons, great sand bars and is practically inaccessible, but to the west side is a town which has given its name to one of the most remarkable discoveries in the history of Egyptology. Rosetta (Canopus or Rashid), the most important Egyptian port on the Mediterranean coast, was founded in the first millennium AD and is still a major port. Just 64km (40 miles) east of Alexandria, Rosetta is now famous for the discovery — during Napoleon's 1799 restoration of Fort Rashid — of the stone which assisted French historian Champollion to decipher the language of Ancient Egypt. Engraved on a black slab, now in the British Museum, are inscriptions in three languages; demotic Egyptian, Greek and Egyptian hieroglyphs — key to the secret of the mysterious script of the Pharaohs. Little can now be seen of the fort where the stone was recovered, just outside the town.

As Rosetta was once a rich trading centre it is also famed for the number of well-preserved monuments of a different age, its historic grand houses including those gems of early seventeenth-century Egyptian architecture such as El Fatairi's House and the Arab Keli Museum which is preserved because of its finely carved woodwork. The design of both the houses and important mosques in and around Rosetta comply to a typical Delta style. Most impressive of the town's mosques is the double mosque of Zaghloul, founded around 1600, with its imaginative perspectives created by 300 columns. By the river, recognisable by its towering minaret, is the Mohammed al-Abbasi Mosque which dates to 1809 and, back in the town, the decorative façade of the Al Amaciali mansion is of the same period. Also not to be missed in Rosetta are the colourful bazaar stalls which mirror the continued prosperity of the town at the head of the Nile.

## DAMIETTA

The twin town to Rosetta lies 193km (120 miles) to the east. Damietta (Tamiati), lies on the other arm of the River Nile also at the point where it flows into the Mediterranean. Also like Rosetta, Damietta is an important commercial town. Lying between the river and a great lagoon, this port played a fascinating role during the Crusades in the early thirteenth century. Damietta also has many interesting old houses with typical Delta style ornamentation, dating from the times of past prosperity and its several unusual mosques are worth visiting. The town has a long reputation as a cultural centre as the El Madbuliya Mosque and school was built in 1475 — the Amr el-As Mosque is said to be even older. There is also a university in the town. Rosetta and Damietta are Egypt's most northerly towns and these are also the names given to the twin arms of the Nile. At one time there were seven branches of the river. **Port Said**, south-east of

# Places of Interest In the Nile Delta

**Damanhur**
About 32km (20 miles) south-east of Alexandria
Important trading port with long history.

**Damietta**
193km (120 miles) east of Rosetta
Crusader history and town with interesting architecture of El Madbuliya Mosque and Amr el-As Mosque.

**Lake Manzalik**
In north-east corner of the Delta 380km (237 miles) from Cairo.
The most famous lake in the Delta region.

**Rosetta**
64km (40 miles) east of Alexandria
Site of 'Rosetta Stone', ancient port, Keli Museum and Zaghloul Mosque.

**Tanis**
Near San el-Haga
Great Temple of Amun, Temple of Horus, and Royal Necropolis.

**Zagazig**
About 65km (40 miles) north of Cairo
Ancient site of Tel Basta (Bubastis). Remains of temple, underground cat cemetery and Uragi Museum.

Damietta is the same distance from the town as Alexandria is from Rosetta. The symmetry of this phenomenon, with the four towns equally distanced on the triangle of the Delta, forms a perfectly balanced inverted pyramid when linked by an imaginary line between each of the towns with Cairo at its apex, — a tantalising significance!

Lower Egypt with its rich, agricultural Nile Delta, faces the Mediterranean Sea and is bounded on both sides by hostile seas of a different nature. The great Eastern Desert borders the Nile Delta on a line from Cairo to the Suez Canal and the vast Western Desert threatens the Delta on a line stretching from Cairo to the famous port of Alexandria. There are good road and rail links from Cairo to Ismailia and Port Said on the Suez Canal. Likewise there are excellent services between the capital and Alexandria. Many international cruise ships passengers see part of Egypt by using the Suez Canal and connecting Bitter Lakes between Port Said and the Suez, on the Gulf of Suez arm of the Red Sea. Hundreds of cruise liners also include Alexandria as an important stop-over on Mediterranean cruises.

## WADI EL-NATRUN
The 'Wadi of Natron' is a centre of Christian monastic communities located about halfway (90km, 56 miles) between Cairo and Alexandria, to the west of the Route 11 highway. This was the early Roman

## Places of Interest In Wadi el-Natrun

These monasteries are all located on the west side of the Cairo to Alexandria road, after the modern Sadat city, about 100km (62 miles) north-west of Cairo.

**Dier Abu Maqar**
The largest and most important monastery in the wadi. Fine frescoes.

**Dier al-Suryan**
Two excellently preserved churches and many icons.

**Dier Anba Baramus**
Smallest monastery of the four, many ancient artifacts and relics.

**Dier Anba Bishoi**
The only monastery of the four here to be open to the public.

city of Scythiaca and monasteries and hermitages grew up here from the fourth century. Nestling below sea level, this ancient group of monasteries (once totalling more than fifty) is now the seat of the Coptic Pope who resides in exile from Cairo in the largest monastery, Dier Abu Maqar. There are four monasteries still active in the long valley which is strung with salt lakes from which it gets its name.

**Dier Abu Maqar** (St Makarios) one of the earliest has interesting frescoes and is the nearest to Cairo although reached at the southern end of a road from the main highway which passes by the **Dier Anba Bishoi** monastery. This monastery was founded at the end of the fourth century and is the only one of the four open to the public and with permission from the Patriarch in Alexandria. The unusual gateway of the Dier Anba Bishoi monastery is surmounted by a drawbridge which rests on the roof of the main entrance and allows admission into the first storey of the monastery. **Dier al-Suryan** monastery, located near to Dier Anba Bishoi dates from about the sixth century and was purchased 200 years later by a Syrian known as Tekrit. Its main features are its well-preserved buildings, thought to be designed on the basic outline of Noah's Ark, and an exemplary iconostasis in the Church of the Virgin. The smallest monastery is the furthest from the Cairo-Alexandria road and is the **Dier Anba Baramus** (Virgin Mary Monastery). Also possessing a fine iconostasis in the Church of St Mary which dates back to around 370 and the time of the Emperor Valentine, later St Valentine. Relics of St Moses and St Isidora are kept here and carved panels in the main doorway date from the eleventh century.

Monasteries in the Wadi el-Natrun are built with massive ramparts and walls often 12m (39ft) high and more than 3m (10ft) in

*A distinct boundary delineates the fertile land of the Delta from the arid desert*

*Barge transport on the Nile near the barrage*

thickness. Inside the walls was built a keep, fortress (qasr), usually with a drawbridge; courtyards, gardens, cells for the monks, chapels and several churches. The Coptic church is generally divided into three parts consisting of a sanctuary (haikal), a choir and a two-section nave. The haikal is divided by a wooden screen, often carved or richly painted which forms a curtain in front of the altar. Sometimes used in foot-washing ceremonies like that at the Dier Anba Bishoi monsastery, some churches will have a foot bath (lakan). Exquisite icons are often a particular feature of Coptic monasteries.

---

## THE RIVER NILE

'Egypt is the Gift of the Nile', wrote Herodotus in 465BC, and the lotus flower shape of Egypt's benefactor still stands testimony to the Ancient Greek historian's observation.

The world's longest river flows 6,695km (4,150 miles) from its source in Lake Victoria to the shores of the Mediterranean Sea. The Nile is unusual in that it runs northwards from the equator, across the Tropic of Cancer to an estuary which is almost in Europe. The Nile comprises several major river systems long before the main stream enters Egypt to become a single river; Victoria Nile, the Bahr el-Jebel (Somerset River); Bahr el-Abiad (White Nile) which is joined by the Bahr el-Azrak (Blue Nile) and the Atbara (Black Nile). Four cataracts drop the Nile through gorges encircling the Nubian desert, the third of which is now submerged beneath the waters of Lake Nubia. The Sudan (Egypts border) runs across the waters of Lake Nubia just north of the second cataract near Wadi Halfa. This line almost follows the line of the Tropic of Cancer. Linking Lake Nubia with the artificially created Lake Nasser, is the Sadat Canal. Lake Nasser was formed when the Aswan High Dam was opened in 1970. The fourth cataract became submerged the following year when the dam was completed. The 3,600m (11,808ft) span of the Aswan High Dam, and the 1960s hydro-electric dam together hold back 5,180sq km (2,000sq miles) of valley water. From here the Nile wanders through granite islands smoothed by the force of flood waters. At this point the river is only around 90m (300ft) above sea level but its great build up of water drives it northwards another 1,100km (700 miles) to the Mediterranean Sea.

The Nile is littered with islets along its length from the great loop at Kena to its exit into the sea, but once it was much wider than today's average width of just over 400m ($1/4$ mile). The river's valley is wide and comparatively straight after El-Minija, making its way through cultivated lowlands, alluvial-rich water margins and reed beds towards Cairo, the great Delta and then the sea. A short distance before the Nile begins to divide at its Delta into numerous tributaries, an offshoot — like a stalk from the main stem of the lotus-like river — forms the basin of the Fayyum, and Birket Qarun, an expansive lake in the large, fertile area of the Fayyum, supports a productive agricultural community. The river's silty flood plains once extended out into the desert from their July flooding river banks. Today they are deprived of their annual replenishment of soil and are gradually contracting since the Aswan High Dam retains much of the rich alluvia. The fertile strip which runs down each side of the Nile from Edfu — just below the dam to the vast Delta — once held the secret to Egypt's riches. This abundance of arable soil which was regularly washed by the Nile's fresh waters, gave the country a constantly replenished agricultural region amounting to an area the size of England. However, vast deserts to the east and west constantly threatened to encroach on this valuable asset. Now the valley plains have diminished in width and fertility as the amount of water and silt filling the irrigation channels and renewing the land's richness becomes more restricted. A certain amount of the water, which flows all the way from the equator to the Mediterranean, evaporates from the wide expanse of Lake Nasser but the water that does flow down through the dam's outlets contains little of the silt and nutriments which is needed to maintain the quality of the soil essential for adequate cultivation along the river's banks.

To add to this erosion of resources, many of the younger farmers are giving up their living on the land because of the diminishing supply of organically rich water to their land which is now held back by the dams, making it increasingly difficult to raise crops. In growing numbers these land workers, which make up an eighth of Egypt's population, are heading into the towns and cities in search of alternative work. The phenomenon of Egypt's arable land contracting with the reduction of Nile waters can best be seen in modern satellite photographs of the Nile's watercourse. These show an almost 50 per cent reduction in cultivated land each side of the river over the past century, although much of this has been due to the attitude of farmers who are increasingly abandoning their land to the desert's ravages in favour of more lucrative work in the metropolis. The faint outlines of fields and arable plots, once productive in centuries gone by, show up much further into the desert than the present line of cultivation.

The effects of almost 100 years of damming the Nile floods has made an impact as far north as its great Delta. Here, insufficient fresh water from the river has resulted in the salty waters of the Mediterranean encroaching on the fertile Delta. There is no single outlet of the Nile into the sea through this vast area of fields and marshes. The Delta forms a huge triangle of fertile flatlands and great lagoons from Alexandria in the west to Ismalia in the east, and reaching as far south as Cairo. Like fingers of a giant hand or veins in the opening lotus flower, the river forks into a hundred waterways. Shoreline lakes like Idku, Burullus and Manzalik are sanctuaries for migratory birds and create bays and mudflats from the Rosetta Mouth to the Damietta Mouth. Action to improve the irrigation further upstream has deprived the Delta region of water and silt and both man-made and saline pollution is encroaching on the fertile area, undermining the ecological balance of this rich and varied region. Much of Egypt's population live and derive their livelihood from the Delta, the oasis of the Fayyum which derives much of its water from the Nile, and the 10km (6 mile) wide fertile strip along the river banks. However, the Fayyum, and its large lake, is not the only oasis which supports cultivatable land. In the Western Desert there are three main oases; Bahariya, to the north, the Kharga Oasis in the south, and the Dakhla Oasis out towards the Libyan border. All three desert oases, and the Fayyum, have gradually declined in production since ancient times but the most noticeable shrinkage of cultivatable land is that which is part of the Nile waterway system. Authorities are now making efforts to correct the imbalance created by the long-term effects of the dam and pollution to their rich agricultural resource.

The river however, still provides work for the majority of Egypt's people and agriculture remains the mainstay of the Egyptian economy with rice, cotton, wheat, maize, sugar cane, barley, beans lentils, millet and onions making up the major crops. Large fields of these crops can be seen from the many steamers which carry passengers from Aswan to Cairo and the Mediterranean coast. The people who work alongside this great river and ply its waters in a variety of craft are known as the Fellahin. These riverside folk are at home either on land or on the wide Nilotic waters. On some stretches of the river the visitor will see all manner of water-borne transport; from an inflated buffalo skin propelled by paddle (like a giant rubber dinghy) to the tall masted, elegant felluccas, the graceful Nile dhows or the more unusual *dahabiyas* — a name once used for the gilded barges of Egypt's Islamic rulers. Whether paddled, sailed or engine-driven, the riverboats are working boats, employed as ferries, fishing craft, long distance haulage containers or tourist pleasure boats. Every-

*Many Nile feluccas now carry sightseers instead of cargo*

thing has its purpose either on land or on the river and a variety of implements have been devised over the centuries for use both on land or water and for use between the river and the fields. Camel, oxen, donkey or a combination of two will often be seen ploughing the fields with tools identical to those depicted in carvings on tomb walls of thousands of years ago. The Fellahin's methods of cultivation are still generally as primitive as they were in Ancient Egyptian times although mechanisation is slowly overtaking some of the more obscure implements and irrigation devices. However, the early mechanics used to extract the Nile's precious 'lifeblood' are as effective as they need be and irrigating the riverside fields provides work for a large percentage of Egypt's population. Most celebrated among the methods of drawing water is the *tanbur*, or Archimedes' screw, a hollow spiral placed slantingly in the water and revolved to raise water. The *shaduf* is a counterbalanced bucket on a long, turning pole, often seen worked by two men along the riverbanks. The large waterwheels, a common sight on most canals and waterways and consisting of several buckets turned by a donkey, ox or sometimes by a camel, are known as *saqiyas*. Finally, in competition to the tried and tested methods of irrigation used on the Nile for millennia the long, snaking hoses seen emerging from the waterside are connected to recently installed, mechanical pumping units now placed at regular points along the river. Today, Herodotus' 'Gift' is moving with the technology of modern times!

# 4
# *ALEXANDRIA*
# *AND THE NORTH-WEST*

The part of Egypt's coastline between the Nile Delta and Alexandria has a fascinating history which dates back to ancient times. This seaboard was one of the most strategic areas in the country as it faced the Mediterranean countries of empire-builders such as Greece and Italy. Greek triremes, Roman quadriremes, quinqueremes from Assyria and Phoenecian galleys were seen off this coast and its history of sea warfare has made this part of Egypt famous.

Between Rosetta and Alexandria lies the seaside resort of **Abukir**, more famous for its past than its present attractions of seafood and sandy beaches. On 1 August 1798 Admiral Lord Nelson brought the English fleet into engagement with the French defending Abukir Bay. Napoleon's ships were routed in a 2-day battle commonly known as the 'Battle of the Nile'. Still lying on the seabed, the ships of the French navy are destined to be raised soon by a recently implemented project. A year after this great sea battle, with Napoleon as commander, a huge Turkish landing force was defeated in Abukir by the French. In 1801, prompting the French withdrawal from Egyptian occupation, Sir Ralph Abercrombie led the English on a final victory over Napoleon's forces. Few ancient sites exist in the small town of Abukir but just a short walk south-west takes the visitor to the remains of what was once the majestic Temple of Serapis erected during Ptolemaic times in the now ruined city of **Kanopus**. Linked with the Egyptian God Aphis and connected with Π dark underworld perversions, this city once dominated a major outlet of the Nile. Here also can be seen the original location of Fort Tewfikieh and the site where several monuments to Ramesses II were excavated. Back in Abukir, with its gaily painted fishing boats bobbing in the bay, eucalyptus trees shading the towns narrow streets and its excellent fish restaurants, there is little to remind one of the past glory of this ancient centre. Other sites in Abukir are the  El Saba Fort on the coast, north of the main road and opposite the railway station. Another fort, El Rami, stands east of the town on Abukir Bay itself. There is one hotel here, the Abukir Hotel.

Visible from the eastern outskirts of Alexandria, Abukir stands out on a point north of Ma'muora, a suburb of the famous city. **El Ma'muora Beach** is the furthest east of Alexandria's fourteen famous resort beaches. It is the golden sands of this part of Egypt's Mediterranean coast which attract thousands of Cairo's holiday-makers to vacation here. Alexandria's many hotels and beach complexes accommodate the annual influx of visitors to this, Egypt's second most important city. Trainloads of holidaymakers either stream to the beaches off the excellent express train service, pack the bus service from the city's international airport, or arrive by road from the capital. There are two routes from Cairo; desert, via Giza, or through the Delta on the north road, about 225km (140 miles). Few bother to stay aboard the train as far as the main station in the city centre as the four top hotels, the Ma'moura (in Ma'moura Palace), the Alexandria Sheraton, the Palestine and El Salamlek (in the Montazah Pavilion) are located to the east of the city around Montazah.

Lying 16km (10 miles) from the ports of Alexandria, **El-Montazah** is famous for its highly ornate, royal palace. Verracci, an Italian architect, created this neo-Byzantine edifice in its beautiful gardens for Khedive Abbas II. This became one of King Farouk's palaces and is the site of his abdication in 1952. The building is undergoing one of its many alterations and is therefore not open to the general public. However, visitors are missing little save the vast frescoes on its cathedral-like walls and grand chandeliers. The Montazah Palace is best viewed from the outside. Montazah can be reached either by road from the city centre, with regular bus services, or by rail to its own station or Mandara, just outside the gardens of the palace and near the beach of the same name. Montazah has its own beach and is one of the more famous resorts but there are 13km (9 miles) of excellent beaches between the palace with its two attendant hotels and the city. Numbered among the more popular public beaches east of Alexandria are Sporting, Stanley, Glim and Sidi Bishr, not to mention those with romantic names, Caesar's Camp (Camp Shizar), Cleopatra Beach and Miyami Beach. On the west side of Alexandria, within easy reach of the city, are two beaches, Agami and Hanoville.

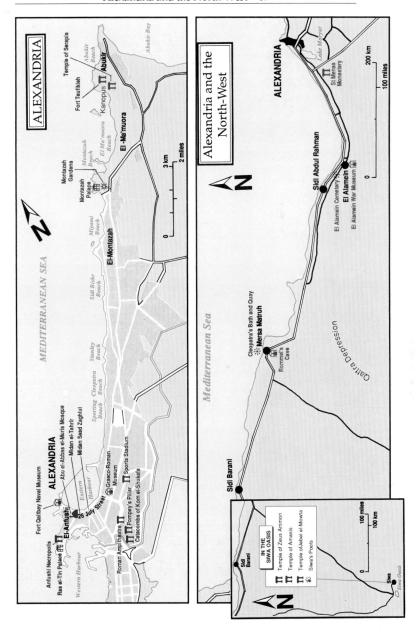

ALEXANDRIA

MEDITERRANEAN SEA

Temple of Serapis
Abukir Beach
Abukir
Fort Teufikieh
Kanopus
Abukir Bay
Montazah Gardens
El Ma'muora
Montazah Palace
Montazah Beach
El Ma'muora Beach
El-Montazah
Miyami Beach
Sidi Bishr Beach
Stanley Beach
Cleopatra Beach
Sporting Beach
Eastern Harbour

Fort Qaitbay Naval Museum
Antushi Necropolis
Ras el-Tin Palace
El-Antushi
Abu el-Abbas el-Mursi Mosque
Midan el-Tahrir
Midan Saad Zaghlul
ALEXANDRIA
26 July Street
Sports Stadium
Graeco-Roman Museum
Pompey's Pillar
Roman Amphitheatre
Catacomba of Kom el-Shukafa
Western Harbour

3 km
2 miles
0

N

Alexandria and the North-West

Mediterranean Sea

Lake Maryut
ALEXANDRIA
St Menas Monastery
Sidi Abdul Rahman
El Alamein Cemetery
El Alamein
El Alamein War Museum
Cleopatra's Bath and Quay
Mersa Matruh
Rommel's Cave
Qattra Depression
Sidi Barani

200 km
100 miles
100 km
0

N

IN THE SIWA OASIS
Temple of Zeus Ammon
Temple of Amasis
Temple of Jebel el-Mowta
Siwa's Pools

Sidi Barani
Siwa
Siwa Oasis

100 miles
100 km
0

N

# A Conqueror's City

The magic that Alexandria has conjured up over its turbulent history can never be underestimated. Its founder, Alexander the Great, crossed from Europe into Asia in 334BC, cut east, down the Tigris and Euphrates rivers (deep into Persia), out to the Hindu Kush, Bukhara and Tashkent and then across India as far as the tributary of the Indus known as the Beas. In his wake as conqueror of the known world, Alexander left a string of cities named after him — one in Iran, three in Afghanistan, two in Pakistan, four in the USSR and one in Egypt. During his campaigns lasting 11 years, Alexander had immortalised himself in stone and mortar in as many cities. Only one, however, was to thrive through the centuries and still stands today as testament to the power of the Macedonian leader more than 2,300 years after his death — the city of Alexandria in Egypt.

❋     **Alexandria** is said to be the world's longest continually inhabited city. This is the site of one of the Seven Wonders of the World, brainchild of one of the world's greatest military figures, site of the most famous library ever, home to Anthony and Cleopatra, base for the spread of Christianity and ultimate target for caesars, emperors and kings, including the legendary King Chosroes of Persia. This city has an identity of its own, separate from the familiar image of Ancient Egypt's Pharaohs and pyramids. In Alexandria lies a completely different facet of Egypt's varied history.

This city is the Greek, Roman and Christian face of Mediterranean Egypt. Founded in 331BC by Alexander the Great when he was just 25 years old, the military leader selected this site as a melding of Greek and Egyptian cultures to celebrate his newly-acquired territory, the Empire of Egypt. Alexander stayed long enough, in what was then the tiny fishing village of Rhalotis, to prepare for his pilgrimage to Siwa, in the Western Desert. He envisaged a fabulous city on the site and instructed his army of masons and sculptors to build a golden city in his name with great colonnades, huge temples, magnificent palaces and a great sea harbour overshadowed by a giant lighthouse, the Pharos. Remaining at the site only long enough to sketch out the plans of expansive, straight roads, avenues and broad promenades, Alexander bid farewell to a city that he conceived but was never to see built. Mysteriously, the conqueror headed off into the desert with a small retinue in order to receive a sacred blessing on what was to be his 8-year rule of Egypt. Never to see a single building erected in the city which bears his name, Alexander was to return here in 322BC, entwined in a golden shroud and encased in a glass sarcophagus, to be buried in a still undiscovered tomb.

As soon as Alexander the Great had completed his curious desert pilgrimage he left Egypt from Memphis, the then capital of Egypt, on his conquering travels around Asia. What had drawn him to the site of his Greek outpost on the Egyptian coast was its strategic position, an ideal climate, its excellent harbour, the protective Isle of Pharos and its links with the River Nile. The city has changed considerably since Alexander's times but a great deal is known about this historic capital. The Greek king's vision of a glorious new city on the coast materialised over the centuries and some of the most marvellous structures of the Greek and Roman Empires were built in Alexandria. Probably one of the most famous monuments of all was the second of Egypt's two wonders of the world. Completed around 280BC and situated on the tip of Pharos Island which Ptolemy II had linked to the city by the Heptastadion causeway, the Great Lighthouse, or Pharos, was a white, limestone tower said to be 180m (590ft) high. This highly ornate column supported a giant cedarwood brazier whose light was reflected by mechanised mirrors and some sort of camera obscura device making it visible from great distances. It has long since disappeared after successive earthquakes and its eventual destruction in 1302 by the Mameluke ruler, El Nasir. When Sultan Qiatbay built his fort on Pharos in 1480, much of the remains of the lighthouse were incorporated in the massive walls. Since the construction of this father of all lighthouses, subsequent lighthouses around the world have adhered to the name 'Pharos'.

One of the most significant of early Alexandria's monuments was the famous library which once housed almost a million papyrus scrolls. This fabulous collection, known as the Alexandria Library, was burned by the Caliph Omar in AD642 as he believed it contained writings contrary to the Islamic faith. Other magnificent edifices of Ancient Alexandria included; the Graeco-Roman Museum; temples to the Egyptian goddess Isis, those to the Roman goddess Artemis and also to the only man-created god, Serapis; a huge stadium, gymnasium, a spectacular theatre and a great royal palace. Artists, writers, philosophers, mathematicians, scientists and religious leaders flocked to Alexandria from the corners of the Ancient World and the city became the birthplace of a wealth of ideas and inventions.

Throughout its charmed and enlightened history of almost 2,500 years, Alexandria has hosted a pageant of personalities throughout the march of time since Alexander the Great dictated that his architect, Dinocrates, begin his 'city of dreams'. The Greek scholar Strabo

*Alexandria — 'A magnificent entry into history'*

left detailed descriptions of the city when it was just in its 300th year. Euclid, Hero and Eratosthenes all studied at the great Ptolemaic library, often considered the first university in the world. Anthony lived for 12 years with Cleopatra in the city from 42BC to 30BC. After the Battle of Actium, where Octavian (Augustus) defeated Anthony and Cleopatra (last of the Ptolemies), the great Caesar strolled down the cities triumphal way. Hadrian, the Roman emperor, visited Alexandria and St Mark first preached in the Jewish quarter of the ancient city. Egyptian born astronomer and geographer Ptolemy walked the length of the famous Roman-Greek columned main street, the Kanopic Way, from its ancient Moon Gate to the Gate of the Sun. Homer refers to Pharos Island in his *Odyssey* even before the Alexandrians had made it the hub of their famous city and, almost 3,000 years later writers like the local poet, Constantine Cavafy, Lawrence Durrell and E.M. Forster enthused over the magic of this timeless city once christened the 'Bride of the Sea'.

### EXCURSIONS IN ALEXANDRIA
Unlike Cairo, Alexandria is not difficult to see in a day's intensive sightseeing. However, a tour which incorporates most of the impor-

*Alexandria's Eastern Harbour*

tant city sights necessitates the use of taxis rather than the buses or trams as the city centre is a good 5km (3 miles) across. It is logical to start a tour at the tip of what was Pharos Island, on the western arm of the Eastern Harbour, a good taxi ride from the better class hotels.

The furthermost edifice on the harbour arm is Fort Qaitbay. This magnificent structure, built by Sultan Qaitbay in 1480, now houses Fort Qaitbay Naval Museum and is built on the site of the ancient Pharos. Nearby, fish of the Nile and the Red Sea can be seen in the Aquarium at the Hydrobiological Institute. Pharos Island is no more, since the city has encroached across the narrow isthmus which was originally the covered causeway to the island. Today the city is fused to the islands which has now become the Arab and Turkish quarters. Apart from Fort Qaitbay there are several other significant sites on this peninsula which should be viewed before visiting the monuments in the city.

The El-Anfushi residential district here is named after the second century BC Ptolemaic necropolis. This collection of Greek rock tombs, decorated in Graeco-Egyptian styles, can be visited with a guide and is reached from the El-Atta Fort by taking the Ras el-Tin road west. El-Atta Fort lies off to the right of the road overlooking the

Mediterranean and cannot be visited. Beyond the necropolis one can see the Ras el-Tin Palace (Cape of Figs), one of the oldest Egyptian palaces. Built in the first half of the nineteenth century by Mohammed Ali, it was from this 300-room palace that King Farouk sailed away in his yacht after abdicating in 1952. The building at the tip of the point is the Turkish-style Mohammed Karim Mosque and the modern port, the Western Harbour, can be seen in the background. Retracing one's steps towards Fort Qaitbay again, a right turning leads to a large square named after the mosque which stands in its centre, dominated by a highly decorative mosque. The Abu el-Abbas el-Mursi Mosque is built over the tomb of the thirteenth-century saint, Abu el-Abbas and was constructed by the Algerians in AD1767. The smaller mosque of Ibrahim Turbana is even older, built in AD1685. Other mosques in this Turkish part of El-Anfushi are the little Sidi Daoud Mosque and the modern Bouseiri Mosque.

Running alongside the Bouseiri Square is the famous 26 July Street. This is a promenade running the entire curve of the half-moon-shaped Easter Harbour — the main ancient port. The remains of some of Cleopatra's palaces have been discovered in the harbour silt recently but in order to see what actually remains of Ancient Alexandria above water, 26 July Street should be followed in an arc. This passes the turning on the right which leads to Midan el-Tahrir or the old city square, with its statue of Mohammed Ali on horseback.

Continue on to Midan Saad Zaghlul (Zaghlul Square). Long distance buses terminate here and so does the city tram. Dominating the square is the statue of the post-World War I nationalist leader, Saad Zaghlul, but its ancient history goes back to the temple built here in Roman times in honour of Julius Caesar which once sported two huge and ancient obelisks. Today those 'Cleopatra's Needles' grace the Embankment in London and Central Park in New York. Midan Saad Zaghlul is located on 26 July Street and it is from here that the city sites can be easily reached by first taking a taxi to the furthest of sites, the **Catacombs of Kom el-Shukafa**. This is an underground wonderland of ornate carvings and paintings mixing Roman and Egyptian designs. It is the largest Roman funerary complex in Egypt and dates from the second century AD. Passages on three levels lead to an assortment of burial chambers. Near this site is the original location of the ancient Sports Stadium. A short distance from the catacombs is the centre of Alexander's original city of Rhakotis. Site of the Greek's citadel and the Roman's acropolis, this mount, once the city centre of Ancient Rhakohs, is now surmounted by the wrongly-named 'Pompey's Pillar'. The Aswan

## Places of Interest
## In and Around Alexandria

**Abu el-Abbas el-Mursi Mosque**
Following corniche around towards
Fort Qaitbay
Famous ancient religious shrine.

**Abukir Bay**
East of the town and Abukir Point
Site of Napoleon's naval defeat by
Lord Nelson.

*Temple of Serapis*
In the ruined city of Kanopus
Erected during Ptolemaic times.

**El-Anfushi Necropolis**
Reached from El-Atta Fort by tak-
ing the Ras el-Tin road west
Ptolemaic rock tombs.

**Fort Qaitbay**
Far end of Eastern Harbour
Ancient fortress with Naval
Museum.

**Graeco-Roman Museum**
Off Saleh Mustapha Street, north
of main railway station
Many exhibits of Ancient Alexandria and gardens.

**26 July Street**
Esplanade around the ancient port
area.

**Midan el-Tahrir**
Garden and equestrian statue.

**Midan Saad Zaghlul**
Site of Roman temple.
Catacombs of Kom el-Shukafa
Curiously decorated Roman rock
tombs.

**Montazah Palace**
Far east of Alexandria in El-Montazah area
Ornate old royal palace on beachside.

**Pompey's Pillar**
In Karmus district south of main
railway station
Ancient column on hill overlooking
city.

**Ras el-Tin Palace**
North tip of Western Harbour
Early sumptuous royal residence.

**Roman Amphitheatre**
Amir Abdel el-Kader Street, north-
west of main railway station
Remains of baths and amphitheatre
complex.

granite column — which may have been topped by an equestrian statue because Alexandrians call it the 'Horseman Pillar' — was erected to the memory of the siege-breaker, Diocletian in AD292, and is flanked by sphinx. This is also the ancient site of Mark Anthony and Cleopatra's second Alexandria Library and the mysterious cult of Serapis' temple, the Serapeum. Today, a third great library is planned to be built in Alexandria, 2,300 years after its foundation. A joint venture between UNESCO and the Egyptian authorities, this building will house books on Pharaonic, Phoenician, Coptic, Islamic

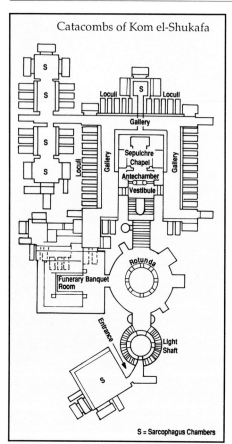

Catacombs of Kom el-Shukafa

S = Sarcophagus Chambers

civilisations and also on ancient and medieval sciences. Due for completion in 1995 and designed to house 8 million volumes and documents, the library will be the most important centre for studies of regional civilisations.

One should now return by taxi to the Graeco-Roman Museum passing, en route, the city's main rail station, the Cecil Hotel (made famous in Durrell's *Alexandria Quartet*), the site of the Roman Amphitheatre and baths near the area known as Kom el-Dikka. It is possible that this is the site of Alexander the Great's massive tomb, described in 641 by the Arab Caliph Omar when he entered the city

*26 July Street, or Corniche, almost encircles the Eastern Harbour*

by the Sun Gate of the Kanopic Way. He said that the two most impressive monuments he noticed either side of the columned avenue was Alexander's Tomb rising to the left and the Pharos pillar to the right. The Kanopic Way is now Gamal Abdel Nasser Street running along the north flank of Kom el-Dikka hill from west to east. It is just across Gamal Abdel Nasser Street that one finds the city museum. Many of the exhibits in the Graeco-Roman Museum in-  clude frescoes, coins, mummies, papyrus, vases and urns and a large number of sculptures — sphinx, statues and columns. The beautiful gardens of the museum contain a variety of reconstructed tombs. Other places of interest in Alexandria include the Fine Art Museum, near the main railway station and St Catherine's Cathedral, also not far from the station.

## WEST FROM ALEXANDRIA

Few travellers have time to make the excursion along the coast, west from Alexandria, but to some the locations of El Alamein, Sidi Abdul Rahman, Mersa Matruh and Sidi Barani have become historic monuments in their own right. Without the naval exploits of An- thony and Cleopatra, and without the great feats of Field Marshall

Montgomery's Eighth Army and Rommel's Afrika Korps in the Western Desert during World War II, these tiny coastal outposts would have remained largely forgotten.

A car should be hired in order to make the entire trip which can be quite arduous. The journey of about 370km (229 miles) from Alexandria to Sidi Barani can be a long day's trek but a visit to El Alamein from the city is a comfortable day's excursion. The road out through the port area of Alexandria passes a track to **St Menas Monastery**, named after a Christian who was martyred and buried here in AD296. The ruins were only discovered early this century and now the site of a nearby fifth-century town is being excavated. **El Alamein** is 100km (62 miles) from Alexandria and is of importance because of the battle fought here in late 1942. A vast British war cemetery, a yellow-bricked German memorial, a white marble Italian memorial and the El Alamein War Museum are monuments to the fierce fighting during the autumn battle in which more than 80,000 troops died. Do not stray off the track here or visit the beach as live mines from the wartime offensive are still being unearthed.

For beach-lovers and for day-trippers from Alexandria the sands at **Sidi Abdul Rahman**, another 24km (15 miles) further west are a great attraction. This tiny resort, named after a Bedouin holy man (Abdul Rahman), has a large, popular hotel, the El Alamein, a tiny mosque and a glorious white-sanded beach. Another beach resort, 233km (144 miles) from Alexandria is **Mersa Matruh** (Paraetonium), a large town with a fascinating history. Apart from the sandy shore, rocky coves and delightful little harbour, there are the newly-excavated sites of Cleopatra's quay-side used by her Egyptian fleet, and to the west of the harbour lagoon is Cleopatra's Bath, a pool sheltered by a high cliff supposedly used by the Ptolemaic queen. Alexander the Great, on his pilgrimage to the desert oasis of Siwa, passed through here after instructing his architect to build his famed city at Alexandria. Mersa Matruh has remained, since Alexander's time, a busy and flourishing market town and port. Its fine beaches have given Mersa Matruh the title of 'Egypt's Riviera'. A remnant of World War II, Rommel's Cave, used by the Field Marshall to plan his desert campaigns, is now a museum containing contemporary relics and personal items belonging to the German 'Desert Fox'.

For those few who wish to travel even further west there are more fine beaches at Abyad, Ageeba and at Sidi Barani. One of Cleopatra's palaces is said to lie along the road at Qasr and in Ok Rakhaam there is evidence of a temple dating to the times of the Pharaoh Ramesses II. However, the one main attraction in this part of the country is that

## Places of Interest In North-West Egypt

**El Alamein**
On the coast, south-west of Alexandria
Location of the World War II conflict, museum, cemetery and memorials.

**Mersa Matruh**
On the coast, halfway between Alexandria and Libyan border
Cleopatra's quay, Cleopatra's Bath and famous beach resort.

*Rommel's Cave*
Short walk from Mersa Matruh

harbour. Base for the German World War II campaign, museum and trophies.

**Sidi Abdul Rahman**
On coast, west of El Alamein
Popular beach resort and interesting coastal town.

**St Menas Monastery**
West of Alexandria, south of main road
Second-century AD site recently excavated.

which brought Alexander the Great here almost 2,500 years ago. The oasis of Siwa, a long hard trek deep into the Western Desert, was once the site of the revered Temple of Zeus-Ammon a religion which combined Greek and Egyptian beliefs. By being blessed here, Alexander cemented his belief that his was a God-King and had moulded the Egyptian religion to that of Greece. Once crowned with the sacred ram's horned diadem, Alexander left Siwa to conquer much of Asia. The parts of two temples survive in this isolated oasis and there are a number of rock tombs to explore. A visit to the area of the Siwa Oasis requires a permit obtainable from the governor at Alexandria, the Frontier Corps in Cairo, or the governor at Mersa Matruh.

## SIWA OASIS

Before one travels the 300km (186 miles) from Mersa Matruh, or even the 600km (372 miles) from Alexandria to the isolated town Siwa, a permit to stay in the oasis should be sought as this almost forgotten attraction lies far out in the North-West Frontier Province near the Libyan border. It is advisable to travel the good road south across the desert from Mersa Matruh in convoys of two vehicles or more but there are two buses a day from the coastal resort. There are a couple of reasonable hotels and two not so palatable establishments in Siwa, but it does have a good tourist information office. The 5-hour journey by bus, or the 4-hour trip by taxi or car, is worth the dust and heat for the numerous sites to be visited in this enigmatic oasis which was the

*Alexandria's Roman Amphitheatre, once the centre of Mediterranean culture*

*Siwa Oasis, inhabited by both the Berbers and Bedouin tribes*

goal of a pilgrimage made by Alexander the Great when he was 25 years old, the furthest west the conqueror was ever to travel.

This mysterious journey made with a small retinue was, some historians say, a mission by the all-powerful, all-physical general into the realms of witchcraft and the supernatural. This extraordinary place was the centre of an obscure cult, that of Ammon. Alexander thought that by consulting the Oracle of Ammon, the Libyan god which had powers in at least three important national religions, he would unify his empire. The power of this strange Oracle had been proved less than 200 years earlier when the invading Persian army was swallowed up by a 'divinely conjured' sandstorm. The Siwa cult mixed three pagan gods; the Libyan, with Ammon; Egyptian, in the form of Amun and the Greek religion with their god Zeus. Alexander hoped that visiting the Oracle of Ammon, would allow him to unite the political powers through spiritual and divine means and so sought confirmation from the priests of Ammon of a secret belief that he was in fact the son of Zeus. After his visit to the Oracle of the ram-headed god Ammon he had his head, portrayed with the horns of the ram, stamped on Greek coinage. It is thought that the young general went through some sort of initiation ceremony in which he attained divine powers. Another of Alexander's motives for this curious pilgrimage was his need for a sacred blessing on what was to be 8 more years of conquest.

It had taken Alexander and his men 8 days trek from Mersa Matruh to reach the Sanctuary of Ammon. The modern visitor will note that little could have changed in the two millennia since that time. The villager's huts are still on salt-caked mud and palm trunks and the Siwa women still conform to so many restrictions that it is rare to see a female in the street. The Berber dialect has probably changed little, but the object of Alexander's pilgrimage has. On the craggy hillock of Aghurmi stands the scant ruins of the Sanctuary of Ammon, an acropolis dating from around 650BC. This was the hub of a religion once so powerful that it magnetised one of the greatest commanders in the world to make a 800km (496 mile) desert excursion to consult its Oracle. This site is the Temple of Amasis; twin of the Temple of Umm el-Ubeydah, sometimes called the Temple of Ammon although actually that of the Pharaoh Nectabo II, built around 350BC. Further on are the remains of Old Siwa, situated on a rocky bluff and overlooking the modern town of Siwa.

There are about 200 natural fresh water springs in the Siwa Oasis and two have orginial names, Cleopatra's Pool and the Pool of Fatnus, located in the middle of a salt pan. Of major importance in Siwa are the ancient rock tombs, more of which are being discovered. These are the Tombs of Jebel el-Mowta, dating from the Twenty-sixth to the Thirtieth Dynasties, about 660BC to 350BC. These ancient tombs are gated but unlocked by the local keeper — a torch is needed to see the fine reliefs and murals, especially those in the Tomb of the Crocodile and that of Si-Amun. The necropolis here is honeycombed with tombs, some dating from the Ptolemaic and Roman periods.

## THE QUEST FOR THE CONQUEROR'S CASKET

Alexander the Great was born in Pella, Macedonia, in 356BC, succeeded his father, King Philip of Epirus, when he was 20 years old and established himself Champion of the Greeks. His education at the feet of Aristotle and his devotion to the writings of Homer, convinced him that the superior interlect of the Greeks should overpower any barbarians. Proving this theory he swept through

## Places of Interest In the Siwa Oasis

**Siwa's Pools**
Surrounding the hill village of Siwa town
A number of strikingly beautiful freshwater oases.

**Temple of Amasis**
An hour's walk west of Siwa town
Said to be the site of Alexander's Oracle of Ammon.

**Temple of Zeus Ammon**
An hour's walk west of Siwa town
Twin of the famous sanctuary of the Oracle.

**Tombs of Jebel el-Mowta**
Just outside village of Qaret el-Musabberin
Interesting late dynastic, Greek and Roman rock tombs.

half of the world subduing the Persian and Syrians and overran Egypt in 332BC when he was aged just 24.

The next year Alexander led his army west from Memphis on the Nile, towards what is now Libya. On a pilgrimage to visit the Temple of Zeus Ammon, the heroic general, for some reason that historians find hard to explain, passed by what is now the site of the city of Alexandria. Pausing only to dictate that a great city should be built in his honour on the shores of the Mediterranean Sea at that point, he continued on his strange mission.

Alexander never returned to see the city he founded — his travels led him back from Siwa to the Nile Valley and on into Asia Minor where he again routed the Persians. In 324BC, when he was 32, the conqueror of the ancient world died in the city of Babylon after a fever which lasted 11 days. Alexander's army brought his body back to Egypt and presented it to the Egyptian priests at Luxor. Willing to embalm and enshrine the king, the acolytes refused to bury the body in the Temple of Luxor where Alexander had built a chapel known as the Sanctuary of Alexander the Great. The priests said that to bury the king on the sacred grounds of their gods would bring bad luck.

In great pomp and ceremony the body was brought down the Nile to Memphis, the ancient capital of Egypt. It was here, or so the story goes, that the embalmed body of Alexander was encased in solid gold, the famous ram's horned diadem of Zeus Ammon was placed on his head and he was laid in a glass sarcophagus. The skill of producing glass, especially in large flat pieces, was an art still to be discovered at the time of Alexander's death. Possibly the narrator referred to some construction of rock crystal? Nevertheless, the priests of Memphis also refused to let the king be buried in their own sacred cemeteries and the entire cortège then made its way up the

Nile, through the Delta, into the Mediterranean and along the coast of Egypt to Alexandria — the city which the king had founded 7 years earlier but had never seen.

A gigantic tomb was erected at the crossroads of the great central avenue, Kanopic Street and Soma Street. Between the Gates of the Sun and the Moon, halfway along a causeway of columns, Alexander's mausoleum dominated the city skyline. Alexander was interred in the massive tomb and henceforth revered as the city's diety. For 965 years, the tomb was Alexandria's focal point and as famous a landmark as the Pharos. The Caliph Omar, first of the Islamic caliphs to rule Egypt, swept into the city through the Gate of the Sun, and down the grand colonnaded avenue. The year was 641 and the caliph described his first impressions as he looked towards the harbour. On one side, he said, rose the great mausoleum of Alexander and to his right, across the harbour, rose the Pharos, two great monuments to the city's glory. The Muslim caliph was affronted by the exhuberance of the city and immediately went to work to destroy Alexandria's magnificent monuments, converting the giant Pharos into an Arab fortress and surmounting it with a crescent, burning the most famous library in the world and desecrating temples and tombs. Alexander's mausoleum was torn down and today no trace remains of where it stood.

Some historians believe that the sarcophagus containing the remains of Alexander the Great was spirited away by the proud Alexandrians into a maze of catacombs below street level, before they could be desecrated by the fanatical Arab ruler. It is also thought that a good deal of the papyrus and manuscripts from the nearby library were also rescued from the pyre and hidden in the deep cellars near the Paneum (Park of Pan), now the hill called Kom el-Dik. For centuries the mystery of where Alexander's body lay, puzzled antiquarians and devotees of Ancient Egyptian history. However, the rumour was put about during the end of the nineteenth century that, in 1850, a dragoman exploring under a mosque erected near the Kom el-Dikka, broke a hole in a door leading to one of the thousand passages and chambers below the mosque. Inside, he says, he saw the image of a man dressed in gold, sitting on a type of throne encased in a sort of glass cage. On the seated man's head was, he relates, a large crown and piled on the floor of the chamber were the remains of what looked like thousands of books, scrolls and parchments. Could it be that the guide, an assistant at the Russian Embassy, had glimpsed the face of the world's conqueror, ignominiously interred in the cellars under his great city?

# 5
# *SUEZ*
# *AND THE CANAL TOWNS*

E ast, across the the wide Delta triangle from Alexandria and the architectural miracles performed at the instigation of Alexander the Great, lies a similarly dramatic project etched onto the Egyptian landscape. As Alexander's successors raised enormous temples and palaces where there was once a tiny fishing village so, about 250 years earlier, great schemes were afoot to tame the waterways of the Eastern Delta. The Achaeamenid Emperor Darius I, king of Persia, who ruled this part of Egypt around 500BC, constructed a canal from the once important city of Zagazig (Ancient Bubastis) to Ismailia at the head of the Bitter Lakes. He later linked these with the Red Sea so connecting an arm of the Nile with the Red Sea. This was not an original project as, 100 years before, Herodotus reports that the Pharaoh Necho lost a force of 120,000 slaves while attempting a similar project. Even earlier attempts to create canal links in this part of the country were said to have been made during the Seventh or Eighth Dynasty, around 2100BC.

A gigantic feat of engineering for its time, the original plans for a Suez link suffered variously over the millennia. Greeks, Romans, Arabs and even Venetians toyed with the idea of developing the waterways. At times these canal links were infilled, at times deepened, widened and improved until, during Emperor Napoleon's sorties in Egypt between 1798 and 1801, it was again suggested that a channel could be cut from the Red Sea to the Mediterranean. For the first time in the 2,500 years since Necho tried linking the Nile with the Red Sea to bring the Eastern lands that much closer to his domain, Lepere (a Frenchman), in 1798 put forward a scheme that would link all the countries of the West with those of the East.

Due to miscalculations and unforseen economic and political hiccups it was not until early in 1856 that Lepere's fellow countryman, Ferdinand de Lesseps, obtained permission to start work on the one communication route which would change the face of trade, commerce and travel for most of the world. Work on the canal did not begin until mid-1859 and it was on 17 November 1869 that the great project was finally opened. For a total of 171km (106 miles) the Suez Canal ran north from the town of Suez, through Ismailia to the artificially created city of Port Said, linking an arm of the Indian Ocean with an extension of the Atlantic Ocean. The inaugural celebrations were spectacular and included attendance of the Empress Eugenie by invite of the Khedive Ismail (after whom Ismailia was named) and the first performance of Verdi's *Aida* in Cairo. The empress's yacht *Aigle* was one of the first ships to sail the entire length from Port Said to Suez. Economic problems forced Egypt to sign away its shares in the canal to Britain which contributed to the British occupation of the country in 1882. Several battles, including those of the World War I and II, led to the Canal Zone being the subject of bitter fighting over a 50-year period until, between 1967 and 1975, the waterway was blocked by sunken ships and mines due to the war between Egypt and Israel.

Today the Suez Canal is wider and deeper than ever and around 100 ships at a time pass through on their 15-hour journey from sea to sea. Seen from a distance, the convoy of ships passing along the canal between sand dunes on either side, look like fairyland mirages of whole cities moving across the arid, blazing desert. Freighters, container ships, passenger liners and oil tankers wind through the Little and Great Bitter Lakes which comprise part of the canal system and ease through the 200m (656ft) wide channels which link Port Said with Ismailia and the Bitter Lakes with the town of Suez.

Few visitors to Egypt will see much of the isthmus of Suez, the Canal Zone and its three townships unless on a special excursion or journeying the length of the canal by passenger ship. There is however, the opportunity for the traveller to join a cruise which sails the route of the canal from the port of Suez to Port Said or travel by a road and rail route which follows the entire course.

## SUEZ

The nearest and easiest accessible part of the Suez Canal from Cairo, is the town of Suez itself. An air service and a rail route connects the capital with the southern opening of the canal and an excellent highway, 137km (85 miles) links Cairo with this town of around 500,000 people. The motorway runs straight across wadi-scoured desert with little to see except possibly a detour about halfway to the isolated palace site at Abbassi. Founded in the fifteenth century as a pilgrim's stop-over between Cairo and Mecca, the battle-scarred town is recovering from the action of the 1967 and 1973 wars and is of little interest to the visitor as its main preoccupation is industry. There is a good view of the entrance to the canal from Port Tewfik  Island, a little further out from the town on a short causeway. From Port Tewfik one can take an hour's boat excursion around the canal entrance. Some short distance north of Suez is the airport and the two tunnels which link the Eastern Desert side of the canal with the Sinai Peninsula. There are two hotels in Suez and they are not international standard.

## ISMAILIA
As the town of Suez is built on the Cairo side of the canal at the very tip of the Gulf of Suez, so Ismailia is constructed on the shores of a small lake, Timsah (Crocodile Lake). Ismailia is a clean, pleasant, well laid out port with neat squares, parks and gardens. Colonial, balconied houses look out over tree-lined avenues in this town named after the Khedive Ismail when it was founded as a halfway stop-over on the canal by the architect Lesseps in 1863. The Ismailia Canal, a sweetwater canal built in the late 1850s to supply workers with fresh water from the Nile during the Suez Canal construction, runs parallel to the waterfront between the town buildings and the port area. War damage in the town, inflicted during the two wars in the 1960s and 1970s, still scars many buildings but there are several diversions to take one's mind off the recent past and into a different world. The remnants of ancient grandeur discovered nearby are  displayed in the Garden of the Stelae near Fountain Park and more artifacts are exhibited in the fascinating Museum of Antiquities  adjacent to the two parks. Lesseps House, from where Lessep directed operations during the Suez Canal construction, is on the main promenade (Mohammed Ali Quay) which runs alongside the Ismailia Canal from Fountain Park. Now a museum in its own gardens, many items connected with the French engineer can be seen here including a faded photograph of the grand opening of the canal. The large skyscraper building overlooking the port is the Suez Canal Authority office. There are two small hotels in Ismailia and access to the town from Cairo is via the wide, straight highway (145km, 90 miles), the detouring and longer rail link, or by air.

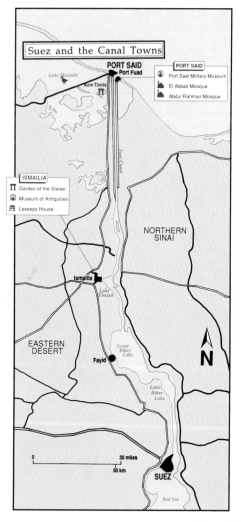

Suez and the Canal Towns

PORT SAID
Port Fuad

PORT SAID
Port Said Military Museum
El Abbas Mosque
Abdul Rahman Mosque

Lake Manzala
Kom Tinnis

ISMAILIA
Garden of the Stelae
Museum of Antiquities
Lesseps House

Suez Canal

NORTHERN
SINAI

Ismailia
Lake
Timsah

EASTERN
DESERT

Great
Bitter
Lake

Fayid

Little
Bitter
Lake

N

0          30 miles

50 km

SUEZ

Red Sea

## PORT SAID

Known to ocean liner passengers as the 'Gateway to the East', Port Said was built as the Mediterranean entrance to the Suez Canal in the mid-1800s. Port Said, named after the Viceroy (Prince), is constructed on an artificially extended promentory where the great lagoons of the Nile Delta meet the marsh and sands of the Sinai Peninsula. On the face of it, Port Said looks like a completely 'modern' town in Egyptian terms. The location, however, has a history which stretches back to the times of the Pharaohs and was a particularly productive agricultural area. Under the Ptolemies the town was called El-Farma. Far to the north-east of the capital, Port Said is 200km (124 miles) from Cairo but is popular with shoppers from all over Egypt for its duty-free goods. Almost a Hong Kong of the desert, the town has little to offer the visitor except a wealth of souvenirs and a small museum. However, it will be noticed that there are many more races represented here in Port Said than in most other Egyptian towns.

Architectural styles vary here and many of Port Said's buildings were damaged in the Suez war but there are four hotels in the town, several good restaurants, casinos and clubs. One outstanding struc-

*Fishing boats at Suez, an important ship refuelling point*

*'Port-Out-Starboard-Home' through the Suez Canal*

# Places of Interest Along the Suez Canal

**Suez**
137km (85 miles) east of Cairo
Fifteenth-century history, now modern port at head of canal.

*Ismailia*
80km (50 miles) south of Port Said

**Garden of the Stelae**
Near Fountain Park
Remnants of ancient relics.

**Museum of Antiquities**
Adjacent to Garden of the Stelae and Fountain Park.
Sphinx found during the cutting of the canal and artifacts from canal engineering. Mosaics and terracottas from the Graeco-Egyptian period.

**Lesseps House**
Mohammed Ali Quay
Home of the architect who constructed the Suez Canal.
Now a museum

**Lake Manzala**
In the Delta region of Egypt, near Port Said
Giant inland lake and bird sanctuary. Ancient site of Kom Tinnis.

**Port Said**
200km (124 miles) north-east of Cairo
Nineteenth-century bustling trading town with modern history and military museum.

ture combines arches and green domes and is the Suez Canal Authority building. One cannot miss the great obelisk of the 'Martyr's Memorial' on the green and the catholic cathedral on 26 July Street. There is also an interesting Coptic church in the town known as the Mari Gergis. Near the railway station, on one side of the Commercial Harbour, a ferry can be taken to Port Fuad (Bur Fuad), the side of the canal which sports fine beaches and botanical gardens. Walking down the quayside waterfront known as Palestine Street from the ferry, the two buildings which are of most interest to visitors are the Ministry of Tourism office and the Casino Palace. At the north  end of Palestine Street is Port Said Military Museum in its large square. Two mosques in Port Said which are worth visiting are the  El Abbas Mosque on the corner of the gardens facing the governorate building, and the Abdul Rahman Mosque. Out on the New Corniche there are resort beaches and it is possible to make a boat trip from the  town to the bird sanctuary on the vast **Lake Manzala**. Also on this famous lake, the largest in the Delta region of Egypt, there is the  ancient city site of Kom Tinnis located on a small island. Special arrangements can be made to take a tour out to this ancient site or one can reach it by taking Route 7 road west of Port Said to El-Matariya. Kom Tinnis lies to the left of the highway which leapfrogs the lake.

# 6
# *THE SINAI PENINSULA*

Only a fortieth of the land area of Egypt and shaped like an elongated triangle similar to that of the Nile Delta, this is part of the country rarely visited on tours of Egypt. Barren and waterless, mostly desert and mountains, this wedge of inhospitable territory represents the land link between Asia and Africa. Sinai stands between Islamic Egypt and Israeli Judaism and is the site of one of the most famous Christian monasteries. In ancient times its mineral wealth gave it the name 'The Turquoise Land' and mystics referred to Sinai as the 'Land of Enchantments'. As the Lord told Moses in the Bible, the ground he was standing on was 'Holy Ground', and it was in this dry wilderness that Old Testament wonders, including the saga of the 'Burning Bush' and the 'Water from Rock' episodes were enacted. Over many millennia the great wasteland has been witness to the passage of fleeing tribes, invading hordes, early mineral prospectors, groups of religious recluses and today's oil prospectors. It has also provided the scenario for battles between modern armies and been the centre of archaeologist's attention when examples of the earliest written alphabet the 'Cananaean Inscriptions' were found in Sinai.

For short term vistors to Egypt the prospect of visiting many sites in the Sinai is limited. There is the question of the long distances to be covered from Cairo or Suez, the need for adequate provisions for food, water fuel and sleeping facilities while travelling in the mountains or deserts and the time it takes to make the treks to the various points of interest. It takes about 5 hours to drive from Suez, through the Ahmed Hamdi Tunnel, down the western side of the peninsula and across to St Catherine's Monastery — the roads are clear of traffic and in excellent condition. Although one of Egypt's outstanding,

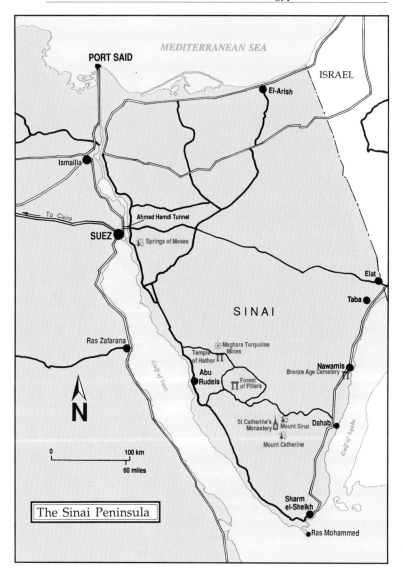

The Sinai Peninsula

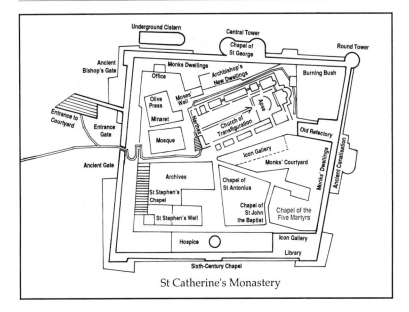

St Catherine's Monastery

interesting and awe-inspiring regions, the time allowed for including Sinai in the itinerary of an average tour of Egypt prohibits all but a fleeting visit to one of its best-known attractions — St Catherine's Monastery. Access to the peninsula is either by road, from Cairo east to Suez, or through the Ahmed Hamdi Tunnel under the Suez Canal just north of the town. Remember that the journey from Cairo to the monastery and back is around 885km (549 miles).

Alternatively a regular air service from the capital links Cairo with the Mount Sinai Airport where accommodation is available at Hotel Isis. This is by far the easiest of routes to take as Egyptian companies organise excursions from hotels to the monastery and back.

In the centre of the apex of the inverted triangle shape of Sinai, **St Catherine's Monastery** (a fortress-like settlement) is hidden deep in the southern mountains, isolated from all but the most determined traveller or fanatical pilgrim. Biblical occurrences connected with the location of the monastery are the delivery to Moses of the tablets of the Ten Commandments, from Mount Sinai (Gebel Musa, Mountain of Moses), and the 'Burning Bush' incident which started the notion of a church erected to cover the site of the miracle. A place of pilgrimage for centuries before, the empress St Helena (Constantine the Great's mother), had the first chapel built here in AD342. The Emperor Justinian I, in about AD527, officially founded the original fortified monastery which now contains the remains of St Catherine and St Stephen of Eilat. Instead of the traditional basket-and-pulley method of entry into the complex, today's visitors enter by a small doorway. Inside its 15m (49ft) walls are chapels to St Antonius, St George, St John the Baptist and the Five Martyrs of Crete. There is also a tiny twelfth-century mosque for Muslim visitors to the monastery. In the Church of the Transfiguration there are chapels to eleven more saints and the very special Burning Bush Chapel. Jewelled chests standing outside the carved doors were donated by the Russian rulers, Empress Catherine during the seventeenth century, and Czar Alexander II in the nineteenth century. Inside the chapel a silver plate marks the supposed site of Moses' bush and rich adornments, a golden ceiling and blue-tiled walls surround the actual altar niche. Shoes must be removed before entering the chapel and, should visitors wish to view some of the 2,000 icons in the museum or enter the celebrated library, permission must be obtained from the Greek Orthodox prelate in Cairo before travelling. The Charnel House, or ossuary, at St Tryphon's Chapel, outside the citadel, is a particularly grisly part of the monastery tour as the skulls of former monks are piled high in one section while limb bones are stacked separately.

It takes about half a day to see the monastic buildings and another half to climb the heights of Mount Sinai, but the rewards of visiting the various sites 'Fountain of Moses' and the view from the chapel of the Holy Trinity on Mount Sinai's summit, are worth the toil. Steps are carved into the cliff face and, as there are 3,750 up and down, it is better to take the lesser inclined route up and the steps down. Camels can be hired to make the trek easier on the feet — but not on the seat! **Ras el-Safsaf** (Hill of the Willow), is the mount where Moses is said to have cut himself a staff and is another good viewpoint. More of a challenge is a day's hike up **Mount Catherine** (Gebel Katherina) crags, the highest mountain in Egypt at 2,642m (8,667ft). The Chapel of Aaron, two monasteries and King Fuad's Pavilion are passed on the ascent and the Chapel of St Catherine, whose headless corpse was supposed to have been transported to heaven from the mount, is located at its summit. It should be remembered that it can take a good hour's drive back from this spot to the west coast.

Few travellers will have much time to visit other sites in the great peninsula but in the west, nearer to Suez, are the **Springs of Moses** (Ain Musa) a group of hot springs connected with the story of Moses

## Places of Interest In the Sinai Peninsula

### El-Arish
190km (118 miles) north-east of Ismailia
Largest town in Sinai Peninsula

### Geziret el-Faraun
Short drive down the Sinai coast road south-west of El Aqaba
Ancient settlement with ruins of crusader castle.

### Mount Sinai
In the south of the peninsula
'Mountain of Moses', important chapel and fine viewpoint.

### Nawamis
On the Gulf of Aqaba coast
Bronze age burial site

### Ras el-Safsaf
Near to St Catherine's Monastery
Ancient site connected with Moses and the Exodus.

### Sharm el-Sheikh
Important town and ferry terminal at the tip of the peninsula.

### Springs of Moses
A short drive south-east of Suez
Biblical location with ancient hot springs.

### St Catherine's Monastery
In centre of south port of the peninsula
Sixth-century monastery, site of Moses' 'Burning Bush', rich icons.

### Taba
Near Pharaoh's Island
Important resort on Gulf of Aqaba.

### Temple of Hathor
North of Maghara at Serabit al-Khadim, east of Abu Zenima
Twelfth Dynasty site, turquoise mines of Maghara and inscriptions.

and the bitter-sweet spring of Marah. Further out in the mountains is the site of and ancient settlement, Q'lat al-Yundi, and another, Sarabit al-Khadim, near the coastal town of Abu Rudeis. During the Twelfth Dynasty the **Temple of Hathor**, 'Mistress of the Turquoise' was erected on this site at Serabit el-Khadim, north of Maghara in a side valley off Wadi Sidiri. Turquoise was mined here in vast quantities during the Twelfth Dynasty. The turquoise mines of Maghara have many early Egyptian remains and fascinating early Egyptian inscriptions. The scenes carved on stelae and in the rock faces have given historians a valuable insight into early mining techniques and the life and everyday workload of the ancients as far back as the First Dynasty, about 5,000 years ago. A visit to these famous turquoise mines is a popular diversion off the route from Suez to St Catherine's Monastery and is included in the itineraries of specialist excursion operators.

Other excursions and tours of the region might include the

*St Catherine's Monastery, Sinai*

*The Sinai Peninsula is a harsh and inhospitable region*

*Bedouin country near Nawamis, Sinai*

*Pharaoh's Island*

famous Forest of Pillars, Coloured Canyon, the tombs of Sheikh Ukhbus and Sheikh Iqna, a trip to the Rock of Inscriptions, or a visit to the Bronze Age burial grounds at Nawamis. On the opposite coast of Sinai from the port of Abu Rudeis (near the famous resort of Aqaba), is another famed site often visited by travellers entering Egypt from Jordan. This is the **Geziret el-Faraun** (Pharaoh's Island) once inhabited during the Twentieth Dynasty. Today there are the remains of an impressive crusader's castle dominating the rocky granite islet. Nearby, still in Egyptian territory, is the resort town of **Taba**. Up-market accommodation in Taba includes both Hilton and Sheraton hotels. From here one can make excursions either into Israel, via the popular resort of Eilat, or into the Hashemite kingdom of Jordan through the historically famous and popular vacation resort of El-Aqaba. A few of the more ambitious specialist tour companies offer truck or camel safaris into the desert regions of the Sinai and some also provide excursions into either Israel, Jordan or even Saudi Arabia in addition to their Egyptian expeditions.

**El-Arish** is located 190km (118 miles) north-east of Ismailia, 310km (192 miles) north-east of Cairo. It is the largest town in the Sinai Peninsula on the Mediterranean coast and is served by an excellent road from Ismailia and a large airport. Date cultivation and fishing once supported this town's population which now numbers 35,000 but tourism is taking over as more hotels are built along the magnificent beach.

The ancient Ptolemaic name of Rhinocolura refers to the early practice of cutting off the noses of prisoners held at this port. Jacob, according to legend, lived here. El-Arish is also the name of the Wadi which runs through the town — the longest river in the Sinai. Little remains of any original settlement but its history includes being captured by Napoleon in 1799. It was also the site of King Baldwin I of Jerusalem's death in 1118.

# 7

# THE RED SEA COAST

A s with the Sinai Peninsula, many short-term visitors to Egypt may not have the opportunity or time to visit the country's Red Sea coast which includes its western arm known as the Gulf of Suez. Specialist holidaymakers however, particularly snorkel and underwater enthusiasts, flock to several resorts along this shoreline. Archaeology devotees are also attracted to a number of sites of antiquity along the seaboard of the Eastern Desert. There are now some very good specialist tour organisers which include both Sinai and this rather little-known region in their itineraries.

## THE TWIN MONASTERIES

The nearest to Cairo and the most easily accessible of these are the two monasteries of St Anthony the Great and St Paul. It is still necessary to head east out of the capital along the highway to Suez and then south, following the main coastal road to the small port of Ras Zafarana, a journey of 250km (155 miles). A desert track leads out into the desert for about half an hour until a turning on the left is indicated to **St Anthony's Monastery**. The oldest and largest of all Egypt's Coptic monasteries, this walled complex is set on a desert plain below the grotto where the saint isolated himself and was tormented for 20 years of his life. Parts of the monastery date from the third century and the square watch-tower was reconstructed in the mid-sixteenth century on the ruins of a tenth-century site. Frescoes and statues are among the treasures to be seen here but there is evidence everywhere of the Bedouin invasion of 1483. St Mark's Chapel holds the tomb of this saint but the library lost most of its celebrated works in the Muslim raid. Women are forbidden to enter the monastery but the cave of the anchorite saint can be seen a short,

*Divers flock to the clear, prolific Red Sea waters*

*Coral outcrops, an underwater wonderland*

*Angel fish, just one of many species found in the Red Sea*

الثاني ٥٧ ليس

*Sailing off Giftun tourist village*

tough climb up the nearby mountain side. St Anthony was celebrated for his many temptations and is often associated with St Paul,
his contemporary. It is much more difficult to reach **St Paul's**

**Monastery** and one must return to Ras Zafarana and continue along
the coast road south to the turning on the right leading to the
monastery. This is a real desert track and the rough ride can take an
hour or so through stunning mountain landscape. The impressively
situated monastery of St Paul of Thebes is not quite as old as that of
St Anthony as the first church here was built around AD460. The
monastery buildings, which include a watch-tower, the Chapel of
the Virgin, St Mercurius's Church, St Michael's Church and St Paul's
Church, constructed over his anchorite cave (all surrounded by high
walls), date from the fifteenth century. The saint's church, however,
was built in the sixth century.

## HURGHADA

Around 530km (329 miles) south-east from Cairo by the route
through Suez and down the Gulf of Suez coastline, this popular
resort lies on the west coast of the Red Sea itself and can be reached
by a regular hour's flight from the capital. Independent drivers on
the coast road should be warned that there are only two small port
stop-overs on the 400km (248 miles) road from Suez to Hurghada.
Once similar to many of the other little sea ports and fishing villages
along this coastline, this stunningly attractive part of Egypt's Red Sea
shore has been developed into a world-famous tourist resort and a
magnet for those who like diving and fishing. More than two dozen
desert islands and innumerable coral reefs complement the long
stretches of sandy beach and rocky coves. The warm shallow sea,
teeming with a cascade of colourful, tropical fish are a main diversion for boat rides over variegated reefs and diveboats take experts
out to deep drop-offs and underwater caverns for the brilliant
marine life and sea-bed fauna. So important is this location for its
marine interest that the Institute of Hydrobiology has established
their offices here and added the Oceanographical Institute Museum
and Aquarium. At least a score of designated locations for fishing,
swimming, diving, snorkelling and watersports are all within easy
reach of the beachside luxury hotels and the two tourist villages.
Care should be taken when swimming anywhere in the Red Sea as
sharks are prevalent and several species of fish, jellyfish and sea
urchins can be poisonous. Coral can also inflict nasty grazes and all
injuries should receive medical attention in these latitudes. A ferry

## Places of Interest
## On the Red Sea Coast

**Hurghada**
530km (329 miles) south-east of
Cairo
Famous beach resort, beautiful
beaches and coral reefs.

**Mons Claudianus**
Inland, due west of Bur Safaga
Roman temple and extensive
quarry site.

**Mons Porphyrites**
West of Hurghada
Roman remains and ancient
quarry.

**Oceanographic Institute**
10km (6 miles) north of Hurghada
Aquarium and museum.

**St Anthony's Monastery**
Inland, off the Beni Suef road from
Ras Zafarana
Earliest and biggest of all Egypt's
monasteries.

**St Paul's Monastery**
Similar location as St Anthony's
Monastery
Less accessible but better
preserved than St Anthony's.

takes excursions from Hurghada across the Red Sea's Gulf of Suez
arm to the important resort town of Sharm el-Sheikh on the tip of the
Sinai Peninsula.

Excursions can be made from Hurghada into the desert or down
south to the port of Bur Safaga and up to the mountain-ringed
Roman camp of **Mons Claudianus**. Here the ruins of a Roman
settlement can be viewed as can the gigantic excavations made while
the ancients quarried this unusually beautiful white granite for the
construction of monuments as far away as Rome. Another quarry
site which is nearer is that used by the Romans at **Mons Porphyrites**
on the tortuous and difficult track almost directly west of the
Hurghada resort. Few visitors venture much further south than Bur
Safaga and from here one can make a detour across the Eastern
Desert. Take heed of all advice whenever travelling any distance at
all in the desert. Most overland, or cross country desert routes should
be negotiated with a reliable guide and the correct equipment. It is
preferable to travel in convoy, even if the road does look busy and
easily travelled and one should never underestimate the power of
the sun, the unreliability of equipment and hired vehicles, the lack of
availability of fuel and water and especially distances which may
look deceptively short on some maps.

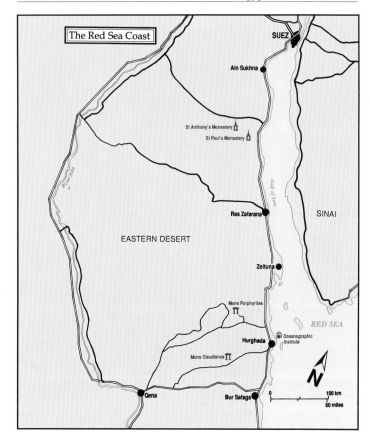

## MARINE LIFE OF EGYPT

One only has to see the beautifully detailed early murals, particularly those in the Tombs of the Nobles like that in the Tomb of Enene in Sheikh Abd el-Qurna in Western Thebes, to appreciate the fact that fishing was an important way of life in everyday Ancient Egypt. Much of the fishing industry at that time was concentrated on the River Nile and its Delta. Since those times the proliferation of fish in the river have dwindled, mainly due to the construction of the Aswan High Dam. Even in the Delta region the annual takings of fish have dropped dramatically.

*El-Arish resort, Sinai*

*Tourism is booming on the Red Sea coast and Gulf of Aqaba*

However, it is not the marine life of the Nile waters which attracts thousands of underwater enthusiasts from around the world to Egypt. With almost 1,135km (704 miles) of Mediterranean coastline in the north, and more than 2,400km (1,488 miles) of Red Sea shoreline, the country commands not only part of the world's longest freshwater river (including the lakelands of the Delta and Fayyum), but some of the temperate Mediterranean's best beaches and an unrivalled stretch of tropical, coral line waters along its eastern coast and that of the Sinai Peninsula.

Alexandria and her new counterpart El-Arish, both on the warm Mediterranean, are today magnets for sun-seekers with beach-lovers migrating, not only from Egypt's towns and cities, but from a hundred different countries, to their sandy seaside resorts. Other resorts being developed along this coastline are the western ports of Sidi Abel Rahman, Mersa Matruh and Sidi Barrani. Alexandria has long been an international favourite for holidaymakers as it is well developed with extensive beach facilities and a plethora of hotels. El-Arish is fast developing as its spectacular beaches become known to tourists and a whole new crop of motels and resort hotels have sprung out of the desert. Alexandria and El-Arish do not attract the serious marine explorer but in the east of the country lie several stars among the internationally acclaimed sub-aqua resorts of the world.

Hurghada and Bur Safaga, on the Egyptian mainland and about halfway down Egypt's east coast, are famed among the diving fraternity for their clear waters and abundant marine life. Several little islets and magnificent coral reefs off the shore make for ideal diving locations and the Hurghada Sheraton Hotel, Club Mediterranean at Magawish and the Giftun Village all offer first class diving facilities. Likened by diving experts to the fabulous Barrier Reef in its abundance of tropical fish, coral-dwelling marine life and clarity of its waters, Hurghada was the first resort to be developed in Eastern Egypt. There are now almost ten hotels in Hurghada and the resort is easily reached by daily flight from Cairo, by road via Suez, or across desert from Kena and Luxor. The Egyptian authorities have established a marine biology station in Hurghada, which was once a quiet fishing port. Most visitors to this part of Egypt will want to spend as much of their time as possible underwater as the Red Sea's marine life is among the most spectacular to be found anywhere.

From an unspoilt beach of sparking coral sand strewn with shells, boats head out for Hurghada's reefs and within minutes one can be snorkelling over crystalline waters or plunging into a wonderland of underwater activity. Lessons for novices, available at most resort hotels, should be taken before attempting a dive however inviting the sparkling waters might look. A variety of off-shore diving sites have been established on some of the thirty islands like the two Giftun islands of El-Kabir and El-Saghir, Abu Ramada Island and Shadwan Island which have snorkelling and diving facilities. At Umm Gammar Island there is a professional diving establishment and the Shaab el-Erg resort offers diving excursions as does Shaab

Abu Shiban. Careless Reef and the House of Sharks off Giftun Village are favourite diving areas as are the locations known as Shasb Saghir Umm Gammae, Sharm el-Arab and Shaab Abu Hashish.

The list of underwater marine life is as endless as the variety of colours below the calm surface of the Red Sea. At most diving shops the visitor can obtain a waterproof card which identifies many of the more common species and diving equipment can be hired in most hotels although the Gobal Hotel is one of the most economical. Once under limpid waters, orange, red and purple elkhorn, stag and brain corals and over a hundred other different types provide a habitat for sea anemones, sponges and starfish. Among pillar coral branches parrot fish graze and multi-coloured chromis dart away from the diver's mask or the shadow of a large grouper, ray or jackfish. The crannies between corals provide sanctuary for damsel fish, trigger fish, butterfly and angelfish, not to speak of the giant moray eel.

Some sort of footwear should be worn as both stone fish and sea urchins on the sea bed can inflict extremely nasty wounds from their spines. Fire coral should also be avoided. Around the fan coral wrasses, puffer fish and lion fish hover in the clear water while in the deeper regions Red Sea sharks and manta ray can be seen. For those visitors who prefer to view this underwater Disneyland, a short distance north of Hurghada town is the Institute of Hydrobiology marine station and marine museum which exhibits a vast range of Red Sea fish and also has a number of rare Red Sea manatees. From the aquarium, glass-bottomed boats (*houris*) can be hired to take groups out over the reefs for a look at the sea creatures in their natural habitat. The waters around Egypt, especially on its Red Sea coast, are as spectacular as the country's ancient monuments and enables its tourism industry to offer combined holidays, where the visitor can wonder at the great works of man in the past and marvel at the great works of nature in the present.

# 8

# CAIRO TO LUXOR
# AND THE OASES
# OF THE WESTERN DESERT

Possibly one of the most romantic and impressive tours anywhere in the world, this ultimate of excursions excites even the most seasoned traveller. Today just about every major tour operator offers either all, or part of this fascinating journey which can be covered in as little as a couple of days or savoured with the respect it is due, over a matter of weeks. Sadly, most visitors from abroad do not have the time to visit even a tenth of the important historical sites along the way, but this short, step-by-step account should briefly explain the many points of interest en route.

The complete Cairo to Luxor journey is around 730km (453 miles) in total. This daunting distance can be covered overland by train in comfortable, economical sleeper carriages and takes about 10 hours. However it is important to book seats in advance at the Midan Ramesses Station, Cairo. From Cairo there are flights daily by Egyptair, an inexpensive domestic service which should be pre-booked. Seats however are allocated on a first come, first served basis. Travelling by bus, from Cairo's Midan el-Tahrir bus station is generally basic in comfort and punctuality unless the Misr Travel group excursion, air-conditioned coach service is used. Taxis are not expensive, and, if a reliable driver is hired, a fare can be negotiated and reasonable tip provided after the trip — your chauffeur may offer to act as a guide. By hire car the journey from Cairo to Luxor is cheap, but best rented with a driver — only the most experienced of international drivers should attempt long distance car travel in

Egypt. Seven major operators based in Cairo run more than fifty large air-conditioned cruise boats but few of these sail from Cairo down to Luxor as most provide services just between Aswan and Luxor.

Along the west bank of the Nile, within easy striking distance of the road, railway or river, are twenty-four major sites of archaeological importance, eight interesting monasteries and two tomb locations which can be visited. Along the east bank, reached by local felucca until the road crosses the Nile at Nag Hammadi are twelve east bank sites of archaeological importance, two monasteries and seven tombs of outstanding note which are officially listed. Some of the monuments concentrated around Luxor can be visited by Nile cruisers which ply the river up as far as Abydos. There are also air services from Cairo to several points along the Nile like El Minya, Asyut and Sohag and the most popular tourist itineraries fly visitors directly to Luxor from where sailboats or steamers visit the more famous points of interest.

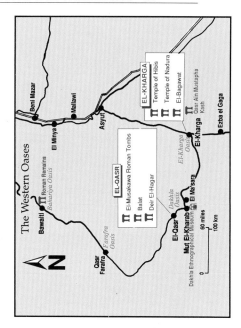

There are so many ancient sites scattered along the river's banks that it is impossible to give each the attention and preservation deserved. However, for the independent traveller with time to devote on the journey from the capital to Luxor, most of the more spectacular monuments can be easily visited either from the rail stations and bus stops or by car, taking advantage of the stop-over points along the way.

# Cairo to Beni Suef

The highway commences in the Giza suburb of Cairo and is joined by taking the left fork on the Al Ahram road to the pyramids. The village suburb of Abu Namrus lies just outside Giza's outskirts and from here the road and rail routes run parallel along the Nile's banks to the small township of El-Hawamdiya. Between here and the next town of El-Badrshein, the ruins of Memphis are passed and it is from El-Badrshein that a detour can be made to most of the monuments to the south-west of Cairo. Doubling back along a secondary road, the pyramids of Zawiyet el-Aryan, the Sun Temple of Abu Gurab, Abusir's pyramids and those monuments at Saqqara can be visited. A good half-day should be allowed to view these and the pyramid of Dahshur, reached by a sand track from Saqqara or from the riverside village of Dahshur a little further down the highway.

After Dahshur quite a long drive continues through palm groves and vegetable fields to **El Lisht** and a group of badly-eroded pyramids and mastabas. These monuments, and a few hummocks, are all that are left of an ancient capital established by Amenemhet I and his son Sesostris I. The two main pyramids are those of the father and son who ruled between 1991BC to 28BC the first two kings of the Twelfth Dynasty. The northern pyramid is that of Amenemhet I and the smaller tombs are those of relations and officials. Imenhotep, the High Priest of Heliopolis is also buried in a mastaba on this site. Ten statues of Sesostris, now in the national museum, were found here. About halfway between Lisht and the next pyramid site a road leads off into the desert from the village of Gerza. A few minute's drive up this track, almost to the edge of the Fayyum district, lie the ruins of the 250BC Greek settlement of **Philadelphia** where numerous 'Fayyum Portrait' funerary masks were discovered.

Back on the highway the triple-stepped **Collapsed Pyramid of Meidum** looms on the horizon to the right after passing through the village of Meidum. The monument is reached from the village of Rikka and is near the road leading into the Fayyum. Two Pharaohs helped create this tomb. Initially it was seven-stepped and built by King Huni. Sneferu, the founder of the Fourth Dynasty, completed the edifice, smoothed the sides and evolved the first true pyramid shape. The other tombs on this site are those of Nefermaat and Rahotep and their wives. From the monuments of Meidum it is a short drive to El Wasta where there is a turning into the Fayyum district.

From Beni Suef there are three important sites of antiquity which create a diversion from the highway. Taking Route 22 north-west from the town, heading towards the Fayyum, a few small villages are passed before reaching the two ruined temples and remains of a New Kingdom town at **Kom Madinet Ghurab** to the left of the road. A little further on, to the right, after the town of **El Lahun**, is the

# Places of Interest
# Between Cairo and Beni Suef

**Collapsed Pyramid of Meidum**
South of Gerza near Meidum village
Ancient famous pyramid and impor-
tant mastabas.

**Dahshur**
2km (1 mile) from Saqqara
Five important pyramids of the ancient royal kings.

**El Lahun**
South-east of Medinet el-Fayyum
Pyramid site of Sesostris II, queens
pyramids and tombs.

**Hawara**
South-east of Medinet el-Fayyum and
north of El Lahun
Important site of Amenemhet III's
tomb and Labyrinth.

**Kom Madinet Ghurab**
South-west of El Lahun, 18km
(12 miles) west of Beni Suef
Two temple sites, the remains of a
town and necropolis.

**El-Lisht**
70km (43 miles) south of Cairo on
west bank of Nile
Remains of ancient capital, two pyramids and tombs.

**Memphis**
22km (14 miles) south of Cairo on
west bank of Nile
Alabaster Sphinx, temple and palace
ruins.

**Philadelphia**
South of Lisht
Remains of a Ptolemaic Greek garri-
son settlement.

**Saqqara**
Inland from riverside site of Memphis
on edge of desert

Famous Step Pyramid and many
other early sites.

*The Fayyum*
**Biahmu**
Short distance north of Medinet el-
Fayyum
'Pharaoh's Chair' and 'The Idol'
monuments and ruins.

**Crocodilopolis**
'Horseman's Hill', on outskirts of
Medinet el-Fayyum
Egypt's largest ancient ruined city site
of Shedet.

**Dimei**
South of Qasr el-Sagha
Ptolemaic island with ruins.

**Dionysius**
Near Qarun town
Large temple and extensive ruins.

**El Hammam**
Southern shores of Lake Qarun
Lakeside settlement ruins.

**Kom Aushim**
Edge of Fayyum, due north of Medi-
net el-Fayyum
Ptolemaic temples and museum.

**Lake Qarun**
On edge of Fayyum north-west of
Medinet el-Fayyum
Egypt's largest natural lake.

**Medinet el-Fayyum**
90km (56 miles) south-west of Cairo
Regional capital and centre of
commerce.

**Qasr el-Sagha**
North of Fayyum area
Ptolemaic temple ruins.

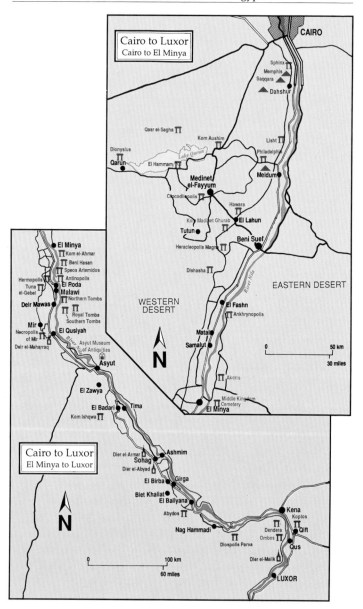

*Ballooning is fast becoming a popular way to view Egyptian sites*

pyramid site of Sesostris II, the queen's pyramid and grave wells of relations where some magnificent funerary jewellery was found. On the same side of the road, just a short drive north, is the site of **Hawara** just after the small town of the same name. Eroded into a huge hummock, the tomb of Amenemhet III is built of mud bricks and is the Pharaoh's second pyramid as he had already constructed one in Dahshur.

A series of courts, passageways and temple rooms (3,000 in all), once maze-like and covered with huge stone slabs, was known in the ancient world as the **Labyrinth**. This network of ruined walls can be seen alongside the canal which passes to the south of the Pyramid of Hawara. Both Strabo and Herodotus wrote of this structure which is now in ruins. The first of many Fayyum portraits (funerary masks painted on wooden plaques and enclosed in the coffins of the deceased) were uncovered in a Roman cemetery near Hawara pyramid. The road from Beni Suef to Hawara runs over many canals and irrigation channels which makes the region so fertile. Amenemhet III developed the major waterway system which fed Nile waters to the Fayyum district and brought life, agriculture and prosperity to the 'Garden of Egypt'.

## THE FAYYUM

This vast, artificial oasis, known as the 'Garden of Egypt', is important not only for its agricultural produce of cotton, vegetables, fruits, sugar cane and livestock, but for the number of ancient sites dotted around its 1800sq km (692sq miles). Originally a marshy 'seep away' of the Nile, irrigation channels and a network of waterways excavated over thousands of years have created an ideal environment for farming. The main features of this region, surrounded as it is by the Western Desert, are Lake Qarun (the largest natural lake in Egypt), the ancient Yusef (Joseph's) Canal which diverts sweet water from the Nile and the large town at the centre of the oasis, Medinet el-Fayyum.

Most visitors will take in the sites of the Fayyum in a day's excursion from Cairo. Two routes lead to the Fayyum from Cairo and the more round-about road is that which runs down the Nile (the Cairo-Aswan highway) through Memphis to either Rikka or Beni Suef where the metalled route can be taken back up to Fayyum's capital. A rail route also follows the course of the highway and River Nile and, by changing at Beni Suef, a train can be taken right through to Medinet el-Fayyum. There is no air service to the Fayyum. The road to the Fayyum is joined at the end of the El Ahram motorway on the edge of the Giza pyramids site. This route cuts straight across the desert, south-west from Giza, a 80km (50 mile) trek through empty desert and into the fertile oasis.

On the very outskirts of the Fayyum is the first of eleven impor- tant ancient ruins scattered throughout this region. **Kom Aushim** is the site of the ancient Greek hill city of Karanis. Little remains of Kom Aushim's past grandeur but there are the ruins of two temples visible and a small museum houses Ptolemaic relics. Further out into the desert, north of Lake Qarun, are the remains of a temple at **Qasr el- Sagha** and even further out, on the northern edge of the lake, are the extensive ruins of the island of **Dimei** (Soknopaios). This Ptolemaic city, known as Dimei, is in a good state of preservation with houses, a temple and statues. This site is best reached by boat from the inn, Auberge du Lac, a 2-hour sail across on the south bank of the lake.

Continuing on into the Fayyum from Kom Aushim, the sudden transformation of terrain from desert sands and bare, rocky outcrops to green plots of vegetables shaded with date palms, is dramatic. Not far from the Aushim ruins is a secondary road leading off to the right which skirts the southern shores of Lake Qarun. Spectacular lakeside views are broken at the end of this small access road by the ruins of **El Hammam**, or the ancient 'baths'. This is very near to Shakshuk where travellers can spend the night. The famous Auberge du Lac, once King Farouk's summer retreat, is on the lakeside here and makes an excellent base for a day's visiting of the Fayyum's fascinat- ing villages and dozen-or-so ancient locations.

Travelling in the Fayyum by conventional car is difficult as most of the roads are just tracks but, returning to the main route which bisects the area diagonally, a short drive from the junction with the Hammam road takes one through the small town of Sennuris. This brings the traveller to the village of **Biahmu** and its adjacent ruins. Locally called the 'Pharaoh's Chair', and 'The Idol', two massive pyramid-shaped blocks here were once the bases for colossi of Amenemhet III who spent a great deal of his reign developing the Fayyum. In the time of Herodotus, who described the statues, these massive monuments once stood in the lake which the Greeks called Lake Moeris.

From here it is a few minute's drive into the region's capital, **Medinet el-Fayyum**. The accommodation in this bustling town is primitive and can be booked up as many Egyptians take their holidays in the Fayyum. This town is famed for its markets and it was here that terracotta was first utilised which may give the visitor an idea for a souvenir. A few interesting mosques, churches, ancient

*Typical Nileside scenery*

*Traditional feluccas transport essential goods*

*'Floating hotels' offer air conditioned luxury and relaxed sightseeing*

waterwheels (typical of the area in the squares) and more markets comprise the sum interest in this town of almost 500,000 people. On 'Horseman's Hill' just on the outskirts of Medinet el-Fayyum are the remains of **Crocodilopolis** Arsinoe, named for the crocodile-headed god Sobek worshipped here during Ancient Egyptian occupation when the huge town was called Shedet, and Ptolemy II's wife, Arsinoe, whom the Greek king named as the city's goddess. The ruins of Crocodilopolis are Egypt's largest ancient site and covers more than 500 acres.

There are six other early locations in the Fayyum region and two of these are quite difficult to reach. The site of Ramesses' **Tebtunis** near the village of Tutun, far on the southern edge of the agricultural oasis, is important for the many papyrus and crocodile mummies found here. Nearby are some interesting Twelfth Dynasty rock tombs. Not far to the west, and equally hard to get to, are the remains of a larger and more spectacular city, Narmouthis, now known as

**Kom el-Medinet Madi.** The main temple here, to Sobek the crocodile-headed god, was established by Amenemhet III. There is another temple to Anubis (the jackel-headed god) and two avenues are
lined by statues of lions and sphinxes — a real zoological medley!

Easier to reach are the ruins in the north-east of the Fayyum, those
up near the western end of Lake Qarun. Driving out of Medinet el-
Fayyum, the first of these three is **Karabat Iret**, once the town of
Theadelphia and now boasting few relics apart from a cemetery and
ruined temple. Ancient Philoteris and Euhemeria lie nearby but the
most spectacular site is at the end of the lake near the town of **Qarun**.
This is the furthest west point of the entire Fayyum oasis and here are
the remains of the old city of **Dionysius**. There are two temple
chambers here and the god worshipped was the ram-headed
Khnum. This is a favourite part of the Fayyum and the hotel and hunting lodge are splendidly located for fishing or boating trips on Lake
Qarun. Note the massive waterwheels and intricate patterns of the
irrigation ditches on the road back to Fayyum's heart. Interesting
villages on the road include El Shawashna and Ibshawai. It is also
possible to link up with the route to Cairo via the village of Sanhour,
joining the road at Sennuris. This road takes traffic down, through
the regional capital, to the main Cairo-Aswan highway at Beni Suef
on the banks of the Nile. As the road heads south-east from Medinet
el-Fayyum, it passes through a narrow swathe of agricultural land
before entering the broad Nilotic wetlands which in shape, creates a
stalk linking the lotus-leaf shaped Fayyum with the stem of the Nile.

## BENI SUEF TO LUXOR

Back on the road to Luxor at Beni Suef there is a short drive to the next
important site of **Heracleopolis Magna**, near the town of Ahnasiya
el-Madina. The road to this Old Kingdom ruins, of which little
remains, leads off to the right of the Nile side highway just after
leaving the town of Beni Suef. If the by-road which runs along the
banks of the Yusef Canal, is taken, a little further along the site of
**Dishasha** contains a number of Fifth Dynasty tombs and murals.
This location can also be reached from the Cairo-Luxor road by
taking a right diversion at the Nile bank market town of Biba. Much
further out in the desert to the south-west, and practically inaccessible, is the monastery of Dier Samwell.

Back on the highway, with the railway line still in attendance
between the road and the river on the left, the town of **El Fashn** is
reached. El Fashn is a popular stop-over for Nile cruises. Should the
visitor be inclined to detour across to the east bank of the Nile by

# Places of Interest
# Between Beni Suef and El Minya

**Akoris**
Between Samalut and El Minya on east bank of Nile
Tombs, temples and ruins of the ancient city.

**Ankhrynopolis**
East bank of River Nile, near El Fashn
Early temple ruins and city wall remains.

**Cynopolis**
On Yusef Canal, near Sandafa el-Far town
Egyptian, Greek and Roman ruins of old Oxyrhynchus.

**Dier Gebel El Teir**
Near Samalut on Bird Mountain, east bank of Nile

St Helen's legendary clifftop monastery.

**Dishasha**
Along bank of Yusef Canal
Collection of ancient tombs with fine murals.

**El Minya**
247km (153 miles) south of Cairo
Museum of El Minya and Middle Kingdom cemetery.

**Heracleopolis Magna**
North-west of Beni Suef
Important Old Kingdom ruins.

**Kom el-Ahmar**
South of Akoris
Royal necropolis of the early Egyptian Hebenu.

means of the bridge here, a temple on the hillside, together with thick city walls and other early Pharaonic ruins, are all that remains of the Greek city of **Ankhrynopolis**. The little village nearby is called El Hiba. Return to the southbound highway which passes through the towns of Maghagha, Abu Girk and Beni Mazzar. From Beni Mazzar a track leads up to the Yusef Canal at the village of Sandafar el-Fa.

Across the westernmost of the two secondary roads which run between the canal and the highway, is the little village of **El Kais**. Here is an Ancient Egyptian site and there are remains of another Greek city, **Cynopolis**. The Ancient Egyptian town here was named after a revered Nile fish and known as Oxyrhynchus. A number of Roman ruins can be seen on the same site which was once a major religious centre. From Beni Mazzar the road runs through the town of Matai and the twin towns of Masaret Samalut and Samalut. By driving through Samalut a short distance on the left is a track to a bridge over the Nile leading to the **Dier Gebel El Teir** on Bird Mountain. This cliff-top monastery, attributed to St Helena, is reached by sixty-six steps hewn into the rock. Between Samalut and the next

*Souks at every stop along the Nile route*

**Π** large town of El Minya the east bank site of **Akoris** can be visited. The best way to reach this interesting site with its tombs, rock carvings, ruins and temples, is by local felucca across the river from the village of El Burgayah.

Any independent traveller who has managed to drive or take the train this far up the Nile Valley might have included an overnight stop in the Fayyum. Medinet el Fayyum to El Minya is a drive of a good 160km (99 miles). Time again to consider resting or taking a break in the journey. **El Minya** has three hotels and is a busy commercial town of almost 160,000 population. This pretty, Nileside market town is a fine base from which to visit at least seven important ancient sites. Some visitors might select to fly direct to El Minya from Cairo and take in the main sites of this area in a day's excursion. There is a long history of this region which dates back to the last Pharaoh of the Eighteenth Dynasty, Amenhotep IV, immediate predecessor of Prince Tutankhamen and ruler between 1364BC to 47BC.

A museum in the town gives a good insight into the importance of this area from early Egyptian times to the era of Greek and Roman occupation. The modern cemetery nearby is notable as this region of Middle Egypt is where the domes and barrel roofs of the hotter

*Camels, or 'ships of the desert' can be hired*

*Nileside villages make picturesque photographs*

regions of the Nile Valley begin to be seen — many of the sepulchres here show the characteristic mud dome. Taxis take visitors to most of the sites but as four of the major ruins and one tomb site lie on the east bank of the Nile, a trip by river steamer from the corniche at El Minya is usually preferred. It is possible to take in at the same time as Akoris, **Kom el-Ahmar** (Red Hill), south of the town, in the east bank hills. This site is surrounded by royal rock tombs and connected with the Ancient Egyptian centre of Hebenu. This Old Kingdom site is near the shoreline village of Zawiyet el-Amwat and Nueirat.

## EL MINYA TO NAG HAMMADI

A steamer trip up the river from El Minya, skirting several small islands and providing magnificent vistas of the Nile's fertile west bank and rugged east bank, first stops at the celebrated tomb site of **Beni Hasan**. Driving down from El Minya the village of Abyuna is passed just before El Fikriyah from where a track crosses the canal, down to the bridge at El Roda or ferry across to the monument road. Beni Hasan village, below the tombs, can be reached from the west bank by means of a ferryboat. The ancient monuments are best visited by hiring a donkey for the tough climb. Beni Hasan is a popular stop-over for Nile tours. This site is a Middle Kingdom necropolis containing twelve magnificently embellished tombs and twenty-seven of lesser importance. The tombs are attributed to the governors of the Oryx Nome and contain chapels within the necropolis. Fine views of the Nile Valley are seen from this viewpoint.

On the east side of the river from the little village of Abu Qurqas, Amenemhet's tomb with its twin-columned entrance cut into the barren rock face is one of the four most important tombs of the Beni Hasan site. Sporting, hunting, battle and religious scenes decorate the walls of Amenemhet's tomb (No 2) and the huge hall is supported by four fluted columns. Tomb No 3 contains a well-restored collection of wall paintings and inscriptions, particularly the lengthy 222 rows of hieroglyphs relating to the activities of Khnumhotep III to whom the columned and handsomely decorated tomb is dedicated. Baket's tomb (No 15), has suffered from vandals and its main pair of columns are missing but several lotus topped columns flank a chamber with exquisite frescoes. More well-preserved paintings decorate the walls of tomb No17, that of Kheti, Baket's son although this tomb has also had its columns removed. Eight more of these rock tombs have wall paintings but these four described are considered superior. The monuments on this site date from the Eleventh and early Twelfth Dynasties about 2040BC to 1840BC.

From the tomb site return to the bridge near El Roda. A little
further south, skirting the cliffs, is the rock temple of the local
goddess Pakhet — the lion, or cat-headed deity. The carved decorations date from Queen Hatshepsut's reign, 1490BC to 68BC, but
Pharaohs have tampered with them. The Greeks called this place
**Speos Artemidos** (Cave of Artemis), a god they associated with
Pakhet. Even further along the same east bank road, past the little
village of Sheikh Timai, is another site of importance — the ruins of
**Antinopolis**, named after the unfortunate Antinous. Known locally
as El Sheikh Ibada, this AD130 city incorporates remains dating from
pre-Dynasty times and a temple here was constructed by Ramesses
II. These fascinating ruins are complemented by several necropolis
sites dating from Egyptian, Roman and Christian times. Once this
site boasted a great arch, colonnades and a Roman theatre, little of
which now remains.

The pretty village of **El Roda** with mosques and an old palace, is
linked with the highway by two roads — either to the north, back
towards El Minya, or south, to the large town of Malawi, via El
Fikriya town and the village of El Rairamun. In order to visit the two
other important historic monuments of this region, Hermopolis and
Tuna el-Gebel, neither of these roads should be taken from El Roda
as a track leads across the highway to link with a side road running
to both sites near the village of **Ashmunein**. Some locals refer to the
sites collectively under the name of the tiny village but they are, in
fact two separate sites divided by hundreds of years. The Ancient
Egyptian city of Khumunu connected with the Moon God, Thoth
(depicted with either a baboon or ibis head) is now under the rubble
which surrounds Ashmunein and nearby **Hermopolis**, really came
into being during the Ptolemaic period. Columns, temples ruins,
pylons and statues (particularly those of giant baboons representing
Thoth), date from the reign of Amenemhet II, Seti II and Amenhotep
III. The Greek Agora is demarcated by re-erected granite columns
and the remains of a Nineteenth Dynasty hall can be seen.

**Tuna el-Gebel**, a short drive west from Ashmunein, is the 300BC
necropolis belonging to the latter city of Hermopolis. On the way a
territorial stele of the Pharaoh Akhenaten can be seen. The funerary
temple of Petosiris, High Priest of Thoth, and the tomb of Isadora are
well worth visiting for the wonderfully preserved carvings, inscriptions, reliefs, fascinating wall paintings and decorated columns.
Other points of interest are the baboon and ibis catacombs. Back on
the highway, the southbound route should be taken to the market
town of **Malawi** where the Archaeological Museum exhibits a fine

*Weathered baboon statue, Hermopolis Magna*

collection of artifacts and relics from each of the nearby ancient locations. These seven sites, grouped around or between the towns of El Minya and Malawi, can all be reached within half an hour's drive of the hotels in El Minya, or a short river steamer trip from the little quayside on the town's corniche.

There are, however, four further ancient sites situated on the east bank of the river south of Malawi. These four rock tomb groups and one early city ruin can also be comfortably fitted into a day's itinerary while boarding at El Minya, or there are regular sailings to them from Malawi. Just a few minutes on the highway out of Malawi the village of **Deir Mawas** should be seen on the left hand it is from here that the historic locations can be visited. There are two bridges across the Nile here, one each side of a small mid-stream island. There is a railway station at Deir Mawas and the ever-present Ibrahimiya Canal runs between it and the river. A donkey should be hired at the ferry landing for the stiff walk to the main attraction which is the famous city of Akhetaten who, with the celebrated Queen Nefertiti, established this 'Horizon of Aten' (Sun Disc) royal residence. Today the site has adopted an Arab name, **Tel el Amarna**. The Royal Palace is generally the first point visited in this extensive city by walking up from the tiny riverside settlement of El Till. The ruins of the Great Temple of Aten, the Sun God, are passed as are the archives in the palace compound. There is a rest-house a little further south of the palace. The summer palace of Pharaoh Akhenaten, who lived between 1364BC to 47BC lies at Maru Aten, just a short walk from the rest-house.

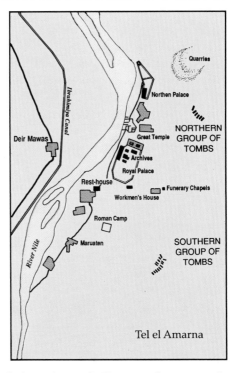

Up in the hills above the palace site are the Southern Group of Tombs. Only sixteen are accessible of the twenty-five so far discovered and are not often included on excursions as the more prolific and interesting group of tombs lie to the north. However, five outstanding graves in the southern group are those of Tutu (No 8), Mahu, the military General (No 9), Commander Mei (No 14), Scribe Enei (No 23) and Ay (No 25). A long trek back through the ruins of the city, passing dignitaries houses, workshops, small temples and palaces, past the main Royal Palace and the Great Temple, leads to the Northern Palace with its adjacent official's residences and workshops. The famous bust of Nefertiti was found in the Northern Palace and is now on display in the Egyptian Museum, Berlin. The Northern Group of Tombs lie north-east of the main Tel el Amarna complex, up in the ridge of cliffs. They look down on both the palaces and comprise nine important sepulchres including those of Huye (No 1), Royal Steward, Merire (No 2), Ahmose (No 3), a High Priest also known as Merire (No 4), Pentu the Royal Physician (No 5) and Visier Panehsi (No 6). The family tomb of Amenophis IV (No 25), lies far out between the two groups of tombs and is rarely visited as there are few remaining inscriptions or wall paintings to view. The superb decorations of this new age of art in the First Intermediate Period, as compared to the simple style of the Old Kingdom, are spectacular and intricate. Hundreds of important artifacts were found throughout this group of tombs, palaces and temples, now on exhibition in museums around the world. About a dozen stelae mark a boundary around the Tel el Amarna site.

Joining the highway south, on the west bank, the road runs through several villages, and near that of Deirut el-Sharif is the ruined monastery of **Apa Apollot**. The road continues on, passing the rail stop town of Dairut on the left and coming to **El Qusiyah** village, well worth a halt as there are ancient tombs and an early monastery nearby. The necropolis of **Mir** contains tombs of Middle Kingdom dignitaries and the frescoes and reliefs here are renowned for their style. Connected with the escapades of the Holy Family's flight in Egypt, the Coptic monastery east of the tomb site is that of **Deir el-Maharraq**. From El Qusiyah (the Ancient Egyptian settlement of Kis) the highway proceeds for a good 15 minutes in a straight line following the route of the canal and the rail track. Halfway along this runway-like stretch of road is the town of Manfalut. Opposite, near Maabda village, is an Old Kingdom necropolis where an extraordinary number of mummified animals and reptiles were incarcerated in the Crocodile Caves and nearby are more ancient tomb sites. This location is best visited by the small east bank road which turns off the highway and crosses the river before one enters historic Asyut. Continuing from Manfalut before a junction, where the El Kharga Oasis road branches off to the right, and just before the airport of Asyut, the Monastery of Dier el-Gabrawi can be seen on the clifftop on the opposite bank of the Nile. The road turns back towards the river at the village of Manqabad and the railway line crosses the highway just before Asyut town.

**Asyut**, once Ancient Lycopolis, now has a population of half a million, a university and many industries including a cement factory, carpet-making, garment weaving and leather goods manufacture. The cotton trade brought wealth to this important centre and evidence of this is seen in the palatial mansions now falling into disrepair. A late nineteenth-century barrage across the Nile here regulates the water from the river flowing into the Ibrahimiya Canal. There is the interesting Museum of Antiquities in Asyut and the bazaar of the Old Town is well worth visiting for souvenirs. However, before leaving the outskirts of Asyut, just after the Old Town, a track leads up the mountain path to an important tomb location,

# Places of Interest
# Between El Minya and Nag Hammadi

**Abydos**
45km (28 miles) south of Girga
Famous capital city ruins of Upper
Egypt. Palaces, temples and wealth
of monuments.

**Antaeopolis**
Near village of Tima
Early Dynastic rock tombs and old
necropolis.

**Anthribis**
South of Sohag on west side of main
road. Early Ptolemaic site.

**Antinopolis**
Outskirts of Sheikh Timai village
Hadrian's city with ruins.

**Apa Apollot**
Near Deirut el-Sharif
Remains of ruined monastery.

**Ashmim**
Short distance east of 'Red Monastery'. Ancient ruins around village.

**Asyut**
378km (234 miles) south of Cairo
Ancient Lycopolis, Old Town houses,
museum.

**Beni Hasan**
On Nile's east bank midway between
El Minya and Mallawi
Ancient necropolis with tomb sites.

**Biet Khaliat**
Out in desert, west of Girga
4,600-year-old funerary site.

**Crocodile Caves**
Near Maabda village
Old Kingdom animal graveyard and
numerous tombs.

**Deir el-Maharraq**
Short distance south of Mir
Legendary monastery site.

**Dier el-Abyad**
Short distance east of 'Red Monastery'. 'White Monastery' ruins.

**Dier el-Armar**
25km (15 miles) north of Sohag town
'Red Monastery' ruins and church.

**Dier el-Gabrawi**
East bank of Nile near Beni Mohame-
diyat town. Early monastery site.

**El Badari**
East bank of Nile near village of same
name. Prehistoric grave location.

**El Birba**
West bank, south of El Mansha
Very Ancient Thinite city location.

**El Zawya**
Short distance into desert south-west
of Asyut. Royal rock tombs.

**Hermopolis**
West side of main road near El-
Ashmunein village. Finely-preserved
Ptolemaic city remains.

**Kis**
On site of modern El Qusiyah
Ancient Cussae, built over by El
Qusiyah.

**Kom Ishqwa**
Between main road and Nile south of
El Sidfa village. Ancient Greek site of
Aphroditopolis.

**Mir**
East of El Qusiyah
Well preserved tombs in necropolis.

**Nag el-Dier**
Opposite Girga on east bank
Prehistoric and Old Kingdom tombs.

**Ptolemais**
West bank of Nile, south of Sohag
Ruins built over by El Mansha.

**Speos Artemidos**
Short distance south of Beni Hasan
Interesting rock temple remains.

**Tel el Amarna**
East bank of Nile opposite Deir
Mawas town
Site of royal city, many tombs.

**Tuna el-Gebel**
West of El-Ashmunein
Temple, basilica and necropolis of
Hermopolis.

near **El Zawya** village, where the rock sepulchres of Hapidjefa I, Hapidjefa III and Prince Kheti can be visited. An extensive local cemetery with characteristic domed tombs is situated nearby as is the Coptic monastery of Dier Rifa.

From the railway station in the main square of El Zawya the road crosses another canal, the Sohagiya, and continues between the railway to the right and the Nile to the left, towards the village of Sidfa where it cuts inland from the river and parts company with the rail track. Taking the secondary turning sharp left, towards the river at this dog-leg's bend in the highway, the village and railway station of **Tima** is on the Nile's west bank. Over on the east bank, up in the far cliffs, are three Fifth Dynasty rock tombs and the extensive necropolis of Antaeopolis. Further north along the east bank road, and near the town of **El Badari**, is a famous prehistoric grave site. Back to El Sidfa on the southbound highway another historic site can be visited. This is the ruined town of **Kom Ishqwa**, the Greek site of the city of Aphroditopolis, on the left of the road. Another 15 minutes drive takes the route through several tiny villages to the important town of **Sohag**. There is a railway station here, an airport, a swing bridge over the river, and a large cathedral. Lying back off the road, in the hills to the west, are the two convents of **Dier el-Armar** (the Red Monastery), and **Dier el-Abyad** (the White Monastery). Opposite the cotton-weaving town of Sohag on the east bank, is **Ashmim**, Ancient Panopolis, where some ruins still exist and a number of old necropoli have been unearthed. Not far upstream is the village of El Mansha, on the west bank, the site of early Ptolemais. On leaving Sohag the ancient remains of **Anthribis** lies to the right of the road just past the village of Rawafi el-Qwasain.

The next important site that could be visited from the route between Sohag and the fascinating ruins of Abydos, lies around the town of Girga on both the west and east banks. Even before the road reaches the Girga vicinity it passes through a small village known as **El Birba** which represents the location of this First and Second Dynasty (Ancient Thinite) dating from around 3000BC. The entire area on the east bank is dotted with very old remains known as **Nag el-Dier**, and date from prehistoric times. Around these ancient tombs are a number of rock tombs built during the Old Kingdom period, some cliff graves of the Nineteenth Dynasty and the site of the ancient city of Lepidoptonopolis. **Girga**, facing this site from the west bank, is reached by means of a service road from the main highway and is an interesting district capital with pretty houses and a railway station. An important mastaba of brick out in the desert west of Girga, at **Biet Khaliat**, dates from the Third Dynasty, around 2600BC. Following the railway track to the left, the road now runs through the town of Minshat Bardis and into **El Baliyana**. This small town with railway station and quayside docking for river cruisers is an important tourist centre as it is from here that most visitors take the short road, out into the desert, to the ancient capital of **Abydos**. However, if the 275km (170 mile) drive from the last hotel accommodation at El Minya, or the rail journey up the Nile route proves too exhaustive to include a visit to Abydos in the same run, it is advisable to continue on and stop at Nag Hammadi, less than an hour's drive further south. The majority of visitors to Abydos will alternatively come from Luxor, either by coach excursion or riverboat trip.

## ABYDOS

The 'City of Osiris' is one of Egypt's most fascinating ancient monuments and its mysteries rival those of the Giza Pyramids, the remains at Karnak and Thebes. Thought to be the original site of the Thinite city of This, possibly pre-dating the El Birba location, Abydos dates from the First and Second Dynasty, around 3000BC. This is the site of the first true capital of Egypt, contemporary with Saqqara, and is in a remarkable state of preservation. The Ancient Egyptian's believed that Osiris, who was reincarnated by his wife Isis, was

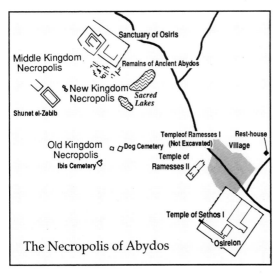

The Necropolis of Abydos

eventually buried in Abydos, and so many came here to die. Another deity associated with Abydos and nearby Asyut was the god of death, the local wolf god Wepwawet. The extensive necropolis here has been the repository for the dead from the earliest Dynasties and offers the visitor a cross section of temples and cemeteries from the Old, Middle and New Kingdoms of Ancient Egypt.

The most impressive structure at Abydos is the Temple of Sethos I (or Seti I) dating from 1304BC to 1290BC — the Nineteenth Dynasty. This is located out of Abydos, past the Osireion, in the desert. Completed by Ramesses II, this seven-chapelled temple was named the 'Memnonium' by the historian Strabo and is famous particularly for the King List which was found here in the Gallery of Kings. The King List of Abydos, engraved on its walls, contain the documented chronology of royal cartouches, or seals, of seventy-six kings and Pharaohs from Menes to Seti I. The walls of the temple's three Hypostyle Galleries are profusely decorated with detailed paintings, inscriptions and religious frescoes. The seven shrines are to the deified Seti himself, Osiris, Isis, Ptah, Amun, Horus and Ra. Two courtyards, with carved incriptions on their walls, fronted the temple. Behind Sethos's temple is the Osireion, a great hall excavated into an artifical mount, sixteen funerary niches, a moat and a secondary hall. This structure was built to represent the stairway to the underworld and is revered as the burial place of Osiris.

Between the Temple of Sethos I and the Temple of Ramesses II, is the unexcavated Temple of Ramesses I, on the outskirts of the modern village of El Arabda el Madfuna (the buried village). Ramesses II's temple with some excellently preserved murals, pillars and columns has some fine reliefs carved on the walls of its chapels and halls. South-west from here is the so-called depository of a number of early cenotaphs of First and Second Dynasty kings. A short walk to the west are the cemeteries of dogs and ibis dating from the Old Kingdom and to the right are two sacred lakes. The ruins of a Second Dynasty palace, Shunet el-Zebib, lies to the west. Between this and the Sanctuary of Osiris are necropoli with little brick pyramids dating from both the Middle and New Kingdoms and traces of the ancient city of Abydos. Little remains of the very early Sanctuary of Osiris. Pre-dynastic remains have been found in Abydos which marks it as one of the earliest and longest-lasting of all Egypt's ancient locations.

## Places of Interest
## Between Nag Hammadi and Luxor

**Apolinopolis Parva**
East bank of Nile, south of Qift
Ancient city ruins on present site of
Qus.

**Dendera**
West bank of Nile, opposite Kena
town
Spectacular ruins including Temple
of Hathor and Isis. Also Roman
and Ptolemaic remains on this
famous early site.

**Dier el-Malik**
South of Dier Mari Buktur
Large monastery complex with
interesting churches.

**Dier Mari Buktur**
North of Luxor on west bank of Nile
Monastic location and church.

**Diospolis Parva**
Modern Hiw, east of Nag Hammadi
Built over ancient city site.

**El Dhaba**
East bank of Nile
Small hillside necropolis.

**Koptos**
East bank of Nile, south of Kena
town
Old caravan station town at Qift.

**Naqada**
Opposite Qus on west bank of Nile
Early Coptic village settlement.

**Ombos**
West bank of Nile, opposite Qus
town
Very early location of capital city of
Upper Egypt.

**Qasr el Banat**
Far out into desert, east of Nile on
Red Sea road
Old Roman watering place on
desert road.

## NAG HAMMADI TO KENA

The track from Abydos leads east to the main Cairo-Aswan highway which continues southwards past many agricultural villages to the Nile side town of **Nag Hammadi** where there is a large hotel. From the accommodation of Nag Hammadi the previously mentioned sites like Abydos, Nag el-Dier and those around Sohag can be comfortably visited, as could the next important location on the Nile Valley excursion, Dendera. Just outside Nag Hammadi, at Hiw, still on the west bank, are the ancient ruins of **Diospolis Parva** of which hardly anything remains. Few visitors take the time to detour to Hiw as, at this point both the rail and road routes change course, crossing the river to the east bank. A minor necropolis from the Sixth Dynasty is to be found in the hills above the village of **El Dhaba** just across the river, but the more exciting monuments of Dendera beckon the traveller as he nears his goal of Luxor.

*Temple of Hathor, Dendera*

A wide strip of cultivated land is traversed as the road follows the course of the Nile almost due east before swinging south in a great curve at the town of **Kena**. There is a large hotel here which is an important railhead, riverside mooring station and junction linking this part of the Nile with Bur Safaga on the Red Sea coast. From Kena a bridge links the east bank with the west. If the next three ancient remains and two monasteries on this itinerary are to be visited by independent transport, it is best for the traveller to continue on the secondary road which runs from the west side of the bridge down the Nile bank to a point opposite the town of Luxor. If the main highway is taken, following the rail route to Luxor, there is little of antiquity to view except the sparse remains of Ancient **Koptos** at Qift, where the old caravan route joins the Nile Valley; Qasr el Banat (Castle of the Maidens), on the old road (Route 88), an Ancient Roman watering hole; the location of several early Egyptian and Greek sites and the ancient city site of Apolinopolis Parva, now Qus.

*Ptolemaic remains*

## DENDERA

Crossing to the west bank and the secondary road by the Kena
bridge, a right turning should be made in order to reach Dendera.
Although heading away from Luxor north, this is the best route to
take when visiting this ancient site unless one keeps on the west bank
from Nag Hammadi continuing on Route 53 through Hiw and El
Waqf. Whichever direction the ruins of Dendera are approached
from the great Temple of Hathor dominates the numerous remains
of ancient buildings. The original Egyptian name for this early city,
thought to date from the Sixth Dynasty (2325BC to 2160BC), was
Yunet Tantare, or Place of the Goddess Hathor. Goddess of the sky,

dancing and love, Hathor wore the head of a cow and her likeness can be seen on the six columns of the temple's façade. The walls of the temple are carved in a frieze of figures and inscriptions and five main chambers lie inside the pylon-like structure.

The spectacular ceiling of the vestibule is decorated with the image of Nut, goddesss of the sky, and her attendant Zodiac symbols. Inside the temple's vestibule are twenty-four further columns depicting the goddess Hathor. The hypostyle hall contains more Hathor-headed columns and the entire building comprises twenty smaller rooms and chapels dedicated to various religious functions. This vast edifice is one of Egypt's best-preserved ancient sites and was constructed on an earlier temple location by the Twelfth Dynasty kings and added to by such Pharaohs as Tutmosis III and both Ramesses II and III.

Behind the Temple of Hathor is the Temple of Isis dating originally from Ptolemaic times but constructed around 27BC. Two other temple ruins have been discovered south of the Temple of Isis as have the tombs of important personages from the Old Kingdom period which dates the complex to around 2600BC. A square sacred lake, now an oasis for palms, lies to the west of the temple compounds and Roman bath houses, a Roman birth-house, a Ptolemaic birth-house and a fifth-century Coptic church stand adjacent to the north-west flank of the main temple. The birth-houses of Ptolemaic Egypt were connected with the rituals of deifying the ruling Dynasties. To the north of the site, next to the entrance, is a Roman gateway, and in front of this and some ancient wells is the rest-house and refreshment room.

---

## DENDERA TO LUXOR

Continuing south on this secondary road, past the bridge to Kena on the left and skirting a high peak, El Ballas, El Zawaydas and Tukh villages are passed before coming on the site of **Ombos** to the right. These ruins are of a very early Egyptian capital and, from the remains found here, indicate a settlement of the prehistoric period. Just a few minute's drive south can be seen a large brick mastaba dating from almost 3000BC, the time of the foundation of the Kingdoms of Egypt. Nearby here is also the ancient Coptic village of **Naqada**. Two very early Coptic churches, **Dier Mari Buktur** and **Dier el-Malik** are located to the right of the road after the village of Danfiq. The latter of these monasteries comprises four separate buildings and its monastery boasts no fewer than twenty-eight domes.

As the road passes Dier el-Malik the awe-inspiring Great Temple of Amun and the columns of the vast religious complex of Karnak can be seen across the Nile waters. Following the Fadiliya Canal, the road passes El Tarif village and Kurna's hospital to the right, reaching a crossroads at the village of New Kurna. Across the Nile is a picture familiar from many guidebooks and postcards — the sedate outline of Luxor to the right and the majestic silhouettes of Karnak's ruins, said to be the world's largest religious complex, to the left. There are two ferry points on the west bank of the Nile both with ticket offices. Before crossing it is worth considering this breathtaking view. Behind, in the brooding mountains, lies the great Necropolis of Thebes, the City of the Dead, and in front, across the placid waters, stands Luxor, its modern hotel buildings mingling with colonial mansions and ancient monuments.

# The Western Oases

### EL-KHARGA OASIS
El-Kharga is Egypt's largest oasis and lies deep in the middle of the vast Western Desert. It is reached by a good, metalled road from Asyut, halfway between Cairo and Aswan, or by air from Cairo. The distance of this oasis from any major town needs consideration. It is about 105km (65 miles) across inhospitable desert from the Nile Valley to El-Kharga, and on any stretch of desert road one should take all the necessary precautions. There is absolutely no habitation, no signs of life, except the occasional passing bus or lorry; no change on the landscape except the shape of wadis and mountain ridges on the interminably long and straight sand-blown road from Asyut to El-Kharga. The first signs that the driver has not been transported to a strip of metalled road across an uninhabited planet will probably be strings of camels in the distance as one approaches the village of El-Mahariq, on the verge of entering the lush green of the oasis proper and before reaching the town of El-Kharga itself.

Surrounded by hills, **El-Kharaga** is a 'text book' oasis. A green ✳ jewel of vegetable fields, fruit trees and date palm groves in a great sea of ochre sand. Kharaga's water is derived by artesian wells and newly introduced irrigation schemes from an ancient subterranean branch of the Nile which flows along a rift called the New Valley. The New Valley runs north-west through the Kharga and Dakhla oases which are also linked. The population of the oasis, with the advent of a new housing scheme, is expanding daily. Accommodation in the oasis is either in the New Valley bungalows (tourist homes), the four-

*El-Bagawat tombs, El-Kharga Oasis*

storey Waha Hotel, or the Kharga Oasis Hotel, opposite the tourist office.

Tourists do not come to El-Kharga for the opportunity of viewing one of Egypt's most advanced re-housing plans, its new duck farms and date groves, or its most modern irrigation systems. Most visitors fly in from Cairo for a few days in order to see the important ancient ruins scattered around the little town and its satellite villages. The old part of El-Kharga town is attractive for its mud-bricked houses and narrow alleyways harking back to Biblical times when this oasis formed an important crossroads for desert caravans bound for Sudan and Nubia. It was around 500BC that one of the region's most famous monuments was constructed. The **Temple of Hibis** was once dedicated to the Egyptian god Amun, but built and rebuilt, first by the Persian Emperor Darius I, then by the Egyptian Pharaoh Nectanebo II and later by several of the Greek Ptolemies. The sanctuary, colonnaded courtyard, hypostyle hall, Chapel of Osiris and imposing entrances are now restored and display interesting friezes dating from about AD40. Within walking distance is the **Temple of Nadura**, built on a hill in about 150. Also only a short walk from the Temple of Hibis are the remains of the Ancient Roman city of Hibis. Other

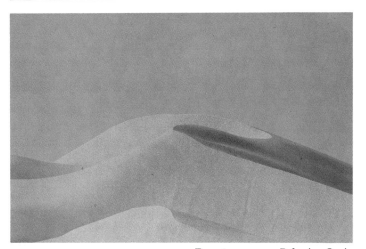

*Desert scene near Bahariya Oasis*

sites include the Christian necropolis of **El-Bagawat**, a veritable 'city of the dead' in which the tombs resemble small houses laid out around a wide street with mud-brick arches, pillars and domed ceilings dating from the fourth to the eighth centuries. A guide lives nearby and will show visitors around the grim mausoleums and its ruined, fifth-century church. The Temple of Hibis, the ancient city, the Temple of Nadura and the El-Bagawat cemetery are grouped conveniently around El-Kharga but it takes a short drive from the town to reach the Roman fort of **El-Dier**, to the north-east. Here the fort's towers and small temple are quite spectacular, isolated as they are in a great waste of shimmering desert sand. Near the town is the brick-built, ruined fourth-century monastery of **Qasr Ain Mustapha Kashif** still in reasonable enough repair to make out the various sections of its construction, like the cells, chapels and out buildings. Further interesting sites not to be missed while visiting El-Kharga are the fortress ruins of Qasr El-Ghueida and Qasr Ain El-Sayyan with their adjoining ancient temples. To the south of the oasis is the Roman Temple of Seraphis and Isis near the village of Qasr Dushi.

## DAKHLA OASIS
Located even further out in the inhospitable Western Desert than El-Kharga Oasis, Dakhla Oasis is reached from Kharga by the road 162km (100 miles) to the west. The modern town in this oasis is called

Mut El-Kharab and contains little of interest to the tourist except a few indistinct remains of ancient structures and the Dakhla Ethnographical Museum. Mut has three hotels, a tourist office and several government rest-houses in the oasis. The main attraction in Dakhla is El-Qasr, a 'dream city' surrounded by lavender-tinted mountains which gives the valley its nickname 'The Pink Oasis'. With ochre-coloured mud-brick minarets, plaster domes and ancient ruins thrusting up through a bright green forest of feathery date palms amid the ocean of burnished orange-gold sand, El-Qasr looks like something out of Sinbad's travels. Its medieval appearance belies the fact that this oasis, like El-Kharga, is now the focus of a new development programme to increase its 55,000 population and raise deeply seated prehistoric water from the desert to expand the agricultural capabilities of the Dakhla region.

Visitors to Dakhla are rare but those that do make the exhausting journey are not be be disappointed by the lack of atmosphere and true oasis life, or the region's ancient sites. Amid the rural bustle of El-Qasr's main town are traces of architectural features which date back to the Pharaohs and the Romans. Out in the deserted Old Town with its fascinating early dwelling and tiny alleyways there are the remains of the Temple of Thoth and an ancient castle. Nearby is a Graeco-Roman cemetery and the El-Musakawa Roman Tombs with some fascinating funerary murals. Other attractions in and around this oasis are; the historic village of Balat with its Ancient Egyptian Temple of Mut, Sixth Dynasty mastabas and Graeco-Roman tombs. A short drive from El-Qasr, in the north part of the oasis, is a first-century Egyptian temple known as **Deir El-Hagar** (Monastery of the Rock) as it was latter used as a monastery by Coptic monks. Pylons, hypostyle hall, pillars, courtyards and sanctuary are all decorated in typical Roman style. For the shopping tourist the Dakhla Oasis is famed for its attractive pottery and wonderful rugs and carpets.

## FARAFRA OASIS

Only really accessible by good road from Cairo, 500km (310 miles) to the south-west, via the oasis of Bahriya, Farafra Oasis is a very ancient and isolated settlement with two rest-houses and the President Sadat Hotel. There is an inferior road running the 210km (130 miles) to the Dakhla Oasis in the south but this route is not recommended. This is the smallest of Egypt's inhabited oases and the houses of its town, Farafra, stand out against the brilliant yellow-white flat desert sand and rock. There is little of interest to the tourist except that it is exceptionally picturesque and has many interesting

## Places of Interest In the Western Oases

**Bahariya Oasis**
334km (207 miles) south-west of Cairo

*Bawaiti*
Many New Kingdom, Greek and Roman remains, temples and tombs.

**Dakhla Oasis**
170km (105 miles) west of El-Kharga Oasis

*El-Qasr*
Ancient half-inhabited town with medieval and Roman ruins. First capital of oases.

*El-Musakawa*
Early Roman tombs with exceptional decorations.

*Balat*
Egyptian temple ruins, mastabas and Graeco-Roman tombs.

*Deir El-Hagar*
Ancient Egyptian temple once occupied by Coptic monks.

**El-Hais Oasis**
Short distance south of Bahriya Oasis. Once a Roman settlement with several remains.

**El-Kharga Oasis**
100km (62 miles) south of Asyut

*Temple of Hibis*
Reconstructed ruins of temple with mixed origins and Roman city.

*Temple of Nadura*
First-century ruins near the town.

*El-Bagawat*
Ancient Christian 'city of the dead'.

**Farafra Oasis**
350km (217 miles) north-west of Dakhla Oasis. Picturesque settlement but of little historic interest.

old houses, narrow alleyways and also a small museum of art.

### BAHARIYA OASIS
Larger than Farafra Oasis and on the same road running south-west from Cairo, this oasis is more populated and more developed with new water technology expanding the agricultural region around this ancient trading stopover. **Bawaiti** has about 25,000 inhabitants and is neat and picturesque with gaily painted houses, three ancient  temples (those to Amasis and Apries and one to Alexander the Great), a Roman archway, a Nineteenth Dynasty necropolis and some Twenty-sixth Dynasty catacombs. There are many ancient tombs in this oasis around the main town. Bawaiti's older twin town, **El-Qasr** (once the oases capital), secretes the ruins of a Roman  settlement and the tiny El-Hais Oasis nearby was once a sizable Roman town.

# 9
# *LUXOR AND KARNAK*

## Luxor

On this tour Luxor and Karnak are viewed first from the west bank
of the Nile. The main Nileside road however, follows the east bank
from the crossing at Nag Hammadi, through Kena and passing
within a few miles of Luxor itself. A side road is signposted to the
town. If the 120km (74 mile) drive has been accomplished from the
hotel accommodation at Nag Hammadi, the first thought will probably be to check into one of Luxor's nine hotels which range from the
height of luxury to the basically economic. At the New Kurna
crossroads the left turning should be taken towards the river and the
two ferry landing stages. For those visitors arriving by road on this
west bank route the necropolis will be behind them when the ferry
is taken across to Luxor. Cars must be taken on a specially designated
ferry from the end of the main road. This ferry delivers vehicles to a
point near Luxor museum. Pedestrian passengers can take either the
local or tourist ferries from either landing stage. From the ticket
offices on the river bank the traveller is transported to one of three
public landing points on Luxor's corniche embankment.

   Arriving by rivercraft the setting is just as stunning and those
visiting by train will have the opportunity to take a horse-drawn
carriage from the station taxi rank down to the corniche. Coming
from the airport by taxi or coach the driver invariably takes the
riverside road on the way to the hotels. From the corniche the view
is expansive. Ahead, far across the quarter-mile wide Nile and vast
flood plain up in the majestic cliffs, lies the great necropolis of Western Thebes, the Valley of the Kings and the Valley of the Queens.

   The airport in Luxor is a short drive east of the town which has a
population of around 65,000. The train service delivers passengers

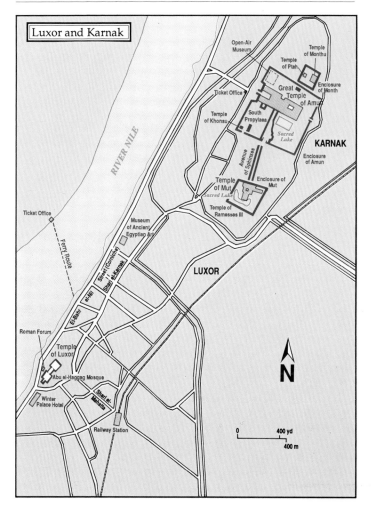

from the railway station in Cairo to the station on the east side of central Luxor, at the end of the Shariah el-Mahatta. Horse-drawn carriages and taxis await in the station forecourt to whisk the traveller to nearby hotels before venturing out to view the fantastic ancient sites or enjoy the splendours of romantic Luxor itself.

It is easy to walk around the main places of interest in Luxor town as most sites are located along the riverside. The tourist board offices are located on the corniche near the Winter Palace Hotel complex. Two main roads run through Luxor, El Bahr el-Nil Street (the corniche) and the Shari el-Karnak. The old Winter Palace Hotel, a special attraction, and an elegant example of nineteenth-century colonial architecture has been added to in the form of the New Winter Palace Hotel. Transport is needed, however, to reach the great complex of Karnak further downstream. Bicycles or horse carriages provide alternatives to taxis. There are few restaurants in Luxor as all hotels provide for visitor's requirements and the only distraction from the magnificent ancient wonders and stupendous natural setting of Luxor, Karnak and Thebes, might be the local souk, tourist bazaar or the town's few souvenir shops. The countryside around Luxor is almost as dramatic as its ancient wonders. A particularly striking feature of the location are the pointed peaks behind the town known as the 'Three Brothers'.

Built on the ancient site of the city of Thebes, Luxor occupies an area on the right bank of the Nile. The town itself surrounds the large ruins of the Temple of Luxor located on the river embankment and the entire region is celebrated as having the largest and most spectacular collection of surviving Ancient Egyptian remains in the country. Luxor is the site of Ancient Thebes, the 'hundred-gated city full of treasure houses' written about in Homer's *Iliad*. It is now known as El-Qasr after the name for a military encampment and the remains of a Roman fortress, built on the temple site, can still be seen. Nearby to the temple is an Ancient Roman quayside, the ruins of the Roman Forum and part of a gateway.

## TEMPLE OF LUXOR

The Temple of Luxor is generally the first of the region's ancient ruins to be inspected by the visitor. This temple, however, was only of secondary importance to the great complex of Karnak. The Temple of Luxor was then linked to Karnak by an almost half-mile long avenue of sphinxes and, at the annual month-long festival of Opet, a religious procession would proceed from Karnak to occupy this temple which the ancients called the 'Harem of Amun in the South'. One of the best examples of religious architecture dating from between 1380BC to 1230BC (Eighteenth to Nineteenth Dynasties), this temple comprises of a large, hypostyle hall; various chapels dedicated to the gods Mut and Khons and the Serapeum, dedicated to Seraphis; the Sanctuary of Alexander the Great; a wide, double-colonnaded courtyard to Ramesses II whose colossal statues stand in

# Places of Interest In Luxor

**El Bahr el-Nil Street**
Embankment boulevard with sites of ancient quays and vista of Luxor's elegant colonial mansions.

**Museum of Ancient Egyptian Art**
North end of Luxor at end of El Bahr el-Nil Street
Four floors of fascinating artifacts and relics from the region's numerous sites of antiquity.

**Roman Forum**
On the landward side of El Bahr el-Nil Street, next to the Temple of Luxor

Outline of ancient theatre and Gate Tower.

**Temple of Luxor**
Alongside the river in the town centre just off El Bahr el-Nil Street
Huge statues, colonnades, chapels, pylon, obelisk, reliefs courtyards and avenue of sphinxes.

*Abu el-Haggag Mosque*
Built in northern part of Temple of Luxor
Nineteenth-century doorway shows original depth of sand encroachment.

one corner; the huge pylon of Ramesses II; the pylon of Amenhotep; the obelisk of Tutmosis II and the remnants of the avenue of sphinxes carved in the shape of rams.

The great pylon forms a main gateway to the court of Ramesses II, and is highly decorated with scenic reliefs as are the outer walls which face the river. Inside the court of Ramesses II is the Abu el-Haggag Mosque built in remembrance of a local holy man. During nineteenth-century clearance of the village which once occupied the temple and subsequent excavations, the ground level has been lowered leaving the mosques door curiously suspended between ground and sky. The only obelisk left on the temple site is one of two originals. The other obelisk, removed in 1836, stands in the Place de la Concorde, Paris, and has evoked comments from numerous personalities, not least Flaubert and Cocteau. The Temple of Luxor is wonderfully lit after dark but this cannot compare with the magical tints cast across the monument by the rays of sunrise and sunset.

## MUSEUM OF ANCIENT EGYPTIAN ART

At the north end of Luxor town, on the corniche, is the Museum of Ancient Egyptian Art. This museum has one of the most fascinating collections of Ancient Egyptian artifacts and monuments outside the Cairo Museum of Egyptian Antiquities. The biggest attraction is the *talatats*, 283 stone blocks with detailed carvings forming a giant wall.

*Temple of Luxor*

Gharry, *or horse-drawn carriage*

*Hieroglyph-enscribed bust in the Luxor Museum of Ancient Egyptian Art*

*Pharaonic head from the Luxor Museum of Ancient Egyptian Art*

*Sphinx avenue, Luxor*

From various sites around the Thebes area over 40,000 such *talatats* have been excavated. Granite and basalt busts and statues of Pharaohs including a colossal stone head are found on the ground floor. Downstairs there are photographs which help the visitor understand the original make-up and purpose of the Karnak complex and stelae, pottery, canopic jars, papyrus scripts, jewellery and furniture are exhibited throughout the museum.

# Karnak

The full splendour of this extensive ancient temple site is best viewed from the river, or the banks of Western Thebes. Its glory lies not only in the great ruins which still stand majestic after many millennia, but also in their original purpose — that of precipitating a line of powerful Pharaohs from the realms of mortality on the east bank of the Nile — into the hereafter in the tombs of the necropolis across the Nile. Most visitors will have glimpsed Karnak from some point on their approach to Luxor and only a stretch of sand north of the suburbs separates it from the town. The most delightful means of travelling this short distance between Luxor and Karnak is by the local horse-drawn carriage, or *gharry*. It can take the visitor a full day to comfortably view the vast ruin complex of Karnak and its numerous temples.

Karnak is the largest ancient religious complex in the world and its focal point, the Great Temple of Amun, underwent various modes of construction during a period of more than 1,250 years. A complicated arrangement of structures evolved between the Eighteenth and the Twenty-fifth Dynasties. Nektanebo I and Nektanebo II (Pharaohs of the Thirtieth Dynasty) were adding to the massive complex as late as 350BC. An avenue of ram-headed sphinxes can be seen as one drives up to the main enclosure and another avenue leads off to the right, to a separate temple enclosure. The sphinxes once linked the Karnak complex to the Temple of Luxor along a processional causeway, only a fragment of which remains. Under the road from Luxor there is said to be intermittent sections of the avenue still surviving. Ten huge pylons act as gateways into sacred areas of the main temple and a vast wall surrounds the twenty smaller temples, shrines, chapels, kiosks and sacred lakes of this extensive site. A moat also encompasses the entire Karnak area.

## THE GREAT TEMPLE OF AMUN

This giant shrine stands at the centre of the Karnak complex and is a most intricate structure. The ticket office to the monument is located on the river side of the Great Temple, near the tiny Chapels

## Places of Interest In Karnak

**Great Temple of Amun**
North of Luxor town on east bank
of Nile
Ten pylons, great halls with many
columns, minor temples, chapels,
colonnades, rows of ram images
and sphinxes, obelisk, sacred lake.

*Other Temples*
Situated around Great Temple of

Amun
Fifteen major sites and monuments
in Temple of Amun complex.

**Open-Air Museum**
Near the ancient quayside and first
pylon
Selection of artifacts.

of Achoris and Psammuthis. From here a short avenue of ram-headed spinxes leads to a pylon-gateway. This huge pylon — the monument's largest and named the First Pylon — guards the entrance to the main body of the temple. A dominant feature of this entrance is the obelisk of Sethos II. A sphinx avenue also leads towards the ancient quay and on the other side of the waters the Temple of Seti I had a matching ram-headed promenade to the western bank of the Nile. Funerary processions linked the two banks between temple complex and distant necropolis.

Inside the Great Temple, which is a series of courtyards, halls and shrines, the first enclosure is the Great Hall, or 'Ethiopian Court'. This contains a number of chapel remains — the Temple of Sethos II and Taharqa's Kiosk which is flanked by a miniature Temple of Ramesses III. At the end of this hall, to the right, is the tenth-century BC Bubastite Gateway. Impressive colonnades and ram carvings embellish the Great Hall which leads through the second pylon into the Great Hypostyle Hall, or 'Hall of the Appearances', lined with 122 incised columns with lotus bud capitals. The twelve central columns with papyrus capitals are so immense that guides say fifty people could comfortably stand on top of the 23m (75ft) columns. This theory is one best not put into practice! The third and fourth pylons lead the visitor past an obelisk to Queen Hatshepsut more elaborately fashioned columns, and then into the Temple of the Middle Kingdom after the fifth and sixth pylons. Note the 'Granite Chamber' or 'Sanctuary of the Sacred Barges'. Behind this courtyard is the 'holy of holies' and a number of chapels can be seen surrounding the Great Festival Hall of Tutmosis III, the Akh-Menu.

To the right of the Great Temple of Amun are the seventh, eighth, ninth and tenth pylons leading past the small Temple of Amenhotep

*One of Karnak's colossal statues*

*Inscribed columns at Karnak*

II. Beyond this temple are the enclosure walls of the main temple complex and rows of sphinxes which form an avenue to the Temple of Mut. Back in the Enclosure of Amun, in the angle created by the latter pylons (known collectively as the South Propylaea) and the main temple, is a sacred lake the size of ten cricket pitches. Alongside the lake is the small Temple of Taharqa and nearby a giant granite carving of a scarab known as the Scarabaeus. On the other side of this oblong lake remains of storehouses for religious offerings have been unearthed and also an aviary where wildfowl were kept. Between the Temple of Amun and the seventh pylon is an area known as the 'Hiding Courtyard' where the Karnak Cache was unearthed.

Other temples inside the Enclosure of Amun include those of the Egyptian gods Osiris, Opet and Khons situated on the Nileside of the South Propylaea. Another Temple of Osiris is situated up against the enclosure wall near the entrance known as the East Gate. Just adjacent to the Northern Gate is the Temple of Ptah. The kiosk of Sestrosis I is also located in the northern courtyard within the surrounding wall. This part of the enclosure is also designated the Open-Air Museum with fragments of statues, friezes and carvings gathered from the Karnak area. Permission should be sought to view the museum's exhibits. Also to the north of the main Temple of Amun is the site known as the Treasury of Chabaka. The remains of Ramesses II's temple can also be found within the Great Temple enclosure just before the East Gate and behind the small eastern Temple of Tutmosis III. As with many of Egypt's great ruins and monuments the intricacies of this entire temple complex are best followed from a floor plan of the area available at the tourist board offices in Luxor.

## OTHER MONUMENTS IN THE KARNAK COMPLEX

Karnak has two other 'domains' apart from the Great Temple of Amun enclosure. These domains, Month and Mut, contain their own temples. Adjacent to the northern wall surrounding the Great Temple of Amun is the Northern Temple precinct encompassing the Temple of Month, the war god. This enclosure also included a sacred lake and to the east of this temple is the location of the Treasury of Tutmosis I. Following the enclosure wall around from the north, and opposite the east gate of the Great Temple enclosure, are the ruins of the Temples of Aton and Amenhotep IV. South of the Great Temple of Amun, and nearer to Luxor, is the Southern Temple precinct with its wall enclosing the Temple of the god Mut and those of the Pharaohs Amenhotep III and Ramesses III. A large sacred lake

*The avenue of rams by the Great Temple of Amun*

*Pharaonic relief, Great Temple of Amun*

*Immense temple columns, Great Temple of Amun, Karnak*

*Roof supports and stone beams at the Great Temple of Amun*

*Funerary scene on the walls of a tomb*

*The gods invite a Pharaoh to the Underworld*

dominates this precinct which is the second largest monument of the entire Karnak complex. The temples of Khonsu and Aphet, with the attendant sphinx avenue, stand facing the river to the south-west of the main temple complex where the enclosure wall begins. In front of the first pylon with its avenue of sphinxes leading to the river, are the remains of the ancient quay. It is from here that priest's religious processions sailed either to incarnation rites in the Temple of Luxor, or from where royal cortèges left for burial rites in the temples and great necropolis across the river on the Nile's west bank.

# 10
# *WESTERN THEBES*

T he eastern bank of the Nile constituted the expressions of mortal life in Ancient Egypt with houses, villas and palaces as living quarters, workshops and storage areas for the labourers, and great temples, chapels and shrines for the worship of living gods and mortal kings. The west bank of the river was its antithesis and epitomised the hereafter and immortality. Consecrated as one enormous necropolis for the burial and worship of the civilisation's kings, queens, nobles and hierarchy, Western Thebes and its many tombs carved into the mountainside is one of the most spectacular ancient sites in the world.

Not only did generations of Egyptians secrete their royal dead in the towering mountains and rugged gorges opposite the settlement of Luxor and Karnak's temples, but also constructed great places of worship on this desert mountain range. No fewer than eighteen mortuary temples were built into the hillsides and at least one Pharaoh, Amenhotep III, had a palace constructed overlooking a lake to the south of the main burial area. More than 200 tombs have been discovered and excavated into the limestone rock while each tomb had its main opening facing the revered River Nile. Apart from temples and tombs, the great crags were home to libraries and schools connected with the necropolis. Here also were the sites of many little villages where the tomb workers lived.

The entire necropolis region of the New Kingdom Pharaohs has been segmented into several areas of principal importance and these include the Valley of the Kings (divided into the Western and Eastern Valleys), and the Valley of the Queens, both of which speak for themselves as royal burial sites lying deep in the mountain range; the Deir El-Medina site near the Valley of the Queens; the Medinet Habu and El-Malqata sites to the south; the Necropolis of Antef and Dra Abu El-Naga on the north-east side of Western Thebes; the central locations of the Tombs of the Nobles: El-Khokha, Qurnet Murai, Sheikh Abu El-Qurna and El-Asasif; the Eleventh Dynasty Tombs to the north (near the great temples at Deir El-Bahari) and the Ramesseum and mortuary temples which skirt the edge of the plateau. A series of suggested tours of Western Thebes follows in order to give a short description of the fourteen sites. For orientation a map of the entire area should be consulted and, for details of each specific monument or tomb, a guide is a wise investment.

It is impossible to see much of the great necropolis of Western Thebes comfortably in a single day's tour and most visitors set aside at least 2 days for excursions into the various valleys where the more important temples and tombs are located. This means that an ideal stop-over in Luxor, in order to see the best sites of the town could be of 3 or 4 day's duration. The best ferry to take from Luxor to Thebes is that which leaves from near the Etap Hotel. The hike up into the necropolis is exhausting and the temperatures and strength of the sun can be relentless. It is important to bear in mind the effort involved in walking, donkey riding or cycling in the heart of the desert. A considerable amount of liquid should be consumed in this exposed location. Some head protection is essential and it is advisable to take a good torch if one is visiting some of the unlit tombs. An early start is recommended as the transport available after the ferry landing on the west bank is soon commandeered by the large numbers of tourists who surge daily through this collection of monuments.

The necropolis is roughly contained in a half-moon, or semi-circular area of the limestone range facing the Nile and Luxor. It lies beyond a wide, flat plain which is criss-crossed with canals and is the site of several new villages like New Kurna, El-Bairat and El-Kom. The road from the Nile ferry points and main ticket offices leads due west across the level desert dotted with acacia trees, thorn scrub and ploughed fields.

## THE COLOSSI OF MEMNON

On the right side of the straight necropolis road the famous Colossi of Memnon stand like giant sentinels to the awe-inspiring monuments in the hills beyond. It was the Greeks who named the great monuments in the belief that these giant images of Pharaoh Amenhotep III were statues representing Memnon of Trojan War fame. The colossi once stood in front of the Temple of Amenhotep III of which little remains. The best preserved of the two, the South

Western Thebes

Colossus, once had a total height of 21m (69ft) but is now only 20m (66ft) high. These lonely guardians were the object of many pilgrimages by incredulous Roman sightseers during the reign of Nero and the celebrated visit of Hadrian and his wife who came to hear the 'singing' of the North Colossus in 130. The North Colossus was famous in ancient times for its strange musical notes it created after being damaged in the earthquake of AD27. It is thought that this 'singing' was the result of the warming of air on sandstone. Today not a murmer issues from the colossus since Emperor Septimus Severus rather half-heartedly repaired the monument. The North Colossus, reponsible until 199 for the dawn phenomenon, has three small images of the Pharaoh's mother, wife and another, unidentifiable celebrity carved into its sides. Little statues are also engraved into the flank of its brother. It is from the location of the Colossi of Memnon that one can get a panoramic view of the layout of the temples and edifices built on the plateau of Western Thebes.

## MEDINET HABU

Little remains of Amenhotep's huge temple, on the right of the path, except rubble but on the left side is the new building of the Antiquities Office which commands the entire necropolis site. It is from here that most visitors will want to take the road ahead towards the Valley of the Queens. However, if the route to the immediate left is taken, Medinet Habu's massive temple complex can be visited. This site is one of Upper Egypt's most spectacular sites and many of its treasures are now displayed in the Cairo Museum of Egyptian Antiquities. Over an extensive area there is a large group of funerary temples — those to Eje and Haremhab, one smaller and one large temple to Ramesses III and the grand Palace of Amenhotep III. In an area running along the southern edge of the Thebean plateau there is also the remains of a royal city — the only attempt during ancient times to construct a permanent royal city. In about 1380BC, Amenhotep III began to build a complex of palaces, festival halls and royal residences to the south of Ramesses III's temple. The largest structure, the Pharaoh's palace, is known as the 'House of Joy'. Today little remains of the ancient city but the modern area is now known as El-Malqata. Also here is the Temple of Thoth, erected in Ptolemaic times, a temple to Tutmosis III, adjacent to that of Ramesses III, the Migdol, and a chapel used by the 'Divine Adorers'.

The grandest structure of the Medinet Habu site is the vast **Temple of Ramesses III** located on a promontory of the plateau. Guards require a LE2 ticket from visitors to this monument which is the most important and best preserved example of all Thebean architectural achievements. Note the double retaining wall and the first great pylon as entrance to the temple's first great court. Inside are fantastic carved columns and figures of Osiris. The second court also is decorated with more figures of Osiris, pillars and columns, festival and processional friezes and military inscriptions. The next court is the 'Hall of Appearances'. Here the Pharaoh's military campaigns and religious devotions are finely depicted on the walls of the maze-like hall. Much of the building surrounding the three-halled temple was devoted to storage space for the abundance of sacrifices needed in the funerary rites. There is the outline of a small palace adjacent to the temple where the king would visit his monument to Pharaonic immortality.

The minor ruins in front of the Temple of Ramesses III are the remains of the mortuary Temple of Princess Ameniridis and the shrines of later wives of the god Amun, personified by Pharaohs of the Twenty-fifth and Twenty-sixth Dynasties. Nearby is the outline of a temple dating from the Eighteenth Dynasty — 300 years older than the Ramesses temple. This was reconstructed during the Thirtieth Dynasty. The great gateway constitutes the Royal Pavilion of the Temple of Ramesses III and is of considerable architectural significance as are the two adjacent pylons and hall. It can take about an hour to tour the Medinet Habu site comfortably and there is a welcomed rest-house to one side of the impressive ruins. Further out, past El-Maqata, is the isolated Roman Temple of Isis at the south end of what used to be the Lake of Amenhotep III, now Birket Habu. Without spending too much time at each monument in this complex, $1^1/_2$ hours should be quite sufficient in which to view Medinet Habu and its adjacent ruins.

## VALLEY OF THE QUEENS

Retracing ones steps from Medinet Habu back to the turning at the Antiquities Office, a separate road leads up to the Valley of the Queens. Remember that a LE1 ticket is required for entry to this valley and its tombs. The valley can also be reached directly by a narrow desert track or on a separate road from the Temple of Medinet Habu. The famous Valley of the Queens, also the last resting place for several princes, is known in Arabic as the 'Place of Beauty'. A stunning setting for a royal graveyard with high, ochre and gold cliffs, this valley is breathtaking in its own right. Note the boldly engraved stelae at the bend in the track as you approach the awe-inspiring valley. Mounds of rubble form miniature hills below the gorges where the tombs are located. Few of these Eighteenth to Twentieth Dynasty tombs, which date back more than 3,000 years, are open to the public. Eighty burial sites have so far been excavated in this cul-de-sac valley, but only the tombs of two queens and those of three early princes are worth visiting if time is limited. Approximately $1^1/_2$ hours should be allowed in order to see the five prominent tombs in this valley.

Probably most famous of the tombs of the Valley of the Queens is that of Queen Nefertari, wife of Ramesses II. Carefully restored after some natural deterioration of the wall paintings, tomb No 66 has some delightful stucco friezes and highly decorated ceilings in its three main chambers. Queen Titi (No 52), is also worth visiting for

*The Colossi of Memnon*

the rich decoration of its corridor, chapel and smaller chambers. The tombs of three of Ramesses III's many sons are also interesting. That of his eldest son, Prince Khaemweset (No 44), has finely painted reliefs as does that of his brother Prince Sethirkhopshef, buried in tomb No 43. The best preserved and most impressive of the princes' tombs is No 55, that of Prince Amenhirkopshef which has a main chamber and corridor, both highly ornate, with the burial chamber at the far end containing the empty granite sarcophagus of the 12-year-old Twentieth Dynasty prince.

## MUMMIES AND DEITIES

Mummification is synonymous with the cults and observances of Ancient Egypt. This practice, perfected by the early Egyptian civilisations, is the process of preserving the dead in as lifelike a manner as possible. It is called mummification, after the Arabic word for a bitumen substance used in the process — *mummiya*. This technique was not unique to Egypt and was used in other ancient civilisations but it was perfected during the Egypt of the first millennium BC. Methods of burial also developed to a high standard with elaborate structures proclaiming the importance of deceased royalty and

*Mummy and coffin from the Twenty-first Dynasty, Thebes*

ornate temples connecting the Ancient Egyptian's complex religion with their dead Pharaohs.

Prior to the times when the pyramids at Giza were constructed in 2575BC, the dead were buried under mastabas. These were flat, platform-like mounds and the complete body was laid underneath, positioned on its side with knees drawn up. As religious dictates developed, it became common practice to dismember the body and bury each piece separately wrapped in cloth. This ritual goes back to the myth of Osiris who was once supposed to have reigned in Egypt after the gods, who originally occupied the country, departed for their separate worlds. Legend says Seth, Osiris' brother, killed him and claimed his crown. Seth cut the body into pieces and dispersed them throughout Egypt. Isis, Osiris's queen, recruited the jackal-headed god Anubis to help her find the body of her king. After a long search she found the remains of her husband. With the wizardry provided by the ibis-headed god Thoth, Isis wrapped the reassembled fourteen pieces of the body in cloth and with incantations and unctions, brought Osiris back to life. Transformed into a god, Osiris took back his throne and later became god of the Underworld and the first deity that departed rulers were supposed to meet in the afterlife.

By Pharaoh Cheops' time, royalty had acquired the added honour of immortality and the death of a king was just a phase of life, a journey across the river of the Underworld to a new life in the hereafter. Royal burials were treated as a veneration of these god-kings who were associated with the deities responsible for death and the afterlife — Seker, Tum, Nephthis, Emewet, Anubis, Isis and Osiris. The bodies of royal personages by the time of the Fourth Dynasty (Old Kingdom) were laid to rest in a prone position and wrapped in cloth symbolic of that used by Osiris. By this time, however, the art of embalming was still quite primitive. The earliest examples of primitive mummification date back to this era. It was not until the reign of Tutmosis I, in the early years of the New Kingdom, that the mummification process was ultimately perfected. This method of the preservation of mortal remains was considered to contribute towards the reincarnation of the dead king to god when his soul, or *ka*, arrived at the Court of Osiris in the Underworld. The best examples of this method of embalment are those of Nineteenth Dynasty Seti I and Ramesses I, two of the best preserved burials among the hundreds in and around Western Thebes and the Valley of the Kings.

Not only Ancient Egyptian royalty underwent mummification as thousands of similarly preserved animals, bulls, cats, ibis, hawks and even crocodiles have been discovered either in Pharaoh's tombs or in separate necropoli. A variety of processes for mummification were used over the many hundreds of years. The earliest mummies were just corpses dehydrated with salt, anointed with oils, encased in bitumen and wrapped in the traditional winding cloth. In later years, seventy mummification stages were performed. These included readings from the *Book of The Dead* whose twelve chapters represented the 12 hours of night; incantations from the *Book of Gates* which described secret ways of passing through the guarded gates between the twelve divisions of the night, and recitations from the *Book of the Opening of the Mouth.* Basic steps of preservation, which took 70 days to complete, included the removal of the brain through the nose; removal of the viscera through the abdomen; packing the preserved entrails in four canopic jars; replacing the heart with a scarab positioned on the thorax; sterilisation of remains; filling the corpse with natron (a dehydrating agent), in a complicated series of rituals; covering the embalmer's incision with a wax plate decorated with a protective 'eye', or udjat motif (this represents the sacred eye of the god Horus); encasing limbs in sand or earth; packing the body with cloth and resin, cinnamon and myrrh and lastly, anointing the remains in sweet-smelling unguents and wrapping the entire body in fine cloth ready for burial. The tools used in this process were quite sophisticated and included a set of ornate instruments used in the 'opening of the mouth' ceremony (during which the body was symbolically brought back to life) a miniature wooden adze and a set of implements used to anoint the embalmed body. It is now thought that the unusual conditions of temperature and humidity created inside the ancient pyramids and tombs contributed to the amazingly perfect state of preservation of some mummies which have survived to this day.

Instead of the basic coffins used in some early mastaba burials, entombments during the New Kingdom period often involved placing the body in a series of coffins — the finest examples are those in which King Tutankhamen's body was encased. This particular burial was typical of New Kingdom interments and accompanied by traditional tomb treasures which have attracted looters and archaeologists over the centuries. The process of mummification was lengthy and complicated, and many coffins in which the body was finally encased were finely wrought in representations of the dead king. The mummy's outer casing consisted of four ornate gold and wooden catafalques fitting within each other and encasing a quartzite stone casket containing the mummy's inner coffins. A sarcophagus surrounded three more coffins. Various materials were used to make sarcophagi and some that have been discovered were made of terracotta, lead, wood and stone. Two of Tutankhamen's inner coffins were richly decorated and made of wood. The third, innermost coffin, which directly encased the shroud-wrapped mummy, was highly ornate and made of solid gold. A gold death mask was then laid over Tutankhamen's face. This magnificent example of the complete process of embalming and burial is the largest and best preserved example of Ancient Egyptian funerary rites ever discovered in modern times. However those mummies of other rulers, such as that of Ramesses I, are in a better state of preservation than that of Tutankhamen. Often images of the deceased were placed in the burial chamber as a substitute for the dead person in the afterlife. In some cases a substitute head made from limestone was also placed near the corpse in case the mummy's head was damaged on its supposed journey to the Underworld.

## A GOD FOR EVERY EVENT

Apart from those Ancient Egyptian gods which were associated with the protection of the dead, like the jackal-headed Anubis, or the falcon-headed Seker, the richly varied panoply of their deities came in a multitude of forms and had widespread responsibilities. Although little is known about the religions of Ancient Egypt, much has been determined from carvings and wall paintings on tombs and temples. Many of the Ancient Egyptian's gods had sacred animal or bird manifestations and were often depicted with these features. Thus Horus, the sun god, and earliest of Egyptian deities, are shown with a hawk's head or as a winged solar disc. The sky goddess, Hathor, is portrayed with a horned cow's head and Bastet, goddess of love, wears the head of a cat. Engravings also show Khnum, the creator god, with a ram's head, Sakhmet, the war goddess with the head of a lion and even one god, Sobek, with a crocodile's head. Thoth, the moon god has an ibis-head. Many gods were depicted with perfectly normal human features like the sky goddess, Nut, an arched, naked girl decorated with stars; Amun, the wind god, represented as a high priest; Maat, the female god who weighs the heart of the dead against an ostrich feather, and Seshat, the female god who holds the tools of the scribe. Death and resurrection in the afterlife was a preoccupation with Ancient Egyptians. More than seventy-five different early Egyptian gods have been identified to date, spanning a wide variety of civilisations over several millennia.

*Contrasting Ancient Egyptian art forms: gods Sobek and Hathor carved in relief in stone and* (below) *the mural of Pharaoh Seti with the god Horus.*

Two of these gods, significantly recurring throughout Egyptian history, are those of Osiris and Ptah, both depicted in engravings, statues and paintings, as mummies.

## DEIR EL-MEDINA

Before returning to the main road to visit the great mortuary temples, it is possible to make a diversion to see the tombs and ancient remains, including that of a Ptolemaic temple at Deir el-Medina. A LE1 ticket is needed to view this site. A track leads due east to the village, the temple and cemeteries from the Valley of the Queens, diverting off the main road. This Eighteenth Dynasty village was where the necropolis workers once lived and the cemetery of its inhabitants, sculptors, masons and artisans, is located to the west and well worth visiting for an insight into the everyday life of the ancients. A brick wall surrounds the main temple which was dedicated to the sky goddess Hathor and Maat the goddess of Truth. This temple was begun during the reign of Ptolemy IV, Philopator, and contains interesting decorative columns and three main chapels. Nearby are two smaller temples and another chapel dating from the reign of Seti I. Many of the tombs in the Deir el-Medina necropolis are of officials who supervised the royal tomb and temple constructions from the Eighteenth to the Twentieth Dynasties. More famous of these rock tombs are those of Sennetem (No 1), which contained a host of funerary treasures now on display in the Cairo Museum of Egyptian Antiquities. The tomb of the sculptor Ipuy (No 217), high up on the rock face has a fascinating frieze of early construction methods and the tomb of Pesedu (No 3) has particularly evocative religious wall paintings. Amenemhet's sepulchre (No 340), nearby is decorated with lively family scenes and that of Anherkau (No 359) is beautifully decorated with religious symbols entwined with vivid depictions of animal life. About $1^1/_2$ hours should be set aside to view the temple of Dier el-Medina, the ancient village and a few of the more elaborate tombs.

## THE RAMESSEUM

Over the course of several Dynastic periods a phalanx of grand temples was constructed facing towards the sacred River Nile, separated from the tombs of the great Pharaohs by deep gorges of the Thebean massif. These are the mortuary temples of regal dignitaries, kings and queens whose tombs lie deeper in the valleys of Thebes. The ancients called the site the 'Mansions of Eternity'. The most spectacular of these temples which were erected on the lip of the rocky plateau, is the 'Ramasseum' of Ramesses II. There are also are a number of medium-sized and small temples in various states of repair.

A LE1 ticket is needed for entry into the Ramesseum. To reach this collection of monuments one must retrace steps to the Antiquities Office. From here a road leads due north, curving around the back of the temples but is not the best route to take in order to see the temples properly. However, a pathway does lead around to the front of the monuments and hugs the edge of the plateau, skirting the remains of Amenhotep III's temple on the right and passing first the ruins of King Merneptah's temple on the left. Merneptah was the only one of Ramesses II's eighty or so sons to survive him. Nearby are the remnants of Queen Tausert's mortuary temple and the only tomb in

this part of Western Thebes — that of Khonsuartais. A small ruin lies
north of this tomb, across a path which leads to the main road, this
is the Temple of Wadjmose. Tutmosis IV built his temple nearby and
this is better preserved than most.

The next massive structure on the left of the path is the Ramesseum itself. A funerary temple of imposing size and grandeur,
Ramesses II's magnificent edifice has made a lasting impression on
each of its visitors down through more than 3,200 years. In the first
century BC the Roman historian Diodorus wrote of the 'Tomb' of
Ozymandias (Ramesses II's tomb is actually in the necropolis of the
Valley of the Kings) and 2,000 years later the early nineteenth-
century poet, Shelley, wrote of the shattered remains of the vast
colossus of the Pharaoh which lies in the first court of the temple, 'My
name is Ozymandias, king of kings'. The colossus is seen to the left
of the second pylon after passing between the gigantic twin towers
of the first pylon. The granite carving of this immense statue which
once weighed 1,000 tons and probably measured more than 17m
(56ft) in height, is remarkable. The first two of the temple's gateways,
including the main pylon, are decorated with reliefs of battles and
military campaigns. In the second court are the headless statues of
the male god Osiris mistakenly referred to by Diodorus as caryatides
(carved architectural supports in the form of draped females).
However the male equivalent of caryatide should be Atlantes. In this
courtyard there is the colossal head of one of the two statues of
Ramesses which stood near the portico. Tall rows of ornate pillars
line the great hypostyle hall and this leads through to two smaller
hypostyle halls. The extensive ruins of Ramesses temple indicated
that most of the rooms of this site were set aside as great storerooms
where sacrificial offerings would have been stored. There is also the
ruin of a small palace where the Pharaoh would stay when visiting
the construction site of his 'Eternal Mansion'.

Continuing along the pathway in front of the Ramesseum, the
next site visited on the left is what little remains of the **Temple of
Amenhotep II**. To the right of the path as it turns, at one side of the
ruin, is a lake. On the same side is a small rest-house where refresh-
ments can be purchased. The track now joins a wider road and
continues around in front of the Temple of Tutmosis III. This structure, built in 1430BC is notable as it is part hewn from the plateau cliff
and part built of Nile mud bricks. On the other side of the road, a little
further along, is the small temple of the Nineteenth Dynasty Pharaoh, Siptah. The next temple along this route is often known as the
Ramesside Temple, that of Ramesses IV. Another lake lies out near

the flat plain by this monument. It is after passing this lake on the right, that a diversion should be made off the road which runs through the village of Dra Abu El-Naga. This track takes the visitor along the side of the plateau, past the mortuary temples of Amenhotep I, Nefertari and that of Nebwenef.

The main object of taking this route is to visit the classic location of the **Temple of Pharaoh Seti I**. A LE1 ticket is needed to view this extraordinary monument. Built immediately opposite the Great Temple of Amun on the other side of the Nile, this temple is thought to have once been linked to the riverside by a processional avenue of ram's headed sphinxes — the extension of which projects to the ancient quay from the Great Temple of Amun. From the east bank quay funerary processions would have crossed the river in great gilded barges and proceeded to Seti I's temple along the now nonexistent avenue. Seti I's temple is the most easterly of all the mortuary temples in Thebes. Its fine reliefs and carvings, executed in around 1300BC should not be missed in this tour of the 'Castles of a Million Years'. Particularly beautiful are the ceiling decorations of winged suns in the main hypostyle hall and nearby the house of the sacred boat of Amun should not be missed. This section of Western Thebes can be walked in about 2 hours from the beginning of the path at the Antiquities Office to the Temple of Seti I.

## THE NECROPOLIS OF ANTEF

To the north of the Temple of Seti I and across the main road, is the settlement of El-Tarif. Most of the village lies alongside the road to Kena but to one side is the little-visited Necropolis of Antef. Known as the Staff Tombs because of the pillared façades common throughout this Eleventh Dynasty mortuary, these large excavations are royal tombs and date back 4,000 years. Little is preserved of the wall paintings and decorations which once embellished these ancient tombs but among the most interesting are those of the Pharaohs Antef I, II and III. Howard Carter, famous for his discoveries in the Valley of the Kings, lived in a house near this necropolis which can be visited by prior permission.

## DRA ABU EL-NAGA

Located to the west of Antef and behind the modern village of the same name, is the necropolis of Dra Abu El-Naga. About forty tombs have been excavated on this site which was first used as a royal cemetery in the Seventeenth Dynasty, then utilised as a tomb site for Eighteenth Dynasty nobles and later by Nineteenth Dynasty priests.

Particularly of significance is the tomb of the High Priest of Amenhotep I, whose tomb (No 19), is decorated with funerary ceremonies.
Tomb No 255, that of the scribe and royal steward Roi, is also finely
embellished with religious rites and divinities. Tomb No 24, that of
an official of the court of Tutmosis III contains an inscribed stela and
fine stucco designs. Other tombs contained the remains of courtiers,
fan-bearers, physicians and other royal attendants.

## EL-KHOKHA
This is the beginning of a suggested tour around the various sections
of a necropolis known collectively as the Tombs of the Nobles, or the
Private Tombs, as opposed to those of royalty. A great deal of time
could be taken in viewing the many tombs scattered through the area
which lies directly north of the row of funerary temples and the
Ramesseum. Many hundreds of these tombs have been opened and
several in each section are open to the public. To describe in length
the details of painting, sculpture and artistry decorating each tomb
would be impractical but several of the foremost tombs have been
indicated at each site. Three LE1 tickets allow visitors to explore the
tombs of Nakht, Menna, Rekmere, Sennofer, Ramose, Userhet and
Khaemhet. Most of these, being the more popular tombs with clock-
watching visitors, are located in the Sheikh Abu El-Qurna section of
the necropolis.

The hill of El-Khokha in and around which rock tombs vie with
modern village houses for space, lies on the opposite side of the road
from Dra Abu El-Naga, near the Metropolitan Museum House. This
site can also be reached by the road which runs behind the mortuary
Temple of Tutmosis III. The western section of El-Khokha, up to the
road, is known as the Lower Enclosure and really forms part of the
Sheikh Abu El-Qurna Tombs of Nobles. The tombs here are those of
high officials from Tutmosis II's time and some from the later reign
of Ramesses II. Of importance are some highly decorative chamber
tombs among which are those of two Eighteenth Dynasty sculptors,
Ipuky and Nebamon (No 181), the richly embellished Tomb of
Amenemhet (No 48), and the complex Tomb of Puyemre (No 39),
with numerous fascinating scenes decorating its several chapels.
Given time, the Tombs of Prennufer (No 188), Keruef (No 192) and
Neferonpet (No 178) should also be viewed.

## QURNET MURAI
This hill, riddled with tombs, is also occupied by modern dwellings
and is reached by continuing back along the road which runs from

Dra Abu El-Naga, behind the row of funerary temples past the Ramesseum on the left. Qurnet Murai is almost opposite the Antiquities Office, up in the hills, and is of little interest as its tombs are no where near as spectacular as those of the nobles at Sheikh Abu El-Qurna just a short distance to the north. Time, however could be taken to view the highly decorated tomb (No 40) of the Governor of Nubia, Huy, who ruled during the reign of Tutankhamen, around 1340BC. One richly painted wall of this tomb is exceptionally detailed and portrays the wealth of the governor.

## SHEIKH ABU EL-QURNA

For a fascinating insight into everyday life in Ancient Egypt, an understanding of religious rites and observances, and an appreciation of early artistic skills, there are few better places for the visitor to see than the Tombs of the Nobles at Sheikh Abu El-Qurna. The area is located directly north of the Ramesseum, next to the El-Khokha Lower Enclosure. The tombs here lie inside the Upper Enclosure's retaining wall and comprise the largest collection of private tomb chapels in Western Thebes. Approaching from the south, the first tomb to visit is that of Rekhmere (No 100), a vizier of Tutmosis III. Processions of tribute bearers decorate the walls and the panoply of offerings is quite fantastic. Climb up from here to view the tombs of Sennofer (No 96B), known as the 'Tomb of the Vines', and that of Ken Amun (No 93), a steward in Amenhotep's court. Note the impressive pillared interior of this tomb.

Between recent buildings, outside and to the south of the main enclosure, are several important tombs. The largest tomb in the Tombs of the Nobles is that of Ramose (No 55), who was governor under Amenhotep IV. Note the huge, hypostyle vestibule, banquet scenes and family groups. Of particular importance are the exquisitely detailed reliefs which show just how beautiful the Ancient Egyptians were. The paintings in this tomb are said to be among the most exquisite examples of Eighteenth Dynasty art yet found. Across the path is the tomb of the royal granary supervisor, Khaemhet. This is tomb No 57 and of particular note are the friezes of harvest tallies and the six funerary statues. Around the north side of the village is the tomb of an Eighteenth Dynasty priest, scribe and astronomer, Nakht (No 52). Country life along the Nile is depicted in great detail with agricultural scenes and all manner of farm and hunting produce. Note the pretty group of musicians and vigorous depictions of Nilotic hunts. The tomb of Djeserkeresenib (No 38), is definitely worth a visit and is not far from that of Nakht. Among the gracefully executed paintings is that of a procession of musicians entertaining at a banquet. Not far away, going back into the Upper Enclosure through the north gate, tomb No 69 is popular for harvest scenes and religious cartoons. This is the tomb of Menna, an estate inspector. An entire day could easily be spent in viewing the Tombs of the Nobles. About twenty-five of the tombs in this part of the necropolis are open to public viewing and most of these are of some significant interest for either their design or the special decoration of their chambers.

## EL-ASASIF

A LE1 ticket is needed to visit these massive brick-built tombs which Π are located to the north-west of the Lower Enclosure and east of the Sheikh Abu El-Qurna site. El-Asasif is the location of the largest tomb in the Thebean cemetery — the burial chamber of Pedmenopet with access by ladders deep into the ground. Other important tombs worth visiting are those of the royal steward Kheruef with its interesting courtyards, that of Puyemre, the double tomb of the royal sculptors Nebamon and Ipuky, Pabasa's tomb with its large staircase and fascinating scenes of ancient everyday life on its walls and columns. Another deep tomb, that of Ibi, is worth a visit as are those of the Twenty-fifth Dynasty Prince Mentemhet and the high-ranking official Peteamenopet. The tombs here date from the Twenty-fifth and Twenty-sixth Dynasties and most of these are in an advanced state of ruination and are kept locked. A guard is generally on hand to admit visitors to the more popular tombs.

## DEIR EL-BAHARI

North of the cemetery of El-Asasif the main road can be joined which Π leads west towards the grand Temple of Hatshepsut. By taking a track leading off to the right just before the vast mortuary temple, one can reach the tombs of the Eleventh Dynasty at the foot of the cliffs surrounding the valley of Deir El-Bahari. These are the private tombs of nobles and royal court officials. In this area, in 1891, the grand sarcophagus of the high priest Amon was discovered and also that of the high priest Khonsu. The valley was evidently used as a hiding place for the most revered of kings in order to finally secrete the mummies from grave looters. Some astounding discoveries were made here in late Victorian times, notably that in 1881 when, from a single grave shaft, the mummies of the Pharaohs Amenhoptep I, Tutmosis II, Tutmosis III, Seti I, Ramesses I and Ramesses III, together with more than forty other royal mummies, were discovered. This last hiding place of some of the most influential Pharaohs

*Temple of Hatshepsut, Western Thebes*

was initially discovered by Maspero, an Egyptologist, in 1876 but the director of antiquities was not informed until much of the funerary artifacts had been removed. The royal remains of the great kings now reside in the Cairo Museum of Egyptian Antiquities. To the north of the valley a mountain path continues around the cliffs passing the Eleventh-Dynasty tombs to the left and continuing on to the eastern gully of the Valley of the Kings. This path gives exceptional views of the grandiose temple complex of Hatshepsut.

Twin mortuary temples, those of Queen Hatshepsut and Mentuhotep II dominate the picturesque valley of Deir El-Bahari. Most magnificent of these is the vast structure of Queen Hatshepsut's funerary temple. Often regarded as the finest Ancient Egyptian monument, this immense building is an architectural miracle, rivalling the works of nature in the great weathered cliffs, lending a dramatic scenario to the location of one of Egypt's most influential queens. Hatshepsut ruled for 22 years at the beginning of the New Kingdom — Eighteenth Dynasty (1490BC to 1468BC). She co-ruled with Tutmosis II who had her image defaced from the great structure and replaced with his own when he succeeded to the throne on her death.

The temple complex is reached from the south-east along the

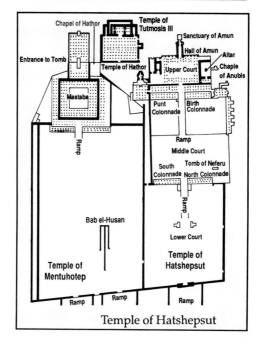

Temple of Hatshepsut

wide valley and ramps lead to the various courtyards and terrace levels. A LE2 ticket admits entry to the entire temple area. Once an avenue of sphinxes led up to the temple but now the approach has been landscaped. Although a ruin and a shadow of its former glory, the Temple of Hatshepsut has been carefully restored as has that of Mentuhotep adjoining it. The pyramid which once surmounted the two colonnaded terraces of Mentuhotep's temple has not been reconstructed. Hatshepsut's temple consists of three terraces cut into the rocky cliffs. The first ramp leads up across the Lower Court which sports some fascinating reliefs and twin colonnades and was originally a garden with fountains, up to to the Middle Court once guarded by stone lions. Great columns, known to the right as the Birth Colonnade and, to the left, the Punt Colonnade face the middle courtyard and the tiny tomb of Neferu. To the right of the twin-pillared Birth Colonnade is a sectioned off altar and the Chapel of Anubis. To the left of the identical Punt Colonnade is a mortuary sanctuary and the Temple of Hathor. The Upper Court, reached by another ramp and built in a square of twin colonnades, is flanked by the Sanctuary of the Sun to the right and the Sanctuary of Hatshepsut to the left. Behind the Upper Court is the sacred Sanctuary of Amun.

Π Linked to the Temple of Hatshepsut and almost fusing the two structures together is the funerary Temple of Mentuhotep. This is the oldest temple known in Thebes and the best preserved of any temples of that era — 2040BC to 1786BC. In front of the temple is a tomb once excavated by Howard Carter at the turn of the century, that of the Eleventh Dynasty Pharaoh Mentuhotep I. Almost entirely devoid of its original superstructure, the temple ramp leads to the first forecourt on which lies the ruins of the second terrace level upon which the mastaba pyramid of the early Middle Kingdom Pharaoh once stood. Behind the ruined colonnades is the entrance to the tomb itself and, to the right of this, the Chapel of Hathor. Between the Temples of Queen Hatshepsut and Mentuhotep II, to the rear, just below the lowering cliffs, are the remains of the Temple of Tutmosis III. Do not forget the spectacular *son et lumière* show held regularly at the temple site.

# Π Valley of the Kings

The famous Valley of the Kings in fact comprises of two valleys, east and west, and is reached by the main road which follows on from that running behind the great temples facing the Nile plain. This route leads from the Antiquities Office north and then sweeps west into the limestone mountain massif and its deeply cleft gorges. The valleys can also be reached by the mountain pathway from the temples of Deir El-Bahari. The fee for entrance to both valleys is LE5 and a full day could be set aside for this tour. There are thirty one important tombs worth visiting in the Eastern Valley and only two in the Western Valley. The tombs of this part of Western Thebes are numbered from one (the tomb of Ramesses VII) to sixty-two (that of Tutankhamen). Located centrally in the Eastern Valley, the famous tomb of Tutankamen is situated in front of a rest-house — a welcome sight after the trek to this remote valley. The tombs here are scattered throughout the crevices, gullies and gorges off the main valley, and small roads lead from the rest-house to the tomb entrances.

These tombs are those of the Pharaohs who reigned during the Eighteenth, Nineteenth and Twentieth New Kingdom Dynasties, from about 1528BC to 1070BC — a period of only 458 years, making some of the tombs more than 3,500 years old. These tombs are carved into the living rock and consist mostly of stepped entrances and long, narrow corridors (usually wide enough only for the tomb attendants to heave the giant sarcophagus to its last resting place). Antechambers were used for funerary rites while offerings were made to the gods in the sacrificial chambers. Side chambers were used for burial rituals and readings from the *Books of the Dead* and storerooms for funerary furniture and grave offerings. The main crypt (or tomb chamber) was where the mummy was lain to rest in the familiar decorated and inscribed coffins and sarcophagi.

## THE EASTERN VALLEY

The eastern gorge of the Valley of the Kings necropolis is the most visited in the entire complex of Western Thebes. Pharaohs of the Eighteenth, Nineteenth and Twentieth Dynasty were buried in the steep-sided network of gullies leading off from the main valley. These Dynasties represent Egyptian rule over a period of almost 500 years and this particular desert location was selected as a cemetery for its isolated location. Still only around a dozen tombs have been installed with electric lighting so a torch is most handy if some of the more remote tombs are to be visited. The Eastern Valley is famous for the number of tombs discovered here (sixty-two in all) and the fact that the fantastic hoard of the boy-king Tutankhamen's treasures were unearthed here. Only thirty-one tombs are regularly open to public viewing, including that of Tutankhamen (No 62). This tomb still contains its golden sarcophagus and the young Pharaoh's mummy, although most of the funerary furniture and grave treasures have been removed to the Cairo Museum of Egyptian Antiquities. Many of the tombs are magnificently decorated with spectacular murals and Tutankhamen's tomb is no exception.

Directly opposite Tutankhamen's tomb is the opening to that of Ramesses VI, one of the more popular tombs with visitors as the ceiling of its vaulted tomb chamber is covered with the famous mural depicting Nut, the sky goddess, embracing with her body the stars and zodiac symbols. Archaeologists call this the Tomb of Memnon. The Tomb of Seti I, also not far from that of Tutankhamen, and near the centrally located rest-house, contains some of the most fascinating decorations including lavish illustrations from the religious books of Ancient Egypt, many representations of gods, goddesses, genii, men, women and mummies in multiples of twelve, elaborate rituals and curious scenes from the Underworld. One important feature is the burial chamber with its astronomical ceiling painted in black and gold. This tomb consists of about ten chambers linked by narrow corridors which drive 100m (328ft) deep into the limestone cliffs. The Tomb of Seti I is commonly known as the Belzoni Tomb after its discoverer.

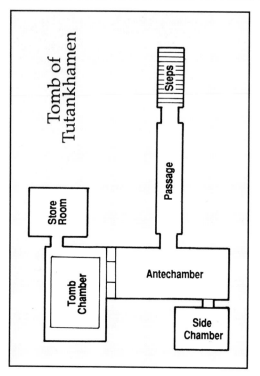

Tomb of Tutankhamen

Steps

Passage

Store Room

Tomb Chamber

Antechamber

Side Chamber

Ⅱ  Further up this high-sided valley is the Tomb of Queen Hat-shepsut where both her sarcophagus and that of her father, Tutmosis I, was found. The queen's fan-bearer, Maherpra, is also buried in the Eastern Valley but along another gulch on the other side of the necropolis. Near to Hatshepsut's tomb is the undecorated Tomb of Tutmosis X. Mentuherkopshef, son of Ramesses IX, is also buried in this part of the valley as is Tutmosis IV. Several tombs, like that of Ramesses X, next to Seti I's tomb, are undecorated. Alternatively, on the other side of Seti I's tomb from that of Ramesses X is the sumptuously painted entrance to the tomb of Ramesses I.

Next to the rest-house is the tomb of Amenhotep III's wife, Queen Tiy and next door to this is the well-decorated, three-corridored sepulchre of Ramesses IX. Almost opposite is the gorge leading to the Tomb of Merenptah with richly decorated corridors and halls and containing a granite coffin lid and the royal sarcophagus cover.

*Western Thebes*

*A Nubian guide*

Ramesses III's tomb is also famed for the vividly decorated walls and ceiling of its twenty-seven chambers and corridors emblazoned with scenes of homage, religious cult figures and various illustrations from the *Book of the Gates*. This tomb is also located quite near the rest-house and on the way to the Tomb of Horemhoreb which also contains spectacular paintings and the Pharaoh's sarcophagus. At the end of this secondary gorge is the Tomb of Amenhotep II. This particular tomb is famous for the detail in its murals and the brightness of the pigments used to decorate the tomb. Amenhotep's sandstone coffin lies in the tomb chamber and a number of other imperial mummies were found stored in this tomb as a precaution against frequent raids of grave robbers.

Continue up the adjacent valley to the oldest tomb in the entire necropolis of Western Thebes, that of Tutmosis I which lies almost at the end of the cul-de-sac and contains an inscribed sarcophagus. On the way to this tomb one passes that of Queen Tausert, wife of Seti II, buried in one of the valley's largest tombs. Across the valley is the tomb of Sitpah which contains some wonderful murals and the royal sarcophagus. Sitpah's chancellor, Bay, is also interred in the Eastern Valley. The furthest tomb in this section of the valley is that of Seti II which contains some intriguing reliefs, beautiful murals and painted scenes from the *Book of What is in the Underworld*. The Tomb of Tutmosis III should be visited. This is the furthest tomb from the rest-house and the southernmost in this valley. The northernmost tomb in the eastern necropolis is that of Ramesses VII, lying in a long gorge just to the left of the road leading to Kurna.

## ℼ THE WESTERN VALLEY

Quite a long trek from the Eastern Valley but located by taking the signposted turning to the right off the main valley road well before reaching the main eastern necropolis. The Western Valley of the Valley of the Kings only holds two tombs of real significance. One of these (No 22) is the royal tomb of the Pharaoh Amenhotep III who reigned from 1402BC to 1364BC. His wife, Queen Tiy, is buried in the Eastern Valley. The other tomb here which is also open to public viewing is tomb No 23, of King Eje (1339BC to 1335BC). This is known as the 'Monkey's Tomb' and the Pharaoh's sarcophagus has been removed to the Cairo Museum of Egyptian Antiquities. Only two other tombs have so far been discovered in the Western Valley.

## CARTER, CARNARVON AND TUTANKHAMEN

'I see wondrous things', gasped the archaeologist Howard Carter as he broke through an ancient doorway under the tomb of Ramesses VI on 26 November 1922. With him was his sponsor, Lord Carnarvon, but their surprise was only feined for the thronging world press. As it was revealed later Tutankhamen's funerary treasures had already been discovered. Both Carter and Carnarvon had visited and robbed the tomb on several occasions since Carter had first discovered the untouched crypt 3 weeks earlier on 4 November. For six seasons Howard Carter had searched in the Valley of the Kings for the tomb of the Eighteenth Dynasty Pharaoh who had ruled Egypt for only 9 years. Convinced, in the face of numerous sceptics, that he would find the 'lost' tomb, Carter had 200,000 tons of rubble removed before the final breakthrough, below a Twentieth Dynasty tomb into a passageway leading to Tutankhamen's grave. The king, aged only 18, had been buried with the usual splendour reserved for more venerable rulers. Breaking the Royal Seal on the walled up entrance, stairs and a passage led the Egyptologists to the ante-chamber, off which led a side chamber, a store room and the burial chamber itself. Each room was packed with a vast array of funerary furniture and goods for the afterlife of the Pharaoh, untouched by grave robbers and looters (except the impatient archaeologist and his patron) for exactly 3,260 years.

More than 5,000 items were found in the four chambers of Tutankhamen's tomb and the job of cataloguing these took 10 years. Only one chamber, the tomb room itself, was decorated, demonstrating a certain urgency in the burial. The grave's largest room was the antechamber and the burial chamber, decorated with religious scenes and post-mortem rites. The burial service and afterlife images contained the intact sarcophagus of the Pharaoh himself. The king's mummy, still inside the tomb, was masked by a rich, solid gold image of the king, that in turn was encased in a solid gold coffin. This was encased in three heavily ornate wooden coffins set into each other and placed in a yellow quartzite casket which lay in a giant sarcophagus. Much of the funerary objects from the tomb's chambers are now a permanent display on the upper floor of the Museum of Egyptian Antiquities in Cairo. Rooms in the tomb were stacked with wine containers, vegetables, clothing, utensils and furniture.

Among the funerary furniture was an elaborately decorated golden throne; a furnerary bed in the form of Hathor; guilded ceremonial beds in the shape of lions and hippopotami and stools and headrests covered in gold leaf. Other treasures found in the tomb included more than 400 *ushbti*, or wooden figures of servants set to look after the king in the afterlife. Many of these were richly ornamented and other models included gold and small statues of the king. Weapons found packed in the small chambers included the first known iron dagger with a gold-decorated sheath; shields, and even military carts, including a state chariot. Toys packed into a corner together with household goods included inlaid board games and there were even two ornate royal walking sticks. Funerary objects included canopic jars, alabaster objects of exquisite design and workmanship, vases, bowls, lamps and ornaments. Rich jewellery items were found around the mummy and on benches and low tables such as a gold pectoral of semi-precious stones and glass representing the 'mystic eye'. Today these treasures are one of Egypt's main archaeological attractions and now often travel on special exhibitions to museums around the world. The wealth of knowledge gained from finding such an intact collection of everyday goods, supplies, decorations, and royal accompaniments has been of

*The tombs of
Tutankhamen and
Ramesses VI*

*The gilded funerary
casket of
Tutankhamen*

*The golden funerary mask of Tutankhamen*

profound use to historians and archaeologists as it represents the largest, and most spectacular accumulation of Ancient Egyptian funerary objects discovered to date.

## Ancient Egyptian Architecture

'No ancient or modern people have thought of art or architecture on such a sublime scale, so vast and so grandiose as that of the Ancient Egyptians'. So wrote Jean Francois Champollion (1790-1832) the French Egyptologist who first deciphered Egyptian hieroglyphics from the inscriptions on the Rosetta Stone.

Before the third millennium BC and Imhotep's revolutionary idea of using stone in construction instead of wood and mud bricks, most buildings were semi-permanent structures subject to rapid erosion and deterioration. Therefore, little remains of those buildings erected in pre-Dynasty times. However, since the first religious and funerary structures were built of stone blocks at Saqqara, the permanence of building material has ensured that many of these magnificent monuments have endured through the centuries, some as long as 5,000 years.

During the early part of the Old Kingdom period 2700BC to 2200BC (at the time of the Third Dynasty reign of King Zoser), the first real pyramids were constructed. Not only did the stone which was employed in the construction of the pyramids resist the sand-blasting effect of the constant desert wind, but the buildings themselves protected the tomb contents from destruction by the forces of nature. The ancients did not have much foresight when it came to predicting human nature. Over the millennia successive waves of invaders, robbers and wilful defacers, damaged and destroyed more of the monuments and their artistic embellishments than the ravages of time could have wreaked naturally over the centuries. The very sand which was so destructive in many cases became the saviour of Ancient Egypt's monuments. Desert winds quickly buried numerous structures from both the eroding sandstorms and the avaricious eye of the grave-robber. In some cases it also concealed a ready-made source of building materials from succeeding generations who regularly cannibalised ancient sites for building blocks.

From the famous Sphinx at Giza, which has been buried and unearthed many times over the centuries, to the great edifice of Ramesses II's temple at Abu Simbel, excavated during the latter half of the nineteenth century, nature has preserved a remarkably large proportion of Egypt's ancient monuments. The countries historic sites have survived in various states of preservation, from outlines of temples traced in the sand, to almost perfectly preserved burial chambers. However, to the casual visitor, the many styles of Ancient Egyptian architecture from classical pyramids to unusual 'pylons', and the terms used to describe parts of monuments, can be confusing.

## Tombs

The Old Kingdom period (2640BC to 2160BC; Third to Sixth Dynasties), was the time of the pyramid builders who had developed the now familiar Egyptian tomb shape from building several 'mastabas', or simple, table-like platforms traditionally erected over grave pits on top of each other in diminishing sizes. Initially the grave pit was located under the entire, solid structure, as in the Step Pyramid at Saqqara and that at Meidum. The pyramid at Meidum was different in that it's steps were smoothed to form the first true pyramid shape. Later, architects built the burial chambers inside the pyramid construction like those at Giza.

Even in pre-Dynasty days, some mastaba burial pits, or *serdabs* were built with an added chamber known as the chapel — a reception room for the deceased spirit, or *ka*. Later architects constructed tombs with passageways, or corridors leading to shrine cellars, often highly decorated. A statue of the deceased was placed in the *serdab* and food and grave furnishings were also left to accompany the dead on the journey to the Underworld. The more complex the tomb's structure became, as in Pyramid of Cheops at Giza, the more accompaniments were placed with the body. The burials became more sophisticated and mummification developed as the preserved body was placed in an elaborately decorated wooden coffin (sometimes in multiple coffins). Often a death mask was painted or placed on the corpse and finally it was laid to rest in a great stone coffin, or sarcophagus. The Middle Kingdom Pharaohs (2040BC to 1650BC; Eleventh to Fourteenth Dynasties), constructed most of their buildings with mud bricks and many have crumbled and disappeared. It was the kings of the New Kingdom (1551BC to 712BC; Eighteenth to Twenty-Fourth Dynasties), who abandoned the building of pyramids and adopted the practice of constructing rock tombs, such as those at Thebes (the Valleys of the Kings and the Queens and the nobles necropolis). This trend not only led to the construction of complex tomb chambers hewn into rock faces instead of being located in structures (like those in the pyramids) but it also led to the building of elaborate 'temples', employed in the funerary rites of royal burials.

## Temples

With the development of the pyramid tomb and the evolution of an extremely complicated religion, Egyptian priests began to dictate that chapels be built adjacent to the pyramids in which the deceased ruler could be worshipped. Royal burial ceremonies, which included

# Places of Interest In Western Thebes

*Colossi of Memnon*
To the right of the road to the temples

**Temple of Amenhotep III**
Also to the right of the road a little
further past the colossi

*Deir El-Bahari*
**Eleventh Dynasty Tombs**
In the hills to the right of Temple of
Hatshepsut

**Temple of Hatshepsut**
At the end of the path due west of the
Ramesside Temple

**Temple of Mentuhotep**
Next to Temple of Hatshepsut

**Temple of Tutmosis III**
Behind and to the left of Temple of
Hatshepsut

**Tomb of Senenmut**
To the right of the track before
Temple of Hatshepsut

*Deir el-Medina*
**Pit of Ostraca**
West of the Ptolomaic temple

**Ptolomaic Temple**
To the east of the ruined village

*El-Asasif*
North-west of Temple of Tutmosis III
next to Sheikh abu El-Qurna

**Lower Enclosure**
In the western quarter of the site

*El-Khokha*
Directly across the track from the
temple of Tutmosis III

**Dra Abu El-Naga**
North of the modern village of that
name and north of Temple of Seti I

**Metropolitan Museum House**
Inside the El-Khokha area

**Necropolis of Antef**
North of the Temple of Seti I near El-
Tarif village

*Medinet Habu*
**Chapel of Divine Adorers**
In front of Migdol

**Migdol**
Next to Temple of Tutmosis III

**Palace of Amenhotep III**
Southernmost of the Medinet Habu
ruins

**Palace of Tutmosis III**
Near that of Amenhotep III

**Temple of Eje and Haremhab**
On the left after the Antiquities Office

**Temple of Isis**
Further south of Medinet Habu, on
the plain at Tel Abu Bital

**Temple of Ramesses III**
Adjacent to those of Eje and
Haremhab

**Temple of Thoth**
Southern corner of Temple of

sacrifices and incantations, took place in the temples and from there, processions would transport the dead ruler from the temple to interment in the tomb. In the case of early kings such as Zoser, whose pyramid is at Saqqara, a mortuary temple containing the *serdab* chamber was built next to their pyramid and a separate temple was erected for worshipping the deceased ruler. An embalming house might be built nearby and a covered, processional causeway often

Ramesses III

**Temple of Tutmosis III**
Next to the Temple of Ramesses III

*Qurnet Murai*
Between Deir el-Medina and Temple of Merneptah

*Ramesseum*
**Ramesseum**
Largest of the terrace temples next to that of Tutmosis IV

**Ramesside Temple**
North-east, across the road from Temple of Tutmosis III

**Temple of Amenhotep I and Nefertari**
Across the lake from the Ramesside Temple

**Temple of Amenhotep II**
Next to Ramesseum

**Temple of Merneptah**
First temple on turning right after the Antiquities Office

**Temple of Nebwenef**
North of The Temple of Seti, towards the El Fadiliya Canal

**Temple of Seti I**
Facing the Nile on El-Fadliya Canal

**Temple of Siptah**
On the plain in front of the Temple of Tutmosis III next to Ramesside Temple

**Temple of Tausert**
Next to Temple of Merneptah

**Temple of Tutmosis III**
Across the track from rest-house

**Temple of Tutmosis IV**
Between the Tomb of Khonsuartais and the Ramesseum

**Temple of Wadjmose**
Next to Tausert's temple

**Tomb of Khonsuartais**
Beside Temple of Tutmosis IV

**Tombs of Ramesses Sitpah and Tausert**
Near that of Wadjmose

*Sheik Abu El-Qurna*
North of the Ramesseum

**Tombs of Nobles**
Upper Enclosure, in the northern part of the site

*Valley of the Kings*
**Eastern Valley of the Kings**
West of Deir El-Bahari

**Western Valley of the Kings**
West of the Eastern Valley

*Valley of the Queens*
Due west of Medinet Habu

linked the mortuary temple to the pyramid entrance. Other smaller temples and sanctuaries were constructed for the worship of deities connected with the dead Pharaoh and over many centuries more shrines and chapels were added to the main temple complex. When the fashion for pyramid burials died out, the temples became even more elaborate and formed vast monuments, many of which remain to this day. It is the mortuary temples and accompanying structures of the New Kingdom which represent the majority of Egypt's most impressive ancient monuments.

Of great complexity in design, the many temple sites scattered along the Nile Valley are bewildering in their layout, construction and original purposes. Initially a main temple would be built some distance from the tomb. During his life, the Pharaoh would worship his gods in the temple and, in some cases, a small palace would be constructed nearby for the king to live in during his pilgrimage to the temple. After his death, the temple would become his funerary temple, and from there his body would be taken for burial in a tomb prepared during his lifetime. With such a diversity of gods in the religion of Ancient Egypt, a Pharaoh might have worshipped a number of deities and would construct other temples to these gods. Some of these temples are immense edifices but most of the more important sites incorporated a number of distinct architectural features.

The basic features of the more famous of Egypt's ancient temples are explained simply by taking the vast temple complex at Karnak as an example because it comprises all the components which were included in traditional temple designs. The main building at Karnak, known as the Great Temple of Amun is made up of a series of courtyards. The courtyards, which were covered in, are divided from each other by vast façades known as 'pylons'. Pylons formed impressive entrances to temples and fixtures. Slots in the pylon's facing wall often held gigantic wooden flag posts. These pylons, ten in all, range down in size from the largest, 43m (141ft) high, 113m (371ft) wide and with walls 15m (49ft) thick and comprising two gigantic towers, one with a staircase, forming an immense gateway into the Great Court. Inside the court, which is lined with huge columns and crouching figures of rams, is a small temple and a small open pavilion known as a 'kiosk' and also used as a place of worship. Statues of the Pharaoh precede an antechamber and vestibule. Through the second pylon is another hall called the Great Hypostyle Hall. 'Hypostyle' means a roof supported by pillars, and this hall is exactly that a 5,000sq m (53,000sq ft) hall crammed with 134 gigantic columns in 16 rows reaching 23m (75ft) high, including 'capitals'.

Columns and pillars in Ancient Egyptian architecture took various forms and their shapes were commonly derived from natural forms — columns could be shaped like tree trunks, stemmed like a lotus with a capital, in the form of either a lotus flower or lotus bud. Capitals were also carved to imitate bunches of palm fronds, a group of various plants, or the leaves surrounding a flower. The stems of pillars were sometimes elaborately inscribed with hieroglyphics.

On the walls of the Great Hypostyle Hall of the Great Temple of Amun are religious carvings, known as reliefs. In other temples these might be carvings celebrating military conquests, economic achievements or everyday life of the royal courts. Found in almost every ancient temple, these reliefs are generally in low, or bas-relief. Sometimes the writings or panoramas on temple walls were carved in sunk relief, or relief *en creux*. Other temple and tomb decorations might be incised, or carved into the stone. Walls might have bands of repeated patterns or pictures, 'friezes' or plaster moulded into embellishments, called 'stucco'. In the Amun temple, another hypostyle hall lies beyond the third pylon and this contains a large tapering shaft of stone called an 'obelisk'. Many of these obelisks have been found in ancient sites all over Egypt and were often used as markers, generally inscribed with the name of the Pharaoh responsible for their erection. Pharaohs had a special design signifying their names known as a 'cartouche' — a line embracing several hieroglyphic characters denoting the royal name. Similar to the obelisk is the 'stele', a carved pillar of stone sometimes covered in hieroglyphs relating to the achievements of the current ruler. The inner temple contains a court and sanctuary and behind this is a festival hall preceding another sanctuary. An enclosure wall covered in reliefs embraces the main temple area and a tiny mortuary temple is attached to this outer wall.

Other features of a typical Ancient Egyptian temple site might include, as at Karnak, rows of 'sphinx' which form processional causeways. A sphinx can often be in the form of a crouched lion with a Pharaoh's head as at Giza, or crouched rams as at Karnak. Occasionally sphinx figures might embrace a carved portrayal of a Pharaoh or god. Another common feature of temple precincts is the sacred lake and store rooms which were often built onto the temple and which held offerings used in sacrifices and blessing rituals. A birth-room or *mammisi*, dedicated to the cult of gods, might be included in a temple complex and another common structure might be a cenotaph, or token tomb in the shape of a small temple. Colonnades, great funerary ramps and wide terraces, which were once gardens of herbs and sweet-smelling spice bushes, were also refinement features of some New Kingdom temples. Among the most significant structures which are prime examples of Ancient Egypt are the magnificent monuments which combine to paint a detailed picture of the development of Ancient Egyptian architecture over a period of more than 2,000 years.

# 11
# *LUXOR TO ASWAN*

It is more than 210km (130 miles) from Luxor, due south, to Aswan and there are several options of transport from Nile steamer, felucca, train, aeroplane, bus, service taxi or by hired car. Leaving Luxor whether by train or road, the main route follows the east bank of the Nile unless one takes the secondary road on the west bank which runs only as far as Edfu. There is a reliable bus service from Luxor to Aswan and a regular air service. Economically speaking, the local taxis are inexpensive and constantly ply the dusty route between the main settlements along the Nile. The felucca trip from Luxor takes just over 3 days and stops at Esna, Edfu and Kom Ombo. However, to continue on the Nileside tour of important ancient sites the trip from Luxor to Aswan is best taken in two stages, breaking the journey at Edfu.

## LUXOR TO EDFU
Few monuments in close proximity to Luxor can usually be visited by felucca or local taxi. The three major sites within easy striking distance of Luxor lie just a short trip south, near the next river bend. On the left of the main road south, before reaching the village and rail station of El Idisat, the Ptolemaic temple of the village of Tod can be seen, although only four broken pillars indicate its location. Known in ancient times as Djerti, or Tuphium, this site was a sacred centre for more than fifteen ancient dynasties until the Romans adopted the ruins and built their own temple. The rich treasures of Amenenhet (Twelfth Dynasty) consisting of gold and silver untensils stored in copper coffers and now on show in the Cairo Museum of Egyptian Antiquities, were discovered here. Across the river, on the west bank, near the village of Armant, is the site of ancient **Hermonthis**.

206

There is little to see here except the sacred Bull Necropolis nearby.

Two other ancient sites lie across the river from each other. These are the sites of **Aphroditopolis**, on the west bank, just south of the curiously-shaped ridge of El Gebelein (Two Mountains) and the location of **Mo'allah** to the left of the main road just after the village of El Shaghab. Near El Gebelein mountain and Aphroditopolis are to be seen the Tomb of Sheikh Musa, the ruins of a temple to the god Hathor and the crocodile cemetery — all that is left of the ancient settlement of Crocodopolis. Continuing along the main east bank road the crossing for Esna should be taken by turning right at the village of **El Deir**. On reaching the river, the road bridge leads over an old dam right into the town centre. From the pretty rural township of **Esna**, horse-drawn carriages take visitors the short distance inland to the **Temple of Khnum**. Only the great hypostyle hall now stands with giant pillars and carved friezes. This temple is well worth the diversion from the Nile's eastern highway. There used to be four temples in this region but the only other remains are those of an Ancient Roman dock and a nilometer.

The road to Edfu can be taken from Esna, along the west bank and this secondary road passes the famous sight of the **El-Kula** pyramid, the southernmost structure of its kind in Egypt. The erosion of the pyramid's cladding has left a stepped outline to the structure.

## Places of Interest Between Luxor and Edfu

**Aphroditopolis and Mo'allah**
Facing each other across Nile.
Mo'allah is on east bank 25km
(15 miles) south of Luxor
Ancient city sites, El Gebelein
mountains and location of Tomb of
Sheikh Musa.

**Esna**
54km (34 miles) south of Luxor on
Nile's west bank
The Temple of Khnum and other
ancient remains.

**Tod**
20km (12 miles) south of Luxor, on
east bank of Nile
Ptolemaic temple, site of important
treasure find.

**Edfu**
105km (65 miles) south of Luxor on
the Nile's west bank
Site of the famous Temple of Horus.

**El-Kab**
East bank of Nile opposite El-Kula
Site of ancient city of Nekhab and
Temple of Nekhbet.

**El-Kula**
West bank of Nile 83km (51 miles)
south of Luxor
Significant pyramid site.

**Hermonthis**
Opposite Tod on west bank of Nile
Ancient city site and Bull Necropolis.

However, if the road is kept to, the highway cuts through real desert, parting company with the railway line for a short distance until, returning to the riverside, the road passes, on the right, the remains of Ancient Nekhab at a location called **El-Kab**. Between the road and the railway, which hugs the riverside, are several ancient remains including that of Amenhotep III (Eighteenth Dynasty) and a striking rock temple, a little chapel and a number of rock tombs of the same dynasty. Some of these tombs are in a good state of preservation and worth visiting. At a point opposite the town of Edfu, the main road hugs the riverside while a secondary road joins it from the left. This is the ancient trading route cutting across the empty desert for about 210km (130 miles) to Marsa Alum on the Red Sea coast. From the village of **El-Ridisiya Bahari**, just after the desert road junction, ferries and a good bridge cross the river which is quite wide at this point. There is also an expansive strip of agricultural land here and two rail stations close together which serve the farming population who supply both Edfu and Kom Ombo with fruit and vegetables.

**Edfu** once was known as Apollinopolis Magna, an important greek capital dedicated to their god Horus-Apollo. However, it is Horus, the Ancient Egyptian's god, who has left his mark on this little market town. This is the site of the magnificent **Temple of Hathor** which has defied the elements since its Ptolemaic architects began the construction in 237BC. Horse carriages ply the dusty track for the centre of Edfu to the temple on the riverside, or motor transport can be taken from the railway station. One of the greatest monuments of Upper Egypt, the temple consists of a gigantic pylon, incised with decorations and leading into a great forecourt edged with palm-capitalled columns. A colossal statue of Horus in his common guise as a falcon, is located by the entrance and its twin lies opposite. Beyond the vestibule is a large hypostyle hall with twelve columns leading through into antechambers and passages which surround the inner sanctum. The reliefs and inscriptions in the temple at Edfu are among the most delightful in any of Egypt's ancient monuments. The actual city site can only just be discerned to the west of the Temple of Horus denoted by the mounds of rubble and signs of recent excavations. Most visitors to Edfu and its spectacular temple stay overnight at one of the town's four hotels as this point is conveniently halfway between Luxor and Kom Ombo.

## EDFU TO ASWAN

A railway runs from Edfu, across the Western Desert, past Aswan and Abu Simbel into the Sudan, but the main passenger train south continues from El-Ridisiya Bahari alongside the main highway on the Nile's east bank. The next site south on this route also lies on the banks of the river and is known as **Gebel Serag**. Just a few minute's drive from Edfu, this hill with its ancient quarries and early Byzantine ruins lies just south of the village. The straight road after Gebel Serag runs due south to Kom Ombo through the village of **Silwa Bahari**, surrounded by ancient quarries containing fascinating inscriptions. Entering an important agricultural region at the township of Kagug where the rail track crosses the road from right to left, there is an important site across the river on the west bank. This is known as **Haremhab** and because of its isolated position, is rarely included on any tour itinerary. Beyond Kagug, however, is the famous site of **Silsila**. A row of hills hide ancient quarries and rock tombs. An unfinished sphinx, stelae, a fascinating rock temple and evidence of intensive excavation work cover the site which lies not far north of the next big town, Kom Ombo.

Once named Ombus the important town of **Kom Ombo** lies in a strategic position inland from the river in a large fertile plan surrounded by wide fields of sugar cane and vegetable plots. The Great Temple of Sobek and Horus is celebrated because of the unusual way

*Temple of Khnum, Esna*

*This painted plan shows a typical ceremonial setting*

*Graphic detail was typical of the ancient's wall paintings*

*Inscriptions explain court scene (above)*

*Paintings depict a royal ceremony*

each architectural feature is duplicated. Double doors lead to double chambers and twin rows of columns supported roofs which extended out over twin lines of passageways. The inscriptions and detailed reliefs of deities and rulers in the temple's halls and on its well-preserved walls are most attractive. Look for the Roman *mammisi* alongside which are two ancient wells. Nearby is the Chapel of Hathor and its collection of mummified sacred crocodiles which may have been kept here for religious rituals. Few visitors attempt to find accommodation in Kom Ombo as it is a short drive south to Aswan and its top-class hotels. Just the market township of **Daraw** is of any real interest on the road to Aswan as it is a traditional centre for Sudanese camel traders. The road from Daraw then runs through a narrow fertile strip alongside the river and railway, through El Aqaba and El Khattara into the famous town of Aswan. A long canal on the left of the road denotes the approaches to Aswan and the railway runs parallel to the main road called El-Sall Street.

---

## READING BY PICTURES

Over the millennia, Egypt has been a melting-pot of languages from those of the Persians, the Greeks and the Romans, to the languages of the Copts and the Arabs. Having undergone a sea-change through the succession of tongues, colonisers and invaders, Egypt eventually adopted the Arab language which, today, is the country's official tongue. Across the years the language of early Egypt had become lost in the mists of time. However, staring down on the panoply of tribes and the procession of races which swept across the Egyptian countryside were the hieroglyphic scripts of the ancients, carved immortally in stone. The language of the Ancient Egyptians lay forgotten for thousands of years but since the recognition of its importance for documenting a civilisation's history, the hieroglyphs have given us one of our greatest legacies — written communication from ages past.

Ancient Egypt has traditionally been considered as one origin of our modern alphabet. The three dozen 'Cananaean Inscriptions' on rock faces in the malachite mines of Sinai and those in Hathor's temple, considered among the earliest of engraved scripts, were first revealed in 1868. Since then, the search for the origins of the written word began in earnest. Writing in Egypt probably began during the reign of the legendary King Menes of the First Dynasty in around 2700BC, before the building of the first pyramids. The Ancient Egyptian god Thoth, was also credited by early civilisations with the

## Places of Interest Between Edfu and Aswan

**Gebel Serag**
East bank of Nile, south of Edfu
Interesting ancient quarry sites and
rock tombs.

**Haremhab**
West bank of Nile, opposite Kagug
town
Early town and temple site.

**Kom Ombo**
59km (37 miles) south of Edfu on
Nile's east bank
The Great Temple of Sobek and
Horus, Roman remains.

**Silsila**
37km (23 miles) south of Edfu, east
bank of Nile
Quarries and rock tombs.

**Silwa Bahari**
30km (19 miles) south of Edfu on
east bank of Nile
Ancient quarries with fascinating
inscriptions.

**Temple of Horus**
South of Edfu
2,000-year-old temple.

invention of writing. At about the same time as the first writing was evolving, the Ancient Egyptian solar calendar, with 365 days, was being developed. This calendar is almost identical with today's but commenced its year with July because before the construction of the great dams in southern Egypt the Nile used to flood annually in July.

Before King Menes united the two kingdoms of Ancient Egypt under one crown, the king of Upper Egypt had adopted the colour white for his conical crown and the symbol of the reed, while the rulers of Lower Egypt chose a red crown and the bee as their emblem. These two royal crests were probably used on the ruler's property and painted on walls and carved on furniture as a mark of possession. Menes, whose alternative name was Narmer, selected sound signs which represented his name — a fish for the first part of his name (nar), and a chisel which was pronounced (mar).

During the reign of the Pharaoh Zoser, 2640BC to 2575BC, a more complex symbol was adopted by royalty. This is known as a cartouche and is similar to a seal — an oval line enclosing one or more emblems. King Zoser's cartouche took the form of twin cartouche surmounted by two hawks — one standing on the symbol of a chain representing gold. Before any written language was established in Egypt the most commonly used symbols were those which represented power; for example an arm holding a spear, shown as a 'z'. This was the symbol of Upper Egypt. Other symbols used in cartouche were a bed of reeds, shown as the letter 's' and door bolt as 'r' in the form of an open mouth. Thus, from a picture of a bee or a reed symbolising a kingdom, representations of objects (ideograms) which had no other translation than to stand for an entity, gradually became adopted into a simple language by adding extra symbols and giving each a sound.

Wherever these cartouche appeared, archaeologists were able to identify a sculpture, an artifact or a column with the relevant Pharaoh. This picture language was generally carved on objects, buildings and walls of tombs. Scribes would also paint stories onto pottery and wooden writing tablets and prepared walls of temples using the language. A great deal of religious significance was given to the scribes and the art of writing. Several of the Egyptian gods (Horus, Amun, Maat and Ra), appeared as hieroglyphs in the alphabet. All sorts of objects and animals were employed in Egyptian hieroglyphics such as a hand, a loaf, a pool, a bull, an owl and a snake. The basic language eventually contained around 1,000 symbols in its alphabet.

These symbols were not always portrayed with absolute accuracy. Scribes and stone workers stylised the characters developing the symbols into a complex written language, not just isolated objects and animals. A snake would be abbreviated into a squiggle, a loaf was represented as a curve, or an owl as two connected 'lightning flashes'. As picture writing became more abstract so characters took on the image of alphabet letters similar to those of the Roman or Arabic alphabets of today. This script was reserved for the use of priests and the Greeks called this 'hieratic', or priestly writing. An even more abstract form of this writing evolved and this became known as 'demotic', or popular.

For more than 3,000 years this picture writing and its derivatives, including the still undeciphered script of Meroitic, was employed by scribes, priests and learned scholars. The latest examples found date from about 395. Egyptologists, possibly over a period of 1,000 years, have been attempting to decipher the Egyptian hieroglyphic language but, in comparatively modern times, records show that some work had been attempted on this subject as early as the mid-seventeenth century. The real exponent of the mysterious language is generally accepted to be the French archaeologist, Champollion, who accompanied Napoleon's extensive expeditions in Egypt in the late 1700s. However, it was not until 1822, 23 years after a French soldier had discovered the 'Rosetta Stone', that Champollion began to translate hieroglyphic text. As the Rosetta Stone fragment had inscriptions in Greek certain symbols in demotic Egyptian and Ancient Egyptian hieroglyphs were easily identified. From this one stone an almost complete alphabet was deciphered.

After the early hieroglyphic language had developed into a cursive form of writing, with joined-up symbols, the Coptic form of writing was adopted. From a recognisable symbol in the form of an eye or bird, single lines simplified the image. This was known as literary script which itself was stylised into what was called hieratic script. In hieratic script the letters were often joined as in the Coptic script. Demotic script, which followed hieratic script, was adopted by the Copts and was linked. This was commonly known by the Greeks and Romans as epistolographic script. One of the first translations of the Book of Psalms, written in an extinct Coptic language and bound in wood and leather, was recovered in 1984. It was found just north of the Greek-named Nile town of Oxyrhynchus in a childs grave, dating around 375. This book is now hailed as one of the greatest literary discoveries.

Recently archaeologists have been deciphering ancient papyrus geological maps of the Eastern Desert found in Deir el-Medina, Western Thebes in 1989 and have reached the conclusion that it was drawn up by a scribe named Amenakhte during the reign of Ramesses IV in around 1150BC. Geologists are particularly excited that this scroll, over 2m (7ft) in length is the oldest known geological map by 2,880 years, and is remarkably accurate when compared to modern charts of the area. This is just one example of communication across the millennia; by the way the ancient chart corresponds to those of today, demonstrating the scientific skills of Ancient Egypt, and by the way modern scholars are able to read the hieroglyphic script on the map, thanks to that scribe who carved the texts on the Rosetta Stone.

# 12
# *ASWAN AND ABU SIMBEL*

At either ends of the vast 5,250sq km (2,018sq mile) reservoir known as Lake Nasser, are Aswan and Abu Simbel, the southernmost locations of Egypt's ancient monuments. Lake Nasser was first created by the construction of the Aswan Dam, and almost 60 years later, by the building of the Aswan High Dam. The first dam ensured a year-long supply of water to the arable lands along the Nile Valley, and the High Dam brought the added attraction of hydro-electric power. The lake itself is 510km (316 miles) in length and straddles the Tropic of Cancer. Because of the distance between Aswan and Abu Simbel, most visitors fly from Aswan. The return journey of about 5 hours gives ample time to view the temples, monuments and ancient ruins. A paved road runs the 275km (170 miles) from Aswan to Abu Simbel and early morning buses make the $3^1/_2$-hour drive daily. Bus tickets for Abu Simbel should be purchased the day before travelling. Alternatively, some hotels lay on special taxi tours to the lakeside monuments.

## Aswan

On entering the town of Aswan the road towards the corniche should be taken turning right at the station. This leads to the larger of Aswan's twenty hotels. These range from the height of luxury to several pleasant middle-range hotels and a youth hostel. Rail visitors should remember that the station lies to the north of town, while most hotels are located in the southern part of Aswan. Several Nile cruise steamers and a fleet of feluccas sail from the quayside on Aswan's beautiful long corniche and the city's airport lies south of Aswan, across the High Dam road on the Nile's west bank. Up to twenty flights per week link the town with Cairo via Luxor, and the same number connect Aswan with Abu Simbel. Aswan is the end of the train service for most visitors as the two branch lines head south across vast desert wastes to Sudan, or east, to the Red Sea coast. Few tourists make the long drive to Abu Simbel from Aswan because of the regular public services.

A sailing excursion on the Nile at Aswan is almost obligatory. The climate here is favourable because of its proximity to the great Lake Nasser. Aswan is a pleasant town and warrants a few hours browsing. You can visit the ancient remains of Syene, wander around the temple and ruins above the town at Qasr El-Mula or see the Ptolemaic Temple near the Cataract hotels. This is by far one of the most pleasant experiences in any itinerary of Egyptian touring.

The beautiful and peaceful island of **Elephantine** lays slumbering in mid-stream among many hump-backed islets which are supposed to have given the region the name of Yenbu (Land of the Elephants) because they looked like a herd of elephants bathing. This island makes a favourite felucca excursion from Aswan's corniche and in an hour or so one can visit the fascinating Aswan Archaeological Museum, wander through the ruins of the Temple of Khnum, its necropolis and adjoining smaller temple, view the Kalabsha Kiosk in the south of the island and wonder at the ingenious nilometer carved out of solid rock. One will notice the profusion of flowers, plants and exotic trees on Elephantine Island but these are put in the shade when one visits **Kitchener's Island** once the property of Lord Kitchener. Recently this island has been re-christened 'Botanical Island'.

The pink sandstone shrine dominating the west bank of the Nile is the **Aga Khan Mausoleum** (forty-eighth imam of the Ismaili, 1899-1957) built by his wife, the begum. Visitors may notice a red rose on the sarcophagus, a token replaced daily when the begum is in residence in Aswan. Further north, in the hills alongside the Nile's east bank, are the infrequently visited rock tombs of the governors and nobels of Ancient Aswan. Known locally as the **Tombs of the Winds**, these go back to the era of the Old Kingdom and are dated from the Sixth to the Eighth Dynasties, around 2300BC to 2000BC. The tombs have fascinating inscriptions on their walls. Between the Aga Khan Mausoleum and the Tombs of the Winds is **St Simeon's Monastery**, high on the rocky hillside. Building began in the seventh century and was a Coptic monastery for 600 years until about 1250. This ruined complex, constructed on two levels, has massive walls, turrets and some interesting frescoes.

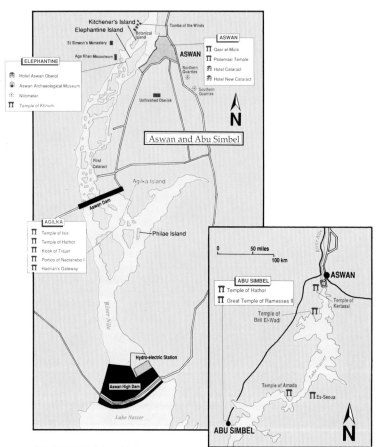

## AROUND ASWAN

Apart from the islands of Elephantine and Kitchener's there are two other main islands, Ambunarti and Sahel, located under the First Cataract, south of Aswan. Most visited of the two is **Sahel Island** with its round dark rocks covered in ancient inscriptions. The 'Famine Stele' is found just above the First Cataract. Nearby is the little Nubian village of **Hazan** and this part of the Aswan is particularly picturesque making a fruitful morning's excursion from Aswan, especially if the tour takes in the massive **Unfinished Obelisk**, 42m (138ft) long, just outside Aswan and the **Southern** and

*Tranquility on the Nile at Aswan*

*Aswan has five major hotels*

# Places of Interest In and Around Aswan

## Aga Khan Mausoleum
Set on small hill opposite Elephantine Island on Nile's west bank
Domed tomb of forty-eighth imam of the Ismaili built in 1950s.

## Agilka Island
6km (4 miles) south of Aswan
The following monuments were moved from Philae Island to Agilka Island

*Temple of Isis*
Largest of six temples on Philae.

*Temple of Hathor*
Particularly decorative example of Philae's temples.

*Kiosk of Trajan*
Exquisite Roman kiosk.

*Portico of Nectanebo I*
Oldest of structures from Philae.

*Hadrian's Gateway*
Ornate lintel and supports on this Roman monument.

## Aswan Dam
About 6km (4 miles) south of Aswan
Early twentieth-century hydro-electric dam.

## Aswan High Dam
15km (10 miles) south of Aswan
Vast hydro-electric dam holding back Lake Nasser's water.

## Elephantine Island
Facing Aswan town
Temple of Khnum, Aswan Archaeological Museum, nilometer, and Kalabsha Kiosk.

## Kitchener's Island
Between Elephantine Island and the Nile's west bank
Lord Kitchener's luxuriant 'Botanical Island'.

## Northern and Southern Quarries
Between $1^1/_2$km (1 mile) and 3km (2 miles) south of Aswan
Ancient quarry sites with some unfinished work.

## Ptolemaic Temple
Near Grand Hotel in south town
Ruins of second-century BC temple.

## Sahel Island
3km (2 miles) south-west of Aswan
Picturesque island with many inscribed rocky boulders.

## St Simeon's Monastery
On Nile's west bank, north of Aga Khan Mausoleum
Fort-like seventh-century Coptic monastery.

## Syene
Scant fragments throughout town
Remains of the Ancient Greek city on the Aswan site.

## Tombs of the Winds
On Nile's west bank north of Kitchener's Island
Ancient rock tombs of governors and nobles.

## Unfinished Obelisk
On southern outskirts of Aswan
Massive half-completed monument and quarry works.

**Northern Quarries** where the granite was obtained for many of Ancient Egypt's temples and pyramids.

## PHILAE

Philae is in a magical location south of the old Aswan Dam in that part of the Nile Valley that was flooded first in 1902, and then deepened in 1912. Of the many islands in between the Aswan Dam and the High Dam, Philae was chosen by the ancients as a sacred place. A great temple complex was constructed at Philae made up of so many beautiful monuments that the island became known as the 'Pearl of Egypt'. Comparatively recent in terms of Egyptian history, Philae's oldest structures date from the reign of Nectanebo I, about 375BC. In the 350 years between the Thirtieth Dynasty Pharaoh and the rule of Emperors Augustus in 25BC and Hadrian in AD130 many temples and monuments were constructed in veneration of a series of gods like Isis, Osiris, Hathor, Khnum and Satet. In much later times the Copts built several Christian churches and a monastery on the island of Philae. The construction of the first of two great dams across the river partly submerged the famous monuments. When the water was later raised concern for the preservation of the treasures mounted. Famous photographs show the magnificent pillars and columns rising from the Nile, reflected onto its shimmering surface. Underneath the surface however, the tides began to etch away at the stonework.

Between 1972 and 1980, using a gigantic coffer dam built around part of the great complex of monuments, UNESCO and government agencies slowly resited all the ancient monuments except two Coptic churches, the Temple of Augustusa, a large Roman gateway and ancient ramp. The site chosen for resettlement of the monuments was the small island to the north of Philae called Agilka. Today a bus takes visitors to a quay just south of the Aswan Dam where a boat can be taken on a tour around Philae, Agilka and their big brother island of Bigga from where the monuments on Agilka make a spectacular vista. A trip to Agilka to see the monuments can be a full afternoon's excursion, and there is a *son et lumière* show in the evening. Many tours include the islands on an excursion to the dams.

The fascinating monuments removed to **Agilka** from Philae include the great funerary Temple of Isis, dominating the site with its central sanctuary, six floral-topped columns of the Hall of Nectanebo I, two great pylons, and wide courtyards flanked by tall, composite plant-capitalled colonnades. Nearby is the little Temple of Haren-

*Kiosk of Trajan, re-erected at Agilka*

dotes and the Hadrian's Gateway, built by the famous emperor. At the end of the long West Colonnade the nilometer can be found down a flight of ancient steps near the water's edge. On the other side of the main body of the Temple of Isis is the Temple of Hathor with its intricately decorated columns and the elegant Kiosk of Trajan, built during the imperial era of Roman occupation. The fourteen columns of this striking kiosk are in an exquisite state of preservation. See also the Portico of Nectanebo I at the southern end of the island — the only pre-Ptolemaic structure still standing. Other structures to view are the Temple of Arsnuphis, the ruins of the Temple of Asclepius and the Chapel of Mandulis.

## BETWEEN ASWAN AND ABU SIMBEL

One of the most important sites within striking distance of the town of Aswan, but a good day's excursion out past the airport on the west bank of the Nasser reservoir, is the **Temple of Kalabsha** built about 28BC during the reign of Emperor Augustus on the site of a 1425BC temple to Amenhotep II. It was moved to this site to prevent submergence in the rising waters of the lake and was once the hub of the ancient city of Talmis which is now submerged. Vast pillars support part of the roof of a wide vestibule and three inner sanctums. A massive pylon forms an entrance to the imposing monument and its colonnaded courtyard.

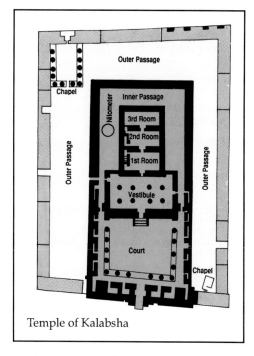

Temple of Kalabsha

Also rescued from the waters of Lake Nasser were the ruins of the **Temple of Beit El-Wali**, to the north of Kalabsha. Hewn from the solid rock, this monument dates from the time of Ramesses II, around 1250BC and sports some fine ancient reliefs. Also north of Kalabsha is the **Temple of Kertassi** with its curious twin columns with their weird Hathor faces stylised into triangles. Little else but the pillars remains of Kertassi but just over 160km (99 miles) south, on the same side of Lake Nasser, are two more rescued monuments. Es-Seoua is not often visited because it is overshadowed in grandeur by its neighbouring complex, Amada.

The rock **Temple of Amada** was built by two Pharaohs, Tutmosis III and Amenhotep II, between 1500BC to 1450BC. Removed to its present position in its entirety, this Eighteenth-Dynasty temple was hewn out of the rock and consists of an inner sanctuary preceded by a large transverse chamber and imposing twelve-columned hypostyle hall. In front of the monument were twin pylons made of brick which have all but disappeared. Built by Ramesses II and saved

## Places of Interest
## Between Aswan and Abu Simbel

**Abu Simbel**
280km (174 miles) south of Aswan
Famous Rock Temples on the western shores of Lake Nasser

**Amada**
200km (124 miles) south of Aswan on west bank of Lake Nasser
Rescued monuments, Temple of Amada, Temple of El-Derr and Tomb of Pennut.

**Es-Seoua**
30km (19 miles) east of Amada on west shores of Lake Nasser
Another rescued monument on

shores of Lake Nasser.

**Temple of Beit El-Wali**
North-west of Kalabsha
This temple has some fine friezes.

**Temple of Kalabsha**
19km (11 miles) south of Aswan on west shore of Lake Nasser
Most spectacular site in this part of Egypt after Abu Simbel.

**Temple of Kertassi**
North of Kalabsha
Little remains of this temple to the goddess Hathor.

by the efforts of the UNESCO rescue operation is the rock **Temple of El-Derr** nearby, containing an inner sanctuary, six-pillared hallway and twelve-pillared hypostyle hall. Also in the Amada complex of temples the rock Tomb of Pennut. This is a Twelfth Dynasty monument of particular importance and was singled out of the now submerged necropolis of Aniba for salvage because of its remarkable wall inscriptions.

# Abu Simbel

Most visitors to Abu Simbel will not spend more than a few hours at Egypt's most spectacular ancient monument site. The aeroplane journey from Aswan takes about a half an hour. The one hotel, the small Nefertari, lies just a short walk from the Rock Temples and the opportunity to spend extra time wondering at some of Ramesses II's greatest works should not be missed. For those staying over at Abu Simbel the bus tickets for the return to Aswan should be purchased a day in advance and for the air service, details should be checked on leaving Aswan.

The site of Abu Simbel, 272km (169 miles) south of Aswan, was named after the tiny town a short drive from the monuments since these massive edifices were removed from their original location 100m (110yd) south of their present positions and 60m (200ft) higher

## Places of Interest In Abu Simbel

**Great Temple of Ramesses II**
Near Abu Simbel airport
Probably Egypt's most impressive
temple site, colossal statues,
friezes.

**Temple of Hathor**
50m (55yd) north of Great Temple
A quarter the size of the Great
Temple of Ramesses II, colossal
statues and inscriptions.

in order to save them from being submerged by the rising waters of Lake Nasser. Re-instated in a dramatic location, set into the impressive pink cliffs on the lake's western bank (almost on the Sudanese border), the two rock temples remain among the greatest wonders of the world. Certainly, if early classical scholars had set eyes on the Great Temple of Ramesses II, there would have been eight Wonders of the Ancient World. However, although many temples, tombs and treasure storehouses were constructed by the Ancient Egyptians in this region, by the time the Greek and Roman empires reached Egypt, the grand monuments had disappeared under the desert sands. Excavated from their millennium-long sandy tomb in the early nineteenth century, the Great Temple of Ramesses II and Temple of Hathor became one of Egypt's most popular spectacles. The original Aswan Dam, built almost 100 years after the temples were unearthed, caused the waters of the Nile above the First Cataract to form a lake. Fifty years later the Aswan High Dam scheme flooded the valley where the temples stood and a 4-year rescue project re-located the temples to their present site at Abu Simbel. Nubia, generally the region south of Aswan into the Sudan, was a favourite site for ancient temples and twenty-three in all were resuced from Lake Nasser's rising tide.

But most famous of all temple sites is that of Abu Simbel and especially the Great Temple of Ramesses II with its four colossal seated figures. The smaller temple, with six colossal standing figures guarding its entrance, is the Temple of Hathor. Both hewn out of the solid rock, instead of free-standing as those further down the Nile, the two temples extend deep into the cliff faces with their intricately-carved façades presenting awe-inspiring edifices in the desert landscape.

The four statues of the enthroned Ramesses II, dominating the east-facing entrance of the main temple, dwarf the entrance door by their 33m (108ft) height. Only three of the statues of Ramesses II

*The Temple of Hathor, Abu Simbel*

*General view of the Great Temple of Ramesses II, Abu Simbel*

retain their heads due possibly to an ancient earthquake and above the central doorway is a relief of Ra the sun god between the god Maat and the jackal-headed User. Above the entire frontage is a frieze of twenty-two baboons. Aligned west to east, the Great Temple of Ramesses II was re-erected on an identical orientation so that it's celebrated phenomenon continued. Each year, on 21 February and 21 October, the rising sun's rays penetrate deep into the temple's interior, highlighting the details inside the huge hypostyle hall with its two rows of square pillars, Osiris figures, wonderful mural reliefs and painted ceiling. Also illuminated are the entrances to eight side chambers which extend far into the cliff and the sacred sanctuary decorated by four giant statues of the king and his deities which are bathed in the golden sunlight only twice a year.

The queen's temple to Hathor was also created by Ramesses II for his wife Queen Nefertari who is represented by two of the six standing statues on its façade. The other four statues are of the Pharaoh and all six stand 10m (33ft) high with a centrally located entrance. Stylised stelae between each statue are deeply engraved with hieroglyphic inscriptions and a frieze of cobras run across the doorway which leads into a hypostyle hall with six pillars, a transverse chamber and a small sanctuary with a figure of Hathor. Rock inscriptions throughout the temple are of religious devotions while those on the exterior are of military significance. This is the general pattern for temple decoration, particularly during the Nineteenth Dynasty when these temples were constructed — 3,500 years ago.

## TEMPLES AND DAMS

For over three and a quarter centuries a wealth of Ancient Egyptian edifices dotted the Nile Valley from the First Cataract along the river banks into what is now the Sudan. Only the shifting sands had begun to threaten the soft stone from which the temples and tombs were carved. Before sand could begin to erode many of the valley's immense desert storms had cocooned many of the early temples in the grasp of its irrepressible tide. In 1813 a Swiss visitor to Abu Simbel, Johan Ludwig Burckhart, noted the colossal heads of the Great Temple of Ramesses II projecting from sand dunes. Four years later the temple was unearthed and many more monuments were discovered over the following decades.

Still nothing threatened the great structures which had survived below the desert sands. However, the need to control the flow of the Nile and the requirement for hydro-electric power instigated the construction of a dam across the Nile above Aswan. The water behind the dam flooded the great valley and submerged several important monuments. Initially, with the construction of the first Aswan Dam in 1902, the island of Philae and its monuments were semi-submerged. Again monuments were rendered lower in the reservoir's waters when the third heightening of the dam was effected in 1932. When the great Aswan High Dam was erected between 1960 and 1971, the threat to even more of Egypt's heritage was of world concern. The waters of Lake Nasser, created by the vast dam, rose quickly, giving a matter of a few years for the teams of government experts, archaeologists, scientists, technicians, photographers and construction engineers to salvage the monuments from submersion. Commencing in early 1963 the operation of carving the great structures into manageable pieces and removing them to a safe level took 5 years. By 1968 the marathon task was completed at a cost of many millions of dollars. In all twenty-three of the hundreds of ancient monuments built in the Lake Nasser area of Egyptian Nubia were rescued from drowning by a massive UNESCO programme.

# Egypt: Tips for Travellers

## Planning Your Visit

## Climate

Blessed with a warm dry climate most of the year, Egypt can get very hot in high summer. The best time to visit the country is between October and March. During this period the nights can get quite cold, particularly in the desert; it is advisable to take something warm to wear. The hottest temperatures occur during June and July and can reach 35°C (95°F) in Cairo and 42°C (108°F) in Aswan. However, the heat is generally dry and bearable in the shade and humidity is relatively low.

*Weather Information — Cairo*

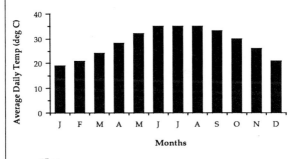

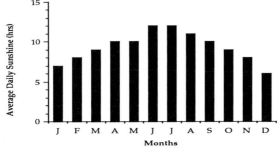

From mid-February to May the sand laden desert wind, or *khamseen*, blows often filling the air with fine particles of dust and sometimes making good photography difficult. There is an average rainfall of 18cm (7in) per annum in the coastal and Delta regions. Precipitation occurs during the period from March to May.

Mineral water is available almost everywhere and one should remember that the average adult should consume about 5 litres (8 pints) per day.

*Weather Information — Aswan*

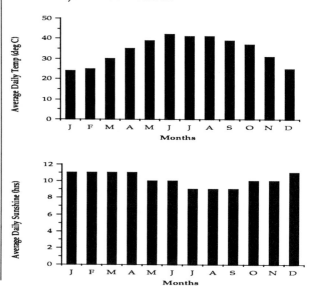

## Currency and Credit Cards

An unlimited amount of foreign currency can be taken into Egypt but no more than 20LE. The Egyptian pound (LE) is divided into 100 piastres. Notes include 1, 5, 10, 20, 50, and 100LE. Coins include 5, 10, 25 and 50 piastres. All money transactions and exchange receipts should be retained. These will help when converting Egyptian pounds back into foreign currency.

Credit cards have not yet become widespread enough in Egypt to make them an essential asset when travelling in the country although the luxury hotels and restaurants in Cairo and Alexandria generally accept internationally recognised credit cards. Traveller's cheques are the best way of taking currency into Egypt, either in US dollars or sterling and are also the safest means of carrying money when travelling. Banks are open Sunday to Thursday, 10am-1pm.

Some banks in Cairo are:
Bank du Caire
5 Salah Salem Street

Bank of America
10 Patrice Lumumba Street

Cairo Barclays International
10 Fawatem Street

Citibank
95, 26 July Street

EAB
Salah Salem Sporting Club

National Bank of Egypt
26 Salah Salem Street

## Customs Regulations

Visitors to Egypt are permitted to enter the country with either 50 cigars or 200 cigarettes or 200 grams of tobacco. Although the laws of Islam forbid alcohol, 2 litres of spirit are permitted to be carried into the country as Egypt is not a 'dry' zone. One litre of toilet water or perfume can be carried in by the visitor and to avoid possible re-export problems it is best to register any valuables on a 'Formulaire 54 KML' form, or a 'D' form. Drugs and firearms, except those registered explicitly for hunting (permission obtainable by writing prior to entry to the Ministry of the Interior), are prohibited. Dog owners should carry a medical and vaccination certificate and there is an entry tax for pets.

No Egyptian currency is permitted to be taken out of the country and all bank receipts of exchange should be retained while in Egypt for presentation upon exit. There is a departure tax of 5LE.

# Documents

*Driving Documents and Regulations*

Few visitors will wish to take a vehicle into Egypt but
details of requirements and restrictions on taking a
vehicle into the country are available at Egyptian
embassies or tourist boards.

An international driver's licence is required in order
to drive in Egypt and this must be valid for at least 90
days from date of entry. Drivers must take out local
insurance in Egypt as the Green Card or International
Motor Insurance is not recognised.

Travel permits are obtainable from the office on the
corner of Sharia Shiekh Rihan and Sharia Nubar, in Cairo
and may be needed for travel on some main routes.
Egyptian driving is on the right and road signs are
inevitably in Arabic. Fuel is known in Egypt as benzene
and is inexpensive but of a low octane content. Fuel
stations are rather thin on the ground outside built up
areas and so journeys must be carefully planned.

If you wish to hire a car in Egypt you must be at least
25 years old. Hire car agencies are based in most hotels;
these include Avis, Hertz, Budget and Bita. Limousines
and cars with drivers are available from Misr Limousine
in Cairo ☎ 25 99813, or Alexandria Limousine, 25 Sharia
Talat Harb ☎ 80 6502.

For those who do drive in Egypt the following addresses
should be noted:

The Automobile Club of
Egypt
10 Sharia Qasr el-Nil
Cairo ☎ 74 3355

The Touring Club of Egypt
8 Sharia Qasr el-Nil
Cairo
☎ 74 3348 or 74 3191

If driving in Alexandria ☎ 96 9494-5
The Touring Club offers a breakdown service on most
trunk roads in the Delta region.

*Passports and Visas*

A full passport valid for at least 6 months is required for
entry to Egypt. It takes around 24 hours to obtain a visa

from the consulate or embassy and these can be applied for and collected from Monday to Friday. Visas are valid for 30 days and are renewable for up to 6 months. Single or multiple entry visas are available.

Visa extensions can be applied for at:
The Passports Office
Mugamma
Palace of the Governor
Room 16
Midan el-Tahir
Cairo

A passport, photograph and the payment of current entry tax are the requirements necessary to obtain a visa and visitors to Egypt must register with the nearest police station within 7 days of arrival in the country.

## First Aid

Medication which is essential includes a diarrhetic of some sort or a strong kaolin or preparation for queasy stomachs in the event of what is commonly termed 'gippy tummy'. Packing an antibacterial remedy is a wise precaution. Salt tablets should be packed as mineral loss via perspiration can cause exhaustion. A mosquito or midge repellant, particularly one with at least 80 per cent diethyl-toluamide, or DEET, might be useful in some regions of the Upper Nile and an antiseptic like TCP is also an important first aid addition.

## Photography

Bring a plastic bag or case to protect the camera from dust. Cleaning cloths for camera lenses are essential; take care of film because of the heat and take unexposed or exposed film in hand luggage when travelling through customs and insist on physical inspection of film instead of X-ray scan.

The re-export of cameras and equipment requires a

completed 'Formulaire 54 KML' form which should be
filled in on entry into Egypt. Most makes of film are
available in Cairo but it is advisable to check expiry
dates. The best film speeds for daytime photography in
Egypt is slow, under ASA 100. *Son et lumière* shots and
night photography require a faster film, like ASA 400-
1000. Processing film locally is quite expensive. Bring a
plastic bag or case to protect the camera from dust. A
selection of filters can be a wise addition to camera
equipment as is a small tripod and flashgun which can
be used in most tombs. Flash photography is not allowed
in the Museum of Egyptian Antiquities and it is forbidden to photograph any strategic establishment, military
installation, industrial region, airport or any official or
military personnel. Always request permission to
photograph individuals although sometimes a few
piastre might smooth the way for better pictures! In
some areas it is the tradition to pay to take photographs.

## Language

Although Egypt is an Arab nation and an African
country, three languages are commonly in use; Arabic,
English and French. Most educated people in Egypt
speak English.

In Egypt language varies greatly from the Mediterranean coast to the depths of the desert. In this guide the
best translations possible have been used, as in the
names of places and objects, but each school has its own
thoughts on translating Arabic into a non-semetic
language. The phonetic translation of words is as
difficult to convert into English as the Arabic script,
which is cursive and runs from right to left.

The following is a short guide to common words and
phrases but a small Arabic/English phrase book or
dictionary is an invaluable asset when travelling in
Egypt.

| | |
|---|---|
| Yes | *Aiwa* |
| No | *Lah* |
| Good morning | *Sab-bah-kheir* |
| Good evening | *Masa-ah-kheir* |
| Hello | *Ahlan wa-salan* |
| Welcome | *Mah-salaam* |
| Goodbye | *Mah-salaama* |
| Greetings | *Mar-har-ba* |
| How are you? | *Keef-ha-lik?* |
| Please | *Min-fad-lik* |
| Thank you | *Shook-ran* |
| How much? | *Bi-kham?* |
| I want | *A-yes* |
| I do not want | *Meesh-awiz* |
| I do not have | *Mah-feesh* |
| Money | *Floos* |
| Where is the toilet? | *Fain al-hammam?* |
| Station/Airport | *Matar* |
| Street | *Sharia* |
| Hotel | *Fun-duk/lok-anda* |
| Restaurant | *Ma-ta-am* |
| Hospital | *Most-ash-far* |
| Water | *Moy-ah* |
| My name is... | *Iss-me...* |
| Your name? | *Iss-mak-aih?* |
| Today | *In-e-harda* |
| Tomorrow | *Book-rah* |
| What is the time? | *Kham-el-sa-ah?* |
| Is it possible? | *Mum-kin?* |

## *Personal Insurance and Medical Care*

Citizens from the UK, USA and Canada do not need vaccination certificates to enter Egypt. Visitors travelling to Egypt from endemic regions must provide a valid certificate of inoculation from yellow fever and cholera. No smallpox inoculation certificate is now required in Egypt. However, it is recommended that visitors obtain vaccinations against typhoid, tetanus, and malaria. A gamma-globulin injection is also recommended to cover against hepatitis which is prevalent now in most hot countries. Malaria is a problem in some parts of Egypt and an anti-malarial course should be considered.

It is essential to take out a personal insurance policy cover for health as medical treatment is expensive in Egypt as is repatriation in an emergency.

## Recommended Maps

Michelin, Bartholomew, Kummerly & Frey, Macmillan, IGN (French), International Communications and the Automobile Association all produce excellent maps of Egypt and that area of Africa and there are many more detailed maps available of the larger towns and cities.

## Tourist Offices

Main Egyptian tourist offices are:

Egyptian General Authority for the Promotion of Tourism
Shari Adly 5
Cairo
Egypt
☎ 92 30 00

Egyptian State Tourist Office
168 Picadilly
London W1
☎ (071) 493 5282

Egyptian Tourist Authority
630 Fifth Avenue
New York, 10111
USA
☎ (212) 246 6960

Egyptian Tourist Authority
Place Bonaventure
40 Frontenac
PO Box 304
Montreal H5A 1B4
Canada
☎ (514) 8614420

Main Egyptian consulates and embassies are:

Consulate General of the Arab Republic of Egypt
19 Kensington Palace Garden Mews
London W8
☎ (071) 937 8050

Egyptian Embassy
2310 Decatur Place NW
Washington DC
20008
USA

1110 Second Avenue          3754 Cote de Nieges
New York                    Montreal
NY 10022                    Canada
USA

## How to Get There

## Land, Sea and Air Travel

Egypt can be entered by land from either Israel or the
Sudan — the Libyan border is closed. Contacts for the
independent traveller are in the 'Driving Documents and
Regulations' section.

The port most used on the Mediterranean coast is
Alexandria, the largest of Egypt's ports. Port Said serves
more as an entrance to the Suez Canal. Cars can be
ferried to Alexandria from several major Mediterranean
ports. Approaching Egypt from the Red Sea by ship the
main ports include Suez and Nuweiba.

Cairo International Airport is linked directly to most
major European and Middle Eastern capitals and to the
USA through Athens or Rome. Egyptair and Air Sinai
are the national airlines. Cairo airport has a good, regular
bus service into the city. Unfamiliar travellers however,
are advised to take the fixed charge limousine service or
negotiate a price with the local taxis. Other airports in
Egypt include Abu Simbel, Alexandria, Aswan, Asyut, El
Arish, Kharga Oasis, Luxor, Sharm al Sheikh, Siwa Oasis
and St Catherine's Monastery.

## When You Are There

## Emergencies

Report any accident immediately to the nearest police
station. Never get out of the car to argue, to attempt to
remove an obstacle or to check on any damage.

# Breakdowns

Many fuel stations have a mechanic at hand but do not always offer a breakdown service. Garages are rather thin on the ground outside built up areas. See 'Driving Documents and Regulations' section for useful addresses.

# Illness and Injury

In an emergency one should consult a doctor or visit one of the many hospitals.

The following addresses should be noted:

**Cairo**
Anglo-American Hospital
On Gezira Island
☎ 34 06163

Al Salam Hospital
3 Syria Street
Mohandessin
☎ 34 07561

Al Salam International
Medical Centre
The Cornish
Maaidi
☎ 35 07878

Cairo Medical Centre
Roxy Square
Heliopolis
☎ 68 0237

**Alexandria**
Al Mossat Hospital
Central Alexandria
☎ 59 72888

Coptic Hospital
4 El Maamoun Moharram
Bay Street
☎ 49 21404

Most chemists are open from 10am to 10pm and will dispense most medicines and prescribe remedies often without a doctor's signature. There are several 24-hour pharmacies.

Take note of the following addresses:

**Cairo**
Attaba Square
☎ 91 0831

**Alexandria**
42 Saad Zaghloul
☎ 80 5154

Rabies is rife in most hot countries; do not attempt to stroke any strange animal, and should one be bitten by any animal, wash the wound thoroughly with soap and clean water and apply alcohol spirit if available. Note the type of animal, go to the nearest police station where you will be directed to the nearest hospital and report the incident.

Snakes rarely attack without provocation but if you are bitten, wipe the bite and cover with a cloth. Apply a tourniquet above the bite if it is on a limb but do not cut off the blood supply. Try to identify the snake and seek medical attention immediately. A scorpion sting, not unusual in Egypt, is best treated similarly to the bite of a snake.

## Legal Advice

Contact your consulate or embassy immediately you require legal assistance. Often the tour operator or travel guide suggest alternatives but insist on seeing a representative of your own country's diplomatic corps.

## National Holidays

Egypt observes the religious holidays of Islam and these include Ramadan, which lasts for 30 days and other celebrations calculated by the phases of the moon. Check the current Muslim calendar dates before you travel. It is unwise to eat or drink in public during the day while the fasting period of Ramadan is being observed. Do not enter mosques during prayer time if you are not a Muslim. Coptic Christian holidays are also observed and these include Sham el Nessim (Easter Monday). National holidays include May Day (1 May), the anniversary of the Egyptian Revolution (23 July) and Egyptian Military Forces Day (6 October).

## Post

The central post office in Cairo is in Attaba Square and is open 24 hours a day. Other post offices open from

8.30am to 3pm every day except Friday. Stamps and postcards can usually be purchased in hotels. Domestic letters cost 3 piastres, Middle East 6 piastres and international postage of letters or cards cost 30 piastres. Packages sent abroad need an export certificate.

## Public Transport

Every 20 minutes buses leave Cairo airport for the city. There are public buses (red and white No 400) from the airport but these are often crowded. Limousine services (blue, fixed rate) and a regular taxi (black and white, negotiable rates) service runs into Cairo. Details of vehicles and destinations are recorded upon leaving the airport.

An excellent rail network runs throughout Egypt and links all principle towns and cities. Main rail stations include Ramesses Station, Cairo ☎ 75 3555; Sidi Gaber, Alexandria and Maydan al-Mahattah in both Luxor and Aswan. Rail travel is inexpensive, regular in service and comparatively efficient. Stations have set windows for the type of ticket issued and women queue on one side, men on the other.

Bus services in Cairo are not recommended as they are uncomfortable and overcrowded, but there is a good coach and bus network across the country and between main towns and cities. Main bus stations can be found at Cairo's railway station, Midan el-Tahrir, Ramesses Street and on Cairo's west bank, Giza Square.

The metro serves Cairo, Old Cairo and Helwan and its main stations can be found at Ramesses Square (Mubarak Station), and a Midan el-Tahrir (Sadat Station). Metro travel is inexpensive but often crowded. In Alexandria there is an efficient and regular tram service with six basic routes running east, as far as Sidi Bishr, from Ramleh main train station, and a local rail service which connects the station with Sidi Gabir, Gabriel, Mandara, Montanzah and Abuqir stations.

# Social and Religious Customs

Egypt is, in the main, a Muslim country and therefore the edicts of the Islamic religion apply and the regulations of that religion should be observed by the visitor. This means that men and women should avoid wearing provocative dress. Improper dress may lead to a refusal at the door of a mosque, museum or public building. The use of common sense in dress avoids disappointment. On board river cruisers, in the desert or on the beaches the normal relaxed attitude to dress applies although topless sunbathing by women is frowned upon. The most comfortable attire to wear in Egypt, by both sexes, is that worn by the locals — the *gellabayah*, ideally suited to Egypt's climate. If women wish to be properly dressed in public they should wear a headscarf.

Women, and occasionally children, may be refused entry to some religious monuments or mosques but this is the norm in a predominantly Islamic country. Shoes should be removed before entering a mosque and carpet slippers are often provided on the door. Mosques should be avoided at times of prayer.

Women and children may also be discouraged from certain clubs and places of entertainment designated especially for the menfolk. They may also be refused admission to the mens coffee or tea rooms.

Muslims do not eat pork or drink alcohol although both are readily available in Egypt. Alcohol should be consumed in moderation in the appointed places and as discreetly as the situation dictates. One should use the right hand to pass food or drink in a Muslim's presence as the left is considered unclean.

# Telephones

There is a good telephone system in Egypt but there are no coin-operated public phone boxes in the countryside. A few hotels have these, some rail stations and a few main town squares. They take a 10 piastre coin for a local call. In the cities and larger towns there are public telephone offices and, when a connection is made, the number is called out by the operator. Long distance calls are best booked well in advance. Many telephone numbers are being changed in Egypt and any seven digit number is a new number — if in doubt with a six digit number, give a prefix of 2 if in Cairo and 3 in Helwan. Alexandrian numbers are still being re-structured and may need prefixes. Check prefixes locally. Shops have telephones which may be used with permission from the shopkeeper. Most hotel rooms in the better hotels are connected with a telephone but reverse-charge calls cannot be made in Egypt. The code to the UK from Egypt is 010 20; to the USA or Canada, 011 20. Direct dialling is not possible from Egypt.

## Tipping

Tipping is known as *baksheesh* in Egypt and it is an integral part of the domestic Egyptian economy.

It is prudent to keep a reasonable amount of small change with you at all times when travelling in Egypt to use as tips and gratuities which become a necessary evil for the slightest service or assistance. The habit of tipping generally works out at 5 piastres for small services; 10 to 20 piastres for each piece of luggage carried by porters; 25 to 50 piastres for a service satisfactorily performed and similarly for guides on top of their set rate. Restaurants generally can expect a tip of between 5 and 10 per cent of the bill.

## Miscellaneous Information

Store signs can be in English, Arabic or French. Shops generally open from 9am to 8pm daily except Friday but these hours vary during the celebrations of Ramadan. Lavatories are scarce throughout Egypt; public toilets are located mostly in railway stations, airports, museums, restaurants and offices. Clean lavatories are non-existant except in the top class hotels and private houses. Always carry a supply of toilet paper.

# FURTHER INFORMATION FOR VISITORS

## PLACES OF INTEREST

Most museums, mausoleums, palaces, pyramids, forts, tombs, particular parts of some mosques and places of special interest charge an admission fee which can vary from a few piastres to 2 or 3 EL or more.

Many small museums and monuments close by about 2pm most days. Although mosques are open all day, tourists should avoid the times of prayer and on afternoons of the Islamic Holy Day (Friday). Some mosques are permanently closed to non-Muslims.

## 1  Cairo — Gateway to the East

### Central Cairo
**Abdin Palace**
Midan el-Gumhuriya
Can only be viewed from outside.

**Art Gallery**
Off 26 July Street in Zamalik region, north Gezira Island
Open: Saturday to Thursday 9am-1pm and 5-8pm. Friday, 9-11am and 5-8pm.

**Ethnological Museum**
El Qasr El-Aini Street
Open: Monday and Wednesday 9.30am-6pm.

**Geological Museum**
Sheikh Rihan Street
Open: Saturday to Thursday 9am-1.30pm.

**Museum of Egyptian Antiquities**
Midan el-Tahrir
Open: Saturday to Thursday 9am-4pm, Friday 9am-12noon, 2-4pm.

**Museum of Islamic Art**
Corner of Port Said and Mohammed Ali Streets
Open: Saturday to Thursday 9am-4pm, Friday 9-11am, 1.30-4pm.

**Postal Museum**
Main Post Office
El-Ataba Square
Open: daily 9am-1pm.

**Railway Museum**
Central Railway Station
Open: Tuesday to Sunday 8.30am-1.30pm.

### Around Central Cairo
**Abu Bakr Ibn Muzhir Mosque**
El-Gamaliya Quarter

**Al-Aqmar Mosque**
Al-Muizz Street

**Al Hakim Mosque**
Middle Galal Street

**Al-Nasir Mosque and Madrasah**
El-Gamaliya Quarter

**Al Rifai Mosque**
Midan Salah el-Din

**Aq-Sunqar Mosque**
Bab el-Wazir Street

**Bab al-Futuh**
Middle Galal Street

**Bab al-Nasr**
Top of el-Gamaliya Street

**Bab Zuwaila**
End Darbel Ahmer Street

**Bulaq Souk**
Bulaq Quarter

**Citadel**
Entrance by Bab al-Qala
Mohammed Ali Mosque, Sultan
Mohammed Ibn Qalaun Mosque,
Joseph's Well, El-Moqattam Tower.

*Military Museum*
Open: Sunday to Thursday and
Saturday 9am-5pm; Friday, 8.30-
11.30am, 1-6pm.

**El-Azhar Mosque**
End El-Azhar Street
Open: Saturday, Sunday to
Thursday 9am-3pm; Friday
9-11am, 1-3pm.

**Gayer Anderson Museum**
Near Ibn Tulun Mosque
Open: Saturday to Thursday 9am-
3.30pm, Friday 9-11am, 1.30-
3.30pm.

**House of Shuhaymi**
El-Gamaliya Quarter
Open: daily 9am-4pm.

**House of Gamal al-Din**
Behind Al-Muizz Street
Open: daily 9am-2pm.

**Ibn Tulun Mosque**
Saliba Street
Open: 9am-4pm.

**Mausoleum, Madrasah and
Wakala of Sultan al-Ghouri**
El-Azhar Street
Open: daily 9am-4pm.

**Musafirkhane Palace**
Darb El-Tablawi in El-Gamaliya
district
Open: daily 9am-4pm.

**Othman Kathuda Palace**
Near Al-Muizz Street
Open: daily 9am-2pm.

**Saleh Ayub Mausoleum**
El-Gamaliya Quarter

**Salih Talai Mosque**
Across from Bab Zuwaila

**Sultan Barquq Mosque**
El-Gamaliya Quarter
Open: daily 9am-4pm.

**Sultan Baybars Monastery**
El-Gamaliya Quarter

**Sultan Baybars I Mosque**
On Al-Guesh Street

**Sultan Hassan Mosque
and Madrasah**
End El-Qa'la Street
Open: daily 8am-6pm.

**Sultan Muayyad**
Near Bab Zuwaila

**Sultan Qalaun Mausoleum
and Madrasah**
El-Gamaliya Quarter
Open: daily 9am-5pm.

**Wakala of Qaytbey**
El-Gamaliya Quarter

*Cairo's Outskirts*
**Abu Sarga**
Near Mar Girgis Station, Old Cairo
Quarter

**Al-Muallaqa**
Near Mar Girgis Station, Old Cairo
Quarter

**Amr Ibn Al-As Mosque**
Sidi Hasan al-Anwar Street

**Ben Ezra Synagogue**
Near Mar Girgis Station, Old Cairo
Quarter

**Coptic Museum**
Near Mar Girgis Station, Old Cairo
Quarter
Open: Saturday to Thursday 9am-
4pm; Friday 9-11am, 1-4pm.

**Fort of Babylon**
Near Mar Girgis Station, Old Cairo
Quarter

**Necropolis**
South-east of Cairo
No visitors on Fridays or during
prayer times.

**Sitt Barbara**
Near Mar Girgis Station, Old Cairo
Quarter

## Islands of Cairo

*Gezira Island*
**Cairo Exhibition Grounds**
*Museum of Sculpture and Art*
Open: daily 9am-3pm.

*Museum of Egyptian Civilisation*
Open: daily 9am-1pm.

*Mogamma al-Fenoun Centre of Arts*
Open: Saturday to Thursday 9am-
1pm, 5-8pm. Not open in summer.

*Papyrus Institute*
On the west bank
Open: daily 9am-4pm.

**Cairo Tower**
Open: 9am-midnight.

**Mohammed-Khalil Museum**
Central on the island
Open: Saturday to Thursday 9am-
1.30pm, 5-8pm.

**Mukhtar Museum**
On the tip of the island

Open: Saturday to Thursday 9am-
1.30pm, Friday 9-11.30am.

*Roda Island*
**Manisterli Palace**
Southernmost tip of island reached
by the Malik al-Saleh Bridge
Open: daily 9am-2pm.

**Manyal Palace and Museum**
Northern point of island
Open: daily 9am-1pm.

**Nilometer**
Southern tip of island

*Cairo's West Bank*
**Agricultural Museum**
End 6 October Bridge
Open: daily 9am-3pm.

**Camel Market**
New city of Imbaba
Open: Fridays 5-10am.

**Cotton Museum**
End of 6 October Bridge
Open: Saturday to Thursday 9am-
2.30pm, Friday 9-11am; 1-2.30pm.

**Museum of Modern Art**
End of El-Sad al-Ali Street
Open: Sunday to Thursday 9am-
2pm, Friday 9am-1pm.

**National Zoo**
End of El-Gama'a Bridge
Open: daily 6am-5pm.

## 2 — Memphis, Saqqara, Giza and the Pyramids

Most of the sites and monuments
in Memphis and Saqqara are open
to the public daily from 9am-4pm.
However, some of the doors to
monuments are kept locked until
visitors arrive and one may have to
wait for a few minutes until a

keeper arrives with the keys. Some guards begin to lock up their monuments at 3.30pm. It is always possible to attach oneself to a guided tour in the more remote Saqqara complexes as orientation from site to site is not easy for the casual visitor. One ticket allows admission to all the monuments which are open in Saqqara.

## Abusir
12km (7 miles) south of Giza
**Sun Temples**

## Dahshur
A short distance south of Saqqara
**'Coloured' Pyramids**
The sites here may be closed to the public.

## Giza
This site is 10km (6 miles) south-west of Cairo. Entrance to the entire Giza site is from the ticket office. The Solar Boat Museum makes an extra charge for entry. All the sites in the complex are open from 9am-4pm although there is no charge for wandering around the outside of the sites.

**Dr Ragab's Papyrus Institute**
Al-Nil Street
Open: daily 8.30am-6.30pm.

**Mortuary Temples**
Located in various sites around Giza complex

**Pyramids of Abu Roash**
North of Giza site

**Pyramid of Cheops**
Dominating Giza funerary site

**Pyramid of Chephron**
South-west of 'Great Pyramid'

**Pyramid of Mycerinus**
South-west corner of Giza site

**Solar Boat Museum**
South side of 'Great Pyramid'
Open: 9am-4pm.

**Sound and Light Auditorium**
South-east side of the pyramid complex. English versions on Saturday, Monday, Wednesday, Thursday and Friday.

**Sphinx**
South-east of 'Great Pyramid'

**Pyramids of Queens and Princesses**
At various locations throughout Giza site.

## Memphis
This site is 24km (15 miles) south of Cairo.

**Alabaster Sphinx**
To left hand side of Saqqara road

**Ramesses II Statue**
Near the road leading to Saqqara

## Saqqara
**Cat Cemetery**
Right-hand side of road from Saqqara town to Step Pyramid.

**Great North and South Courts**
Situated in King Zoser complex

**Mariette's House**
North-west of King Zoser complex

**Mastabas**
South of King Zoser complex
Idut, Nebet, Mehu, Neferherptah, and other early tombs.

**Persian Tombs**
In front of south face of Pyramid of Unas

**Pyramid of Unas**
Situated south of King Zoser complex

**Sekhemkhet Pyramid**
South-west of Step Pyramid
complex

**Serapeum**
Far west side of Step Pyramid

**St Jeremiah's Monastery**
Near entrance to Saqqara site

**Step Pyramid**
Dominating Saqqara cemetery site

# 3 — The Nile Delta

Most of the ancient sites in the Nile
Delta are only open to the public
by appointment through the tourist
boards local offices, are erratic and
often due to the availability of local
guides. Organised tours can be
made with regular excursions
which depart from Cairo by coach.

*Damietta*
193km (120 miles) east of Rosetta

**Amr el-As Mosque**
In cemetery quarter

**El-Madbuliya Mosque**
In town near the river

*Rosetta*
64km (40 miles) east of Alexandria

**Keli Museum**
Off Main Street
Open: Saturday to Thursday 9am-
1pm; 2.30-4pm.

**Rosetta Stone Site**
3km (2 miles) north of Rosetta

**Zaghloul Mosque**
End of Main Street, south of
railway station

*Tanis*
**Great Temple of Amun**
37km (23 miles) north-east of
Zagazig at San el-Haga

*Zagazig*
85km (53 miles) north-east of Cairo

**Lake Manzalik**
Via El-Matariya, 30km (19 miles)
west of Port Said

**Tel Basta Cat Cemetery**
South-east of Zagazig town centre

**Uragi Museum**
Town Centre
Open: Saturday to Thursday 9am-
1.30pm.

Other sites of antiquity discovered
in the Nile Delta are:-

**Buto**
140km (87 miles) north of Cairo

**Hathrib**
42km (26 miles) due north of Cairo,
near Benha

**Tel el-Daba**
105km (65 miles) north-east of
Cairo near Faqus

**Tel Faraun**
Between Tel el-Daba and Tanis
near Shaba

*Wadi el-Natrun*
These monasteries are located on
the west side of the Cairo to
Alexandria road, 100km (62 miles)
north-west of Cairo.
    Only one of the four monasteries
in Wadi el-Natrun is open to the
public.

**Dier Abu Maqar**

**Dier al-Suryan**

**Dier Anba Baramus**

**Dier Anba Bishoi**
Open: Thursday and Friday 10am-
4pm.

# 4 — Alexandria and the North-West

**Abu el-Abbas el-Mursi Mosque**
Between the two harbours to the west of the town

**Aquarium**
On the Eastern Harbour's west arm near Fort Qaitbay
Open: daily 9am-2pm.

**Catacombs of Kom el-Shukafa**
Directly south of the city centre near the Mahmudiya Canal
Open: daily 9am-4pm.

**El-Anfushi Necropolis**
West of town between the Eastern and Western harbours.

**Fine Art Museum**
18 Menasha Street
Open: Sunday to Thursday 8am-2pm,Wednesday 4am-2pm and 7-9pm.

**Fort Qaitbay Naval Museum**
On west point of the Eastern Harbour's west arm
Open: daily 9am-3pm.

**Graeco-Roman Museum**
Off Saleh Mustapha Street
Open: Sunday to Thursday and Saturday 9am-4pm, Friday 9-11.30am, 1.30-4pm.

**Montazah Palace**
Far east of city on coast near Mandara railway station

**Pompey's Pillar**
Near the Catacombs south of the city centre
Open: daily 9am-4pm.

**Ras el-Tin Palace**
West of necropolis on the north arm of the Western Harbour

**Roman Amphitheatre**
Amir Abdel el-Kader Street
Open: daily 9am-4pm.

*In North-West Egypt*

*El Alamein*
**El Alamein Cemetery**
On the left of the road from Alexandria into the El Alamein village. Always open.

**El Alamein War Museum**
Ten-minute walk from cemetery
Open: 9am-6pm.

*Mersa Matruh*
**Cleopatra's Bath, Cleopatra's Quay**
Near the cliffs, 170km (105 miles) west of El Alamein

**Rommel's Cave**
Near the harbour
Open: daily 9am-3pm.

**St Menas Monastery**
Half hour drive or by train south-west of Alexandria

*Siwa Oasis*
A permit is needed to stay in Siwa. The ruins in Siwa can be visited at any time but a guard must be found to unlock the rock tombs.

**Temple of Amasis and Temple of Zeus Ammon**
Both located west of Siwa town

**Tombs of Jebel el-Mowta**
Outside the village of Qaret el-Musabberin

# 5 — Suez and the Canal Towns

Suez tourist information can be obtained from Misr Travel in Port Taufiq ☎ 31 34

*Ismailia*
Tourist information obtainable in Cairo.
80km (50 miles) south of Port Said

**Garden of the Stelae**
Near Fountain Park

**Lesseps House**
Mohammed Ali Quay
Open: Wednesday to Monday 9am-4pm.

**Museum of Antiquities**
Off Mohammed Ali Quay
Open: daily 8.30am-1.30pm.

*Port Said*
Tourist information can be obtained from Misr Travel in Sultan Hussein Street ☎ 46 10
200km (124 miles) north-east of Cairo

**Lake Manzala**
An hour's drive west of Port Said Great inland lake and bird sanctuary.

**Port Said Military Museum**
July 23 Street
Open: daily 8am-6pm.

# 6 — The Sinai Peninsula

The Egyptian tourist board is developing the Mount Sinai region as a new tourist resort. A tourist village is being built near the sixth-century St Catherine's Monastery and is to be linked to a nearby mountain by a 4km (2 mile) long alpine-type cable car route.

**St Catherine's Monastery**
Centre of south port of peninsula
Open: Monday to Thursday and Saturday 9.30am-12.30pm.

**Mount Sinai**
In the south of the peninsula

**Ras el-Safsaf**
Near to St Catherine's Monastery

**Springs of Moses**
South-east of Suez

**Temple of Hathor**
North of Maghara at Serabit al-Khadim

# 7 — The Red Sea Coast

This region, from Suez to the Sudanese border, comes under the Red Sea Frontier District but the tourist office responsible for the area is in Cairo at:

Shari Adly 5
Cairo City
☎ 92 3000

Tourist Police
☎ 91 2644

**St Anthony's Monastery**
Inland of Beni Suef road

**St Paul's Monastery**
Similar location as St Anthony's Monastery

**Hurghada**
*Oceanographic Institute*
North of the town
Open: daily 9am-4.30pm.

**Mons Porphyrites**
West of Hurghada

**Mons Claudianus**
Inland, due west of Bur Safaga

# 8 — Cairo to Luxor

From Cairo to Luxor the visitor passes through seven of Egypts political divisions with diversions to the governorate of El-Fayyum and the Frontier District of the New Valley. Each division has a tourist information office.

The Memphis to Lisht stretch of the Nile Valley which comes under the auspices of the Giza governorate and the Cairo Tourist Office at:

Shari Adly 5
Cairo City
☎ 92 3000

Tourist Police
☎ 91 2644

The Beni Suef governorate extends south almost to the ancient site of Oxyrhynchus on the west bank of the Nile. This region is also looked after by the tourist office of Cairo as is the Fayyum district to the west. This office also administers the ancient sites and places of interest through the governorates of El-Minya, Asyut and Sohag.

For those visitors diverting to the oases of the New Valley the Tourist Promotion Authority for the area of Farafra, Dakhla and El-Kharga is contacted on ☎ 90 1611 and the Tourist Police for the region ☎ 90 1502.

Continuing down the Nile from the site of Abydos southwards, the tourist office of Luxor takes over from that of Cairo. This office is based in the tourist bazaar in the town centre ☎ 22 15, Tourist Police are contacted on ☎ 21 20, and this office's juristiction continues through the Kena governorate as far south as Esna.

From Esna to Aswan the Aswan tourist office is the responsible authority located in the bazaar ☎ 32 97, Tourist Police ☎ 31 63.

## In the Western Oases

Note that most of the ancient monuments and ruins in the Western Desert are open to the public at times which suit the local guardian or custodian. The Tourism Promotion Authority of the entire region can be contacted for up-to-date information ☎ 90 1611 (code for New Valley Governorate 088). The Tourist Police can be most helpful ☎ 90 1502.

# 9 — Luxor and Karnak

*Luxor*

**Abu el-Haggag Mosque**
In northern part of Temple of Luxor.

**Museum of Ancient Egyptian Art**
North end of El Bahr el-Nil Street
Open: 4 -10pm (9pm in winter).

**Roman Forum**
Near Temple of Luxor
Open: daily 6am-10pm, 9pm in winter.

**Temple of Luxor**
Just off El Bahr el-Nil Street
Open: daily 6am-10pm (9pm in winter).

## Karnak

### Great Temple of Amun

Open: daily, sunrise-5pm, winter 6pm, summer 7pm, mid-summer 8pm.

English *son et lumière* lasts 90 minutes Monday, Wednesday and Saturday at 8pm. Friday 10pm.

The fifteen major sites and monuments of Karnak are open at the same time as the central feature, the Great Temple of Amun, as they are part of the same complex.

# 10 — Western Thebes

There are fifty-two major monuments in the Thebes necropolis and tickets to these must be purchased for the individual cemeteries and often to individual temples. These are available from the booking offices on the west bank of the Nile. Prices of entry vary from LE1 to LE5 and the kiosks are open daily from 6am-4pm. All the sites open to the public can be viewed more or less from dawn until sunset. Sites are listed on page 202-3.

# 11 — Luxor to Aswan

## *Between Luxor and Edfu*

### Aphroditopolis and Mo'allah

On either side of the Nile south of Tod
*Ancient city sites*
Open: daily 8am-5pm.

### Edfu

South of Luxor on Nile's west bank

*Temple of Horus*
Open: daily 6am-5pm.

### El-Kab

Opposite El-Kula on east bank
*Ancient Nekhab and Tombs*
Open: daily 6am-5pm.

### El-Kula

West bank of Nile south of Esna
*Pyramid Site*
Open: by appointment.

### Esna

South of Luxor on Nile's west bank
*Temple of Khnum*
Open: daily 7am-6pm.

### Hermonthis

North of Armant on edge of desert
*Bull Necropolis*
North of Armant on edge of desert
Open: daily 7am-6pm.

### Tod

East bank near El Idisat
*Ptolemaic Temple*
Open: daily 7am-6pm.

## *Between Edfu and Aswan*

### Gebel Serag

South of El-Ridisiya Qibili
*Rock Tombs and Quarry Site*
Open: by appointment.

### Kom Ombo

South of Edfu on Nile's east bank
*Great Temple of Sobek and Horus*
Open: daily 6am-6pm.

### Silsila

Near to Kagug town, east bank
*Quarries and Rock Chapel*
Open: by appointment.

For more information on Esna contact the tourist office at Luxor ☎ 22 15. For Edfu contact the Aswan Tourist Board ☎ 23 23/23 97.

## 12 — Aswan and Abu Simbel

*In and Around Aswan*

**Ptolemaic Temple**
Near Grand Hotel
Ruins of temple to Isis

**Syene**
On Aswan site
Remains of Ancient Greek city.

*Elephantine Island*
Facing Aswan town

**Aswan Archaeological Museum**
Open: daily 8am-5pm.

**Temple of Khnum, nilometer, Kalabsha Kiosk**

*Kitchener's Island*
Between Elephantine Island and Nile's west bank
'Botanical Wonderland'.

**Aga Khan Mausoleum**
Opposite Elephantine Island
Open: Tuesday to Sunday 9am-5pm.

**Aswan Dam**
6km (4 miles) south of Aswan

**Aswan High Dam**
15km (10 miles) south of Aswan
Museum Open: daily 7am-5pm.

**Northern and Southern Quarries**
South of Aswan

**St Simeon's Monastery**
On Nile's west bank
Open: daily 9am-6pm.

**Tombs of the Winds**
On Nile's west bank
Open: daily 8am-4pm.

**Unfinished Obelisk**
Outskirts of Aswan
Open: 6am-5pm.

*Agilka Island*
The following list of places of interest were moved from Philae to Agilka. These islands are open daily from 7am-4pm. Tickets are available at the quayside.
*Temple of Isis*
*Portico of Nectanebo I*
*Hadrian's Gateway*
*Temple of Hathor*
*Kiosk of Trajan*

*Between Aswan and Abu Simbel*

**Amada**
South of Aswan

**Es-Seoua**
East of Amada

**Temple of Beit El-Wali**
North-west of Kalabsha

**Temple of Kalabsha**
19km (11 miles) south of Aswan
Open: 6am-5pm.

**Temple of Kertassi**
North of Kalabsha

*In Abu Simbel*

**Great Temple of Ramesses II**
Near Abu Simbel airport
Open: 6am-6pm.

**Temple of Hathor**
North of Great Temple
Open: 6am-6pm.
Unless otherwise stated the monuments, temples and sites of interest in this part of Egypt are accessible only by prior arrangement with the tourist board just near the station in Aswan, on organised excursions or by arrangement with an authorised guide. The tourist office for Aswan and Abu Simbel is located in the tourist bazaar ☎ 32 97.

# INDEX